Interludes and Irony
in the Ancestral Narrative

Interludes and Irony
in the Ancestral Narrative

∽

Jonathan A. Kruschwitz

☙PICKWICK *Publications* · Eugene, Oregon

INTERLUDES AND IRONY IN THE ANCESTRAL NARRATIVE

Copyright © 2021 Jonathan A. Kruschwitz. All rights reserved. Except for brief quotations in critical publications or reviews, no part of this book may be reproduced in any manner without prior written permission from the publisher. Write: Permissions, Wipf and Stock Publishers, 199 W. 8th Ave., Suite 3, Eugene, OR 97401.

Pickwick Publications
An Imprint of Wipf and Stock Publishers
199 W. 8th Ave., Suite 3
Eugene, OR 97401

www.wipfandstock.com

PAPERBACK ISBN: 978-1-7252-6077-1
HARDCOVER ISBN: 978-1-7252-6078-8
EBOOK ISBN: 978-1-7252-6079-5

Cataloguing-in-Publication data:

Names: Kruschwitz, Jonathan A., author.

Title: Interludes and irony in the ancestral narrative / Jonathan A. Kruschwitz.

Description: Eugene, OR: Pickwick Publications, 2021 | Includes bibliographical references.

Identifiers: ISBN 978-1-7252-6077-1 (paperback) | ISBN 978-1-7252-6078-8 (hardcover) | ISBN 978-1-7252-6079-5 (ebook)

Subjects: LCSH: Bible.—Genesis—Criticism, interpretations, etc. | Hagar (Biblical figure) | Dinah (Biblical figure) | Tamar—daughter-in-law of Judah | Patriarchs (Bible) | Women in the Bible

Classification: BS1235.2 K787 2021 (print) | BS1235.2 (ebook)

Manufactured in the U.S.A.   DECEMBER 14, 2020

Table of Contents

Acknowledgments ix

Introduction 1
Chapter 1: Poetics: The Interlude as a Narrative Structure 21
Chapter 2: Hermeneutics: Irony 38
Chapter 3: The Hagar Interludes 85
Chapter 4: The Dinah Interlude 126
Chapter 5: The Tamar Interlude 178
Conclusion 239

Bibliography 251

Acknowledgments

I HAVE HEARD IT said—and I believe it to be true—that being original is forgetting where you read or heard something. What modest claim I can make to originality, then, is displaced by the debt I owe to the many who have influenced my thought and research over the last several years.

I first express my gratitude to a person without whom this study would not have been possible. My dissertation supervisor at the University of Sheffield, Hugh Pyper, assisted my research in countless ways, some more obvious than others. Never short of a recommendation for further reading, eternally curious, and always at hand with a gentle critique, Hugh provided me with invaluable inspiration throughout my study and encouraged independent, innovative thought.

I am also grateful to other instructors whose teaching has kindled my fascination with the biblical text. Special mention must be made of Mark E. Biddle, F. Scott Spencer, Juliana M. Claassens, Melissa Jackson, Sandra Hack Polaski, Donald C. Polaski, and Samuel L. Adams, whose shared love of reading the biblical text undoubtedly nurtured my own.

It would be remiss of me not to acknowledge the academic communities that supported me throughout my studies, including the Department of Biblical Studies at the University of Sheffield and bands of colleagues across the world. Through their welcome and guidance through the corridors in academia—papers, conferences, the joys and travails of PhD life—they provided a firm foundation for my research.

Communities of faith have also sustained me. In particular, Second Baptist Church of Richmond, Virginia, and Gayton Road Christian Church (Disciples of Christ) have kept me near their hearts and emboldened me to pursue my course of research. I am grateful for their love and support.

Close friends contributed to the completion of this project more than they know. Their silliness and levity occasionally made light of what seemed a daunting task—and for that, I can only say, "Thank you." I especially thank Jason, whose transatlantic conversations consistently buoyed my spirits; the Vlads and Reza, Adriana and Itzel, and Nick and Cody, who turned houses into homes; and Svetlana, whose simple words marked my thoughts in profound ways. There are many others, but to continue this word of thanks would take too much space and allow for too many possible omissions.

I close these acknowledgments with a loving embrace of my family—especially my grandfather Verlin C. Kruschwitz, whose enthusiasm for the Old Testament I am honored to have shared; my uncle Robert Kruschwitz, whose generous attention, editorial acumen, and heartfelt encouragement saw me through my final revisions; and my mother and father, Marlis and William, and my brother, Curt, whose listening ears, devoted hearts, and caring words have helped me along the way time and time again.

Introduction

The Strange Stories of Hagar, Dinah, and Tamar: What Are They Doing in the Ancestral Narrative?

The Ancestral Narrative: A Story of Ancestral Identity

COMMENTATORS REGULARLY IDENTIFY GEN 12–50 as a distinct narrative within Genesis. Differentiating it from the more universal, timeless narrative of Gen 1–11,[1] they designate it the "patriarchal"[2] or, as this study prefers, "ancestral" narrative.[3] As its name implies, the ancestral narrative is read as a story about the ancestral family,[4] the forebears of Israel.[5] It

---

1. Fretheim articulates this common interpretive move: "In the study of Genesis it has long been the practice to drive a sharp wedge between Gen 1–11, the 'primeval history,' and Gen 12–50, the 'ancestral history'" (*Abraham*, 1).

2. Westermann explains the reason for this term: "There is no word so characteristic of the patriarchal stories of Gen. 12–50 as *father*" (*Genesis 12–36*, 24).

3. For a selection of commentators who use or acknowledge these common identifications of Gen 12–50, see von Rad, *Genesis*, 164; Speiser, *Genesis*, lviii; Westermann, *Genesis 12–36*, 28; Fretheim, *Abraham*, 184; Wenham, *Genesis 1–15*, 258; Brodie, *Genesis as Dialogue*, 89. Fretheim clarifies the recent trend to exchange "ancestral" for "patriarchal": "The phrase 'patriarchal history' has long been used. The word 'ancestral' makes it clearer that both the men and the women of this story have a crucial role to play in how the story develops" (*Abraham*, 184).

4. Cf. von Rad, *Genesis*, 34; Speiser, *Genesis*, liii; Westermann, *Genesis 12–36*, 28; Wenham, *Genesis 1–15*, 256–58; Brodie, *Genesis as Dialogue*, 25.

5. Many readers of the ancestral narrative focus on how it anticipates Israel's story. E.g., Fretheim, who reads Gen 12:1–3 as the key to Genesis and, moreover, an anticipation of "Israel's later history as a people" (*Abraham*, 32); Westermann, who suggests interpreting the ancestral narrative as a "memory of origin" (*Genesis 12–36*, 23, 29); and Speiser, who highlights the significance of the ancestral narrative for the rest of the Pentateuch (*Genesis*, liii). The term "ancestral" betrays the retrospective focus, as well as the attendant tendency to retroject subsequent narrative elements into

narrates how the ancestral family was born and recounts a diverse range of stories concerning the family as it moves toward the divine promises of offspring, land, and blessing. Indeed, the family's prospects for growth, land, and blessing unify the mix of stories into a coherent narrative. Stories of barren matriarchs, fraternal rivalry, generational transition, sojourning, and confrontation with the inhabitants of the land can all be read to revolve around the ancestral family and its movement toward the divine promises.[6]

According to the conventional reading, the ancestral narrative does not present a finished story—the ancestral family never enjoys the full realization of the divine promises—but rather a portrait of the ancestral family. In other words, what the ancestral narrative really offers is a story of ancestral, if not nascent Israelite, identity. Hence commentators tend to identify the story as a "family history."[7] While the thematic refrains of promised blessing, land, and descendants—the oft-perceived "programmatic" core of the ancestral narrative[8]—never find complete narrative fulfillment, they nevertheless mark three key aspects of the narrative's representation of ancestral identity. They anticipate the development of the ancestral family's relationship with God, its budding relationship with the land and its inhabitants, and its self-defining genealogy.

In accordance with the narrative's nearly exclusive focus on the ancestral family, the conventional reading renders ancestral identity in exclusive terms.[9] The ancestral family stands in a privileged covenantal

---

Genesis, inasmuch as it presupposes the significance of the people of whom Abraham and family are ancestors. Although this study endeavors to avoid such retrojection, it maintains the use of the term "ancestral" for the sake of convenience.

6. Cf. von Rad: "The internal connection between individual narratives can be seen above all in the way in which they are now all subordinated to the theme of the 'promise to the patriarchs'" (*Genesis*, 22).

7. Cf. Speiser, *Genesis*, liii; Westermann, *Genesis 12–36*, 28; Fokkelman, *Narrative Art in Genesis*, 239; Brodie, *Genesis as Dialogue*, 25, 114. Heard, *Dynamics of Diselection* is a relatively recent expression of this longstanding focus on ancestral identity. Invoking the image of the family tree, Heard explores the process of "pruning" by which the ancestral family finds its identity. This process, Heard argues, involves not only genealogy (the biological claim of legitimate heirship) but also a character's relation to the divine plan.

8. Von Rad, *Genesis*, 169. See also Wenham, who explains, "Descendants, land, and divine blessing are the goals to which the stories press" (*Genesis 1–15*, 258).

9. E.g., McAfee, who reads the formulation of an exclusive identity in the story of Abraham: "The desideratum of a chosen people in a chosen land emphasizes separation, distinctiveness, hierarchical relationships and exclusiveness" ("Chosen People

relationship with God, as the future inheritor of the promised land and thus as an implicit opponent of the land's current inhabitants, and as a pure, endogamous lineage distinct from the land's inhabitants. Therefore this reading might be simplified to say that the ancestral narrative outlines an exclusive ancestral identity in three basic aspects: the ancestral family's relations with God, others, and itself.

The Strange Stories of Hagar, Dinah, and Tamar

Obtruding against the unifying force of this interpretation, however, are the stories of Hagar, Dinah, and Tamar, which stray from the ancestral narrative's selective focus on the ancestral family. Readers regularly mark them as outliers of the ancestral narrative. Not uncommonly, they classify them as "interludes" to indicate that they disrupt the natural progression of the larger narrative.[10] Although few readers have yet grouped these three stories together, the possibility has been acknowledged. Mark G. Brett, for instance, brackets these particular stories as potentially subversive toward "the ideology of the Persian-sponsored governors." He contends that they undermine "any version of genealogical exclusivism or moral superiority."[11] Brett's detection of a resonance among these three stories, a resonance that counters the main thrust of the narrative, reflects what might be summarized in more general terms: these stories are strange, and perhaps strangely connected.

One common feature that immediately unites these strange stories is their female protagonists. This shared element extends a particular invitation to feminist criticism. What might the women in these stories share in common? How might their stories be related? How might the female protagonists contribute to or inform the stories' strangeness? While the invitation to feminist criticism is compelling and similar questions have proven insightful to readings of the ancestral narrative, this study

---

in a Chosen Land," 174). McAfee's rhetoric of chosenness echoes the exclusivity that readers have traditionally attributed to ancestral identity. This attribution likely derives, at least in part, from a retrospective perspective that equates ancestral identity with later Israelite identity. For further discussion of readings of an exclusive ancestral identity, see the section "The Divine Program as the Ancestral Prerogative" in ch. 3 (p. 86).

10. For more on the common move to read the stories of Hagar, Dinah, and Tamar as outliers, or "interludes," see the section "A Poetics of the Interlude" in ch. 1 (p. 21).

11. Brett, *Genesis*, 137.

expands its focus beyond a specifically feminist interpretation lest it neglect other strange features of the text. Feminist scholars have already devoted a substantial amount of attention to these stories and their female characters, exploring the limits of patriarchy and the disruptive agency of the female protagonists.[12] While their work doubtlessly informs much of this study's analysis, its comprehensiveness frees this study to look at other aspects of the stories. For instance, how the stories conceptualize outsiderness in terms other than gender—in terms of relations to God, the land, and lineage—will figure into much of the forthcoming discussion. Nevertheless, there does remain what might be identified as a feminist proclivity in this study, insofar as feminism connotes the examination and interrogation of certain assumed binaries. In other words, instead of referring to the special focus on women's characters and voices, or to the challenge on patriarchy, feminism may refer to the broader project of scrutinizing and destabilizing the ways that certain assumptions of what is male and what is female maintain a balance across other binaries in our logic.[13] This study will transpose this brand of feminism to the subject of ancestral identity, as it will explore and interrogate notions of what is ancestral and non-ancestral. It will problematize certain presumed associations that join what is ancestral with divine privilege, an exclusive right to the land, and an endogamously selective genealogy.[14]

If the women protagonists are not read as the distinguishing factor of these stories' strangeness, then the question remains: how exactly are

---

12. In addition to countless scholarly essays and journal articles, a number of feminist-critical monographs devote considerable attention to one or more of the strange stories' female protagonists. For the sake of classification, these book-length studies may be roughly divided into those that confront and counter the patriarchal ideology of the text and those that seek to demonstrate how the text might valorize women and their interests. Works that fall into the former category include Trible, *Texts of Terror*; Exum, *Fragmented Women*; Fewell and Gunn, *Gender, Power, and Promise*; Davies, *The Dissenting Reader*. Works that fall into the latter category include Jeansonne, *The Women of Genesis*; Frymer-Kensky, *Reading the Women of the Bible*; Schneider, *Mothers of Promise*; Jackson, *Comedy and Feminist Interpretation of the Hebrew Bible*.

13. Cf. Culler's discussion of the "third" level of feminist criticism in *On Deconstruction*, 43–63.

14. It is perhaps no coincidence that the strange stories of Hagar, Dinah, and Tamar, which offer alternative perspectives on ancestral identity, feature women protagonists. Niditch notes that women in Genesis "are markers and creators of transition and transformation" ("Genesis," 44). Therefore, while this study does not focus primarily on questions of sexuality and gender, women characters will naturally attract its attention as mediators of identity.

the stories strange? Commentators separate the stories from the ancestral narrative on two basic counts. First, the stories mark a shift in what Seymour Chatman calls the "interest point of view." That is, the cast of characters who are "followed" by the narrative,[15] whose interests determine the focus of the narrative, adjusts to include not only the ancestral family but also, and sometimes even more so, an outsider character. Second, the stories stand in a disjunctive relation to the plot of the surrounding narrative. Heeding the interests of non-ancestral characters, they deviate from the main storyline. They do not advance the plot in a straightforward manner. Von Rad's traditional reading of the stories exemplifies these two points of distinction. For von Rad, Hagar's story is a "cul-de-sac" in the plot,[16] as its attention on an ultimately illegitimate branch of the ancestral family disrupts the progress from promise to fulfillment. Dinah's story exhibits very little interest in Jacob, the main character of its narrative cycle (25:19—36:43), leading von Rad to remark on the story's disjointed relation to the cycle and to speculate whether the tradition from which the story originates even knows of the patriarch.[17] And Tamar's story, which entails an abrupt narrative shift in cast and setting, "has no connection at all with the strictly organized Joseph story" that encloses it.[18]

It might be argued that other stories in Genesis qualify as narrative strangers inasmuch as they distinguish themselves on one or both of these counts, and to an extent, the selection of the stories of Hagar, Dinah, and Tamar *is* an arbitrary one, necessary for limiting the scope of the study. This study would nonetheless offer as a response to this reservation the point that Hagar, Shechem and the Hivites (the Dinah story's main outsiders), and Tamar have captured readers' attention more comprehensively than have other outsider characters, like the kings of Gen 14 or King Abimelech (particularly in Gen 20).[19] The reasons for this

15. Chatman, *Story and Discourse*, 157.

16. Von Rad, *Genesis*, 196.

17. Von Rad, *Genesis*, 330–35. Von Rad also observes the singularity of the story's interest in Dinah, who receives only passing mention elsewhere in Genesis (30:21; 46:15). For von Rad, these differences indicate that the story comes from a tradition other than that which underlies the Jacob cycle.

18. Von Rad, *Genesis*, 356.

19. Another candidate for "narrative stranger" worth mentioning is the story of Sodom and the Plain Cities' destruction. This story disrupts the narrative focus on covenant and the imminent birth of Abraham's promised son. This study distinguishes it from the stories of Hagar, Dinah, and Tamar, however, on the grounds that its central character, Lot, with whom the story begins and ends, is "ancestral"; he descends from

difference in attention are debatable, but this study would point out that the characterization of the outsiders in the stories of Hagar, Dinah, and Tamar is fuller and thus makes their subjectivities more accessible. For the duration of the stories, the ancestral family must share much of the narrative's distribution of subjectivity with an outsider.[20]

The strangeness of these stories elicits the question: what is their purpose or function? How does one make sense of them in the context of the ancestral narrative? Readers have traditionally "naturalized" them[21]—or unified their meaning with the main interests of the ancestral narrative—by treating them as foils that dramatize and throw into deeper relief central aspects of the narrative or as interpretive keys to central narrative concerns. E. A. Speiser's commentary on Genesis exemplifies this naturalizing tendency. For Speiser, the Hagar story is "an interlude of acute suspense."[22] Its incongruity with "earlier hints and expectations"

Terah's line. (Although he ostensibly becomes an ancestral outsider, in the sense that he is not selected as the heir to the ancestral covenant, his character comes from within the ancestral fold, whereas Hagar, Shechem and the Hivites, and Tamar come from without.) This distinction notwithstanding, Gen 19 invites attention to its peculiar interruption of the flow of the narrative. For a reading that attends to the finer details of its thematic integration within Genesis, see Alter, "Sodom as Nexus."

20. Fewell and Gunn define the text's subject as "the point of view whose interest this text expresses, or better, constructs" (*Gender, Power, and Promise*, 16). Bal explains that the outlines of a text's subjectivity might be determined by asking the "simple questions: Who speaks? Who 'sees'? Who acts?" (*Lethal Love*, 21). This study defines subjectivity along similar lines, conceptualizing it as whose side the text is on. The perspective that a text takes, the characters whose dialogue and actions it relays—these help to express the text's own interests and allegiances. That the stories of Hagar, Dinah, and Tamar apportion a great deal of agency and perspective to outsider characters indicates a shift in the text's subjectivity, which normally revolves around ancestral characters.

21. Culler explains, "[T]o naturalize a text is to bring it into relation with a type of discourse or model which is already, in some sense, natural and legible" (*Structuralist Poetics*, 138). While Culler discusses naturalization in the broad context of codes of communication, this study uses it to refer more specifically to thematic comprehension. Here it indicates the way that readers of the ancestral narrative commonly bring the stories of Hagar, Dinah, and Tamar into alignment with the narrative program that they perceive in the main ancestral narrative. This tendency of reading finds expression in Aristotle, *Poet.* 1416a 31–34, which posits the integrity of a story and the necessity of each of its parts. If a part might be removed without consequence to the effect of the story, then it is not essential to the story. One might surmise, therefore, that readers endeavor to interpret the stranger parts as meaningfully related to what they perceive to be the whole.

22. Speiser, *Genesis*, 119.

of Sarah's motherhood renders it "a disappointing anticlimax," one that invites the reader to "wait and see" if Hagar and Ishmael indeed realize the divine promise of an heir.[23] Implicit within Speiser's reading is the common interpretation that Hagar and Ishmael provide dramatic contrast to the true realization of the promise in Sarah and Isaac.[24] The Dinah story "is unusual" in several ways: "it is the only account to concern itself with Jacob's daughter Dinah," "Jacob himself has a minor part" in what is otherwise his narrative, and "there is a pronounced chronological gap" between it and the preceding story.[25] This narrative incongruity notwithstanding, the story helpfully delineates an aspect of ancestral identity as it offers "an all but lost page [on] ethnic interrelations."[26] And the Tamar story is "a completely independent unit" with "no connection with the drama of Joseph, which it interrupts."[27] In its literary context, however, it serves to accentuate Joseph's character and to heighten suspense over his fate by means of his "temporary eclipse."[28] Joseph, in other words, remains the central focus of the narrative, and the Tamar story—apart from its significance as a brief glimpse into the history of Judah's lineage—is thus secondary to the narrative thrust. In each case, then, the strange story and its outsider characters are subordinated to primary themes detected in the encompassing ancestral narrative, which more often than not relate to ancestral identity. The question of the story's significance thus expires before the story's own peculiarity receives full consideration.[29]

23. Speiser, *Genesis*, 119.

24. For more discussion of this common interpretation, see the section "The Hagar Interludes as a Foil" in ch. 3 (p. 92).

25. Speiser, *Genesis*, 266.

26. Speiser, *Genesis*, 266.

27. Speiser, *Genesis*, 299.

28. Speiser implies the effect of suspense by pointing to how the reader's perspective is brought into alignment with the ancestral family's: "as far as they knew," Joseph was gone "forever" (*Genesis*, 300).

29. The expiration of this question, it is worth noting, derives largely from the traditional ways of reading narrative unity. Alter says that these ways subject the text to "tacit laws like the law of stylistic unity, of noncontradiction, of nondigression, of nonrepetition" (*The Art of Biblical Narrative*, 21). Alter offers an alternative view of narrative unity, one that prioritizes thematic rather than plot unity. Cf. Gunn and Fewell: "Meaning is not always the product of cause and effect or of chronological ordering. Meaning sometimes emerges through association" (*Narrative in the Hebrew Bible*, 23). The literary approach that Alter and Gunn and Fewell recommend steers away from shoehorning narratively peculiar episodes into the conventional, plot-centered schema constructed from the main narrative and instead brings into focus how these

The Logic of Narrative Strangeness and the Defamiliarization of a "Familiar" Story

This narrative logic of naturalization or unification, which forces the strange or outside elements to conform to the center, should not go uncontested, for there is a competing logic at work in narrative. Narrative and strangeness are inextricably intertwined. Narrative springs from strangeness. There is no reason to tell a story if it is not somehow strange or different from what a person knows or expects. William Labov and Joshua Waletzky broach this logic in their influential analysis of oral narrative. A story that only "recapitulat[es] experience," they explain, "may be considered empty or pointless narrative."[30] Narrative normally has a point, a point that distinguishes it from what is already known or expected.[31] Thus Labov and Waletzky conclude, "[M]ost narratives are so designed as to emphasize the strange and unusual character of the situation."[32] Although Labov and Waletzky's analysis pertains to oral narrative, their thesis has shaped discussion of narrative in a broader context. "Tellability" has become an important concept by which to explore the seeming necessity of strangeness to narrative.[33]

Although the finer details of the conversation on "tellability" lie beyond the scope of this study, its basic point suggests a way of reading strangeness that is worth considering. If strangeness is the mark of a story, of what makes it "tellable," then the stranger parts of the story are not peripheral; rather, they are central. Thus this study proposes that the interpretive move to unify the ancestral narrative—by subordinating the stories of Hagar, Dinah, and Tamar to the interests of the surrounding narrative—might find a legitimate counter in a reading that treats the strange stories not as outsiders to be naturalized but as a center themselves. Their strangeness flags them as integral to the life of the narrative. Rather than letting the rest of the ancestral narrative determine their

---

episodes often house thematic nuances that engage the main narrative in subtler, and sometimes unexpected, ways.

30. Labov and Waletzky, "Narrative Analysis," 13.

31. The necessity of strangeness to narrative is often manifest not only in the "point" of a narrative, but also in the narrative itself. Thus Aristotle and a longstanding literary tradition following him have privileged complex plots over simple ones—that is, plots that harbor surprise in the form of an unforeseeable twist. Cf. Currie, *The Unexpected*, 41–42.

32. Labov and Waletzky, "Narrative Analysis," 34.

33. Baroni, "Tellability."

significance, this study will explore how they might determine the significance of the ancestral narrative. Whereas traditional readings of the ancestral narrative have relegated the stories of Hagar, Dinah, and Tamar to interludes of secondary status, this study will privilege the stories' strangeness and thus resurrect the question that traditional readings have short-circuited—namely, the question of their peculiarity and its significance. Just what are these "strangers" doing in the ancestral narrative?

An intriguing harmony between two concepts already highlighted—family and strangeness—invites a moment of further reflection. Together these ideas resonate in the Russian formalist concept of "defamiliarization." Popularized by Viktor Shklovsky, *Ostranenie*, or defamiliarization, refers to the fundamental function of art "to make objects 'unfamiliar,' to make forms difficult, to increase the difficulty and length of perception."[34] Defamiliarization militates against habitualization, the phenomenon by which a symbol becomes automatically identified with its referent, such that their identity is taken for granted. "Habitualization," says Shklovsky, "devours works, clothes, furniture, one's wife, and the fear of war."[35] Art as defamiliarization, as a force that works against habitualization, "exists to make one feel things, to make the stone *stony*"; it is meant to "impart the sensation of things as they are perceived and not as they are known."[36]

The ancestral narrative is for many readers a "familiar" narrative—doubly so.[37] It is, first, about a family, the ancestral family: about its role in the divine program, about its relationship to the land and its inhabitants, about its lineage. Second, it is a narrative whose main characters are familiar to readers, many of whom attribute to the narrative an Israel-inclined perspective. As is often the case, familiarity translates to privilege. Familiarity with the ancestral family and its famed lineage entails that its identity is formulated in privileged, exclusive terms: "ancestral" means being divinely elect, having an exclusive claim to the land over against its inhabitants, and being of a pure, endogamous lineage. The strange stories of Hagar, Dinah, and Tamar, however, defamiliarize the narrative. They make strange, or unfamiliar, these thematic elements. Channeling alternative subjectivities and veering from the ancestral storyline, they show God in unexpected roles, the land and its inhabitants in

---

34. Shklovsky, "Art as Technique," 12.
35. Shklovsky, "Art as Technique," 12.
36. Shklovsky, "Art as Technique," 12.
37. Derived from the Latin *familiaris*, the word "familiar" accommodates not only the sense of "well-acquainted" but also the more literal meaning, "of a family."

unimagined relations with the ancestral family, and the family's lineage developing in an unplanned way. They problematize what is "known" about ancestral identity and encourage a reexamination of what might be "perceived." Just as a piece of art might invite Shklovsky to ask "What makes the stone *stony*?" the strange stories might invite the reader to ask, "What makes the ancestral family *ancestral*?" The ancestral family might not be as familiar as one thinks. What is ancestral—according to these stories—might lie beyond the family.

Qualification of Reading

The question of a story's narrative purpose—what are these strange stories doing in the ancestral narrative?—necessarily implies a quest for meaning. Therefore, before proposing this study's answer to the question, it is worth prefacing how this study will seek to arrive at its answer, that is, how it will make the quest for meaning, how it will approach the task of reading and interpreting. This study will operate primarily within the bounds of literary theory and, more specifically, narratology. It assumes the integrity of the text—specifically the Masoretic Text—and demarcates Genesis as an individual narrative. Although it may occasionally take recourse to other biblical texts, it will endeavor to honor the gaps and ambiguities in Genesis. Contrary to the many interpretations that interpolate concepts of biblical or historical Israelite identity or consider potential intertextual allusions, this study will read Genesis on its own terms as much as possible.[38]

In literary discourse, the quest for meaning has proposed numerous sources—most commonly the author, the text, and/or the reader. Biblical scholarship of the last two centuries has sought meaning particularly in relation to some origin. The objective of "original meaning" has been understood in several ways—for example, as an author's original intention or as an original meaning in the words of the text. Although these quests are valid within their own frameworks, this study will take a different approach. After briefly retracing Roland Barthes' and Michel Foucault's well-known cases against locating meaning in the author,[39] and, with the

---

38. This is not so much a decision made on principle but rather for practical reasons. In order to limit its purview to a manageable field, this study focuses on the most immediate content matter, namely Genesis. Worthwhile avenues for the exploration of Genesis' significance surely lie beyond it.

39. Barthes, *Image–Music–Text*, 142–48, and Foucault, "What Is an Author?"

help of Jonathan Culler, extending their argument to include the problem of locating meaning in text and reader, this study will suggest an alternative framework for understanding the search for meaning. This alternative framework will help to clarify the parameters and objectives of this reading.

Against Original Meaning

For many readers, the traditional limit of original meaning is the author, or more specifically the author's intention. On inspection, however, this limit meets with potential fracture. The author and the author's intention represent a variety of things. Barthes, for instance, claims that readers commonly hypostasize the author as "society, history, psyché, [or] liberty."[40] That is, the author (or one might substitute the author's intention) might be constituted as the convergence of certain elements of her society, historical context, singular psychological makeup, or inscrutable free will.[41] The necessary selection and configuration of elements means that each designation—of society, history, psyche, and so on—is subject to further fracture. On the matter of psyche, for instance, Foucault points out that a text is composed not by a unified writing subject, but rather from a multitude of subject positions that any person might occupy.[42] The subject that prefaces a work, for instance, is distinct from that which posits a conclusion. There is no inherent unifying thread that embraces all the subject positions traversed in a text. To talk of the author as an undivided psyche, one must necessarily select and configure among the subject positions read in the text.[43]

---

40. Barthes, *Image–Music–Text*, 147.

41. This study indiscriminately employs both male and female gender pronouns in reference to the abstract reader in order to flag the variability of readerly realization.

42. Foucault, "What Is an Author?" 129–30.

43. Foucault discusses this process of selection and configuration as it relates to the psyche of the author. The author, he points out, reflects not so much a person as a function of reading. That is, the subject positions within a text are measured according to a variety of factors and arranged to constitute the person of the author. Foucault identifies the historical precedent for this in Christian exegesis. He cites Jerome's four norms for determining—or one might say, constructing—authorship. The reader determines, or constructs, the author according to a (1) standard level of quality; (2) a "field of conceptual . . . coherence"; (3) a field of "stylistic uniformity"; and (4) a perceived "historical figure in which a series of events converge" ("What Is an Author?" 127–29). The author, in other words, becomes a function of an arrangement of certain subject

Others would escape the problem of limiting meaning in an author by relocating it to the text, to the words themselves. The text as the locus of meaning, however, falls upon a similar problem, for language is subject to unending displacement. As Barthes explains, "[T]he book itself is only a tissue of signs, an imitation that is lost, infinitely deferred."[44] Simply put, any text is "a tissue of quotations."[45] Thus it is always already intertextual. To locate meaning in the words of a text, one must necessarily take recourse to other texts. That is, one must select and configure among the meanings and relations of words.

Selecting and configuring, whether to locate the author or to determine the original meaning of the words themselves, presupposes a reader who makes these decisions. So while one side of the issue of original meaning consists in limiting the origin, the other side consists in the subjectivity of the reader who performs the limiting. The chronology of a reading experience exposes the latter side of the issue. Rather than the cause (an author or text) preceding the effect (a reader), the effect might be said to precede the cause. That is, reading affects the reader, and then the reader attributes a cause, an original meaning, on the basis of the effect.[46] Original meaning, then, is not a unique object that may be uncovered with the right selection and configuration of elements, but is rather always already a construct of the affected reader.

The reader, however, is no final arbiter of meaning because the reader, abstractly conceived, is not a person but a position or role that is endlessly actualized. And even in each actualization, the reader is not a unified person whose undivided experience can harmonize meaning. As Culler explains, "[T]here is always a gap or division within reading."[47] He illustrates this gap with three basic examples. First, the notion of the "suspension of disbelief" suggests a disunity in the same act of reading between the reader who remains aware of the story's fictional nature and the reader who naïvely accepts it at its word. Second, the reading of

---

positions read within the text. Although Jerome's norms no longer hold in quite the same way, Foucault suggests that the modern idea of the author parallels them, particularly as it posits the author as the perceived unity and coherence in the thought and expression of a work or a corpus of works.

44. Barthes, *Image–Music–Text*, 147.
45. Barthes, *Image–Music–Text*, 146.
46. Culler, *On Deconstruction*, 86–88, expounds on this phenomenon along deconstructive lines.
47. Culler, *On Deconstruction*, 67.

characters reveals a reader who anthropomorphizes and psychologizes them and a reader who treats them as tools of the narrator, as parts that mediate the plot. Third, the appreciation of the suspense in a story whose end is already known indicates that the reader who knows the end nonetheless enjoys the suspense because she reads through the eyes of a reader who does not know.[48] In each case, the reader demonstrates conflicting relations to the text. She believes yet disbelieves, immerses herself in the story world yet stands at a distance, knows yet remains ignorant.

All three traditional sources of original meaning—author, text, and reader—are therefore problematic. The author, as the hypostasis of history, psyche, society, liberty, or a configuration of these elements, is subject to fracture. The text, as "a tissue of quotations," is subject to displacement. The reader, who assumes responsibility for inscribing the limits of author or text, would therefore appear to be the source of original meaning. But even the reader is subject to division, as she simultaneously assumes a multiplicity of reading positions.

A Story of Reading

While the idea of an original, unified meaning—whether in the author, the text, or the reader—entails the potential for conflict, the discourse of interpretation continues to employ it. (It is worth noting here that literary discourse has generally dropped the notion of the author, identifying it as an especially speculative enterprise that distracts from the more immediate players in a reading experience, the text and the reader.) Quite understandably, then, the discourse of interpretation meets with conflict. As Culler demonstrates, the practice of locating an original, unified meaning in one source continually belies itself.[49] He notes in reader-oriented criticism, for example, "how easily text and reader can switch places: a story of the reader structuring the text easily becomes a story of the text provoking certain responses and actively controlling the reader."[50]

---

48. Culler, *On Deconstruction*, 67–68.

49. Culler notes a general "monism of theory" and "dualism of narrative" (*On Deconstruction*, 70–75). In other words, theory tends to situate meaning fully in text or reader or some particular configuration of the two, but then it weaves a narrative of meaning that cannot help but tell a dynamic story of text and reader, a story of two distinct agents in flux.

50. Culler, *On Deconstruction*, 70–73. Culler explores this phenomenon in selected works of Barthes, Umberto Eco, and Stanley Fish.

Rather than disavowing this tendency, however, Culler asserts its necessity. The text and the reader comprise a paradox in which each assumes full autonomy. He explains this by way of an analogy to jokes, which both determine and are determined by the listener's response:

> The listener does not control the outburst of laughter: the text provokes it (the joke, one says, *made me* laugh). But on the other hand, the unpredictable response determines the nature of the text that is supposed to have produced it. No compromise formulation, with the reader partly in control and the text partly in control, would accurately describe this situation, which is captured, rather, by juxtaposition of two absolute perspectives. The shift back and forth in stories of reading is not a mistake that could be corrected but an essential structural feature of the situation.[51]

Interpretation, therefore, is not an objective account of a story's original meaning. It is, rather, itself a story—a "story of reading."[52] It stages text and reader in a dramatic encounter, in which the boundaries of the two are blurred as they tangle with and determine one other, bearing a meaning that is irreducible to the limits of any one origin.

This paradoxical understanding of text and reader informs this study's understanding of its own project. What follows in the analysis of the stories of Hagar, Dinah, and Tamar is another "story of reading," to be added to and compared with the many stories that have preceded it. It will stage a reader, one who is drawn from an experience "divided and deferred."[53] In other words, the reader of this story will find embodiment in past reading experiences, in the conventional ancestor-centered lines of interpretation, as well as in inventive, imagined experiences, in alternative interpretive trajectories. And it will stage a text, one that is drawn both from the ways it has conventionally structured interpretation and from its unforeseeable, defamiliarizing provocations. In other words, the text will emerge both in its traditional guise, with its seemingly incontrovertible interest in the ancestral family, and in an unsettling strangeness, which seems to controvert this same interest. The confrontation between

---

51. Culler, *On Deconstruction*, 73.

52. See the section title of Culler's exploration of theories of the locus of meaning: "Stories of Reading," in *On Deconstruction*, 64–83.

53. Culler articulates the experience of reading as "divided and deferred—already behind us as something to be recovered, yet still before us as something to be produced" (*On Deconstruction*, 82).

multifarious text and reader will propel a story that moves from old to new, from prevailing to pioneering interpretation, from what the reader and text have said in the past to what they insist on now, in light of this study's considerations.

This study's appreciation of the complex textual and readerly factors that contribute to a story of reading, furthermore, will inevitably entail a strategy of reading that privileges the concept of irony, because irony acutely demonstrates the dynamics of any story of reading—the irreducible interplay between text and reader. It illustrates how a text's effect is different from a literal reading, how a reader's interpretation confirms a meaning different from what a text ostensibly says. Like a joke, irony offers a particularly salient demonstration of the play of meaning. Even as one reader might say, "This *text* is ironic," another might say, "*I* read no irony." Irony makes the reason for this paradox of text and reader especially pronounced in a couple of ways. First, as a quotation of a proposition from which the quoter dissociates herself, irony entails a rejection of an apparent meaning at the same time as it encourages the quest for another meaning. Most readers would be reluctant to admit an arbitrary rejection of the apparent meaning; the text, they say, provoked the rejection. But the loss of the apparent meaning demands, in turn, another meaning, one that by irony's definition the text never says. The text, it appears, determines the rejection of a meaning, but it cannot determine its surrogate; only the reader can.[54] Second, in a case of irony, the text evaluatively appropriates a prior discourse: it quotes a previously voiced proposition and hints at the proposition's inadequacy in the current context. By highlighting the reflexivity of discourse, however, it suggests that its own move may be mirrored by the reader, who may just as well reappropriate the words.[55] Thus the line between text and reader is

---

54. Hutcheon, *Irony's Edge*, 7. Hutcheon hints at this phenomenon by pointing out that irony precludes its own explanation. Irony in this regard, she explains, is like a joke. Explanation deflates its effect. Thus irony enjoys a determinative effect but necessarily lacks explanation. The explanation, or interpretation, can only be provided retrospectively by the reader. Cf. Sharp: "Irony demands attention to cues and clues that originate from the text, yet its very presence deconstructs any simplistic construal of intent" (*Irony and Meaning in the Hebrew Bible*, 62). Irony's effect, in other words, seems naturally rooted in the text, yet any explanation of ironic meaning must transcend the text.

55. Sharp explains, "[T]he control of the ironist is actually a parody of control. The ironic authorial voice offers an imitation of control that purposefully undermines its own authority even as it asserts it" (*Irony and Meaning in the Hebrew Bible*, 44). A text's appropriation of a prior discourse uncovers its own vulnerability (as a discourse) to readerly reappropriation.

blurred, and the question of who or what determines the irony is never quite settled.

To summarize this qualification of reading, one might say that this study's appreciation for irony and the interplay of text and reader stems from a broader methodological rule, one that encapsulates the objective of this study and outlines the direction of its story of reading. In an effort to attend to the strangeness of the stories of Hagar, Dinah, and Tamar, to take them on their own terms rather than to subordinate them to the surrounding narrative, this study will exercise an interpretive flexibility, drawing from both attested interpretations of the ancestral narrative and imagined interpretations inspired by the particularities of the strange stories. Together these interpretations offer this study's story of reading, a tale of how conventional readings can be turned inside out. This study will, furthermore, exercise a self-conscious posture that reflects on the justification for its interpretive choices. The methodology of literary, and more specifically narratological, theory will ground this study's interpretive moves and, moreover, situate the study in an established discourse that might evaluate its claims accordingly.

An Overview of This Story of Reading: Of Interludes and Irony

Having introduced this study's question as well as the parameters for answering it, it remains now to outline the proposed answer. In response to the question of the strange stories' narrative purpose, this study submits its thesis: *the strange stories are interludes that ironize ancestral identity.*

By proposing both a structural function for the stories (they are interludes) and a way of interpreting them (they ironize ancestral identity), this thesis embarks on the joint project of advancing a poetics and a hermeneutics. That is, it confronts two interrelated questions. Poetics asks *how* texts mean. Hermeneutics asks *what* texts mean.[56] Poetics is the theory of signification. It examines the text as a cause, investigating the signifying function of its elements, such as words, syllables, and sounds,

---

56. Culler offers a helpful explanation of both terms. "Poetics starts with attested meanings or effects and asks how they are achieved," while hermeneutics "starts with texts and asks what they mean, seeking to discover new and better interpretations" (*Literary Theory*, 61). Culler locates the fundamental difference between the two approaches in their relation to meaning: meanings are the "point of departure" for poetics but the final destination for hermeneutics.

or (more abstractly) settings, characters, and events. Hermeneutics is the theory of interpretation. It explores the results of the text, the interpretations that it can yield. Adele Berlin illumines the distinction with an analogy: "If literature is likened to a cake, then poetics gives us the recipe and interpretation tells us how it tastes."[57]

The relation between poetics and hermeneutics is not easily defined, in large part because reading consists in a sort of infinite spiral from one activity to the other and back again. Literary theorist Tzvetan Todorov explains: "Neither of these two activities takes precedence over the other: both are 'secondary.'"[58] A hermeneutics can only develop within the framework of a poetics, a theory (or less technically, an understanding) of how a story communicates meaning; but that poetics can only develop from the experience of reading stories and making the hermeneutic endeavor to interpret them . . . and so on. The quest for a definite starting point of the reading experience is thus quixotic.

And yet one must start somewhere. The observation of the strangeness of the stories of Hagar, Dinah, and Tamar and the question of their narrative purpose constitutes the starting point of this study. Beginning at this point, this study will first seek out a poetics for the stories. It will consider how the stories are strange and how they might function in their strangeness. Then it will suggest a suitable hermeneutics. It will consider what sorts of interpretations qualify for making sense of the strange stories. Finally, within the framework of this poetics and hermeneutics, it will undertake specific interpretations of the stories to explore how they realize their proposed narrative function. The remainder of the introduction details this progression chapter by chapter.

The Stories as Interludes

Chapter 1 tackles the question of poetics, which is not, it is important to note, a question of poetics proper. Whereas the goal of poetics proper is "to propose a theory of the structure and functioning of literary discourse" as an entirety,[59] this study's poetical question limits the task

---

57. Berlin, *Poetics and Interpretation*, 15. Berlin's reference to interpretation rather than hermeneutics hints at a subtle distinction worth noting. A hermeneutics is a theory of interpretation. An act of interpretation, then, is not identical to hermeneutics but rather instantiates a hermeneutics, that is, a way of interpreting.

58. Todorov, *Introduction to Poetics*, 8.

59. Todorov states that poetics proper seeks the "laws within literature itself" (*Introduction to Poetics*, 6–7).

to identifying and understanding some of the specific literary building blocks that comprise the ancestral narrative and the strange stories within. It concentrates on the literary design that underlies the ancestral narrative and explores how elements like subjectivity, themes and motifs, and plot structure meaning. It asks: how are the stories of Hagar, Dinah, and Tamar strange? How might they function in their strangeness?[60]

Because biblical interpretation commonly identifies the stories of Hagar, Dinah, and Tamar as "interludes," this study proposes the concept of interlude as a model for the poetics of these stories. While scholarship generally applies the term to the stories to indicate that they are intermediately positioned and secondary in terms of narrative significance, the concept itself suggestively harbors a more comprehensive sense. Certain musical interludes, for instance, do not merely interrupt the main work; they also provide a meaningful contrast to it and develop its thematic material. This study configures its poetics of the interlude around the suggestions of these musical interludes and explores how the strange stories may develop primary thematic content. While readers typically allow the primary narrative to determine the significance of the strange stories, this poetics illumines how the strange stories may determine aspects of the primary narrative.

The Stories as Ironic

Having established *how* the strange stories might function—namely, as interludes that contrast to and develop the ancestral narrative's themes of ancestral identity—this study approaches in Chapter 2 the question of *what* they might mean. Berlin elucidates the logic of this analytical progression: "Poetics aids interpretation. If we know *how* texts mean, we are in a better position to discover *what* a particular text means."[61] In other words, poetics offers "a number of useful categories for examining and describing" the textual object of interpretation.[62] It clarifies the story

---

60. That is, this study aims to derive a poetics that attends to how certain literary elements distinguish the stories of Hagar, Dinah, and Tamar from the main ancestral narrative—and how the patterns of these elements inform the relation between these stories and the main ancestral narrative. Berlin explains: "If the same things are said, and said in the same way, often enough, then some general conclusions can be drawn, some poetical principles discovered" (*Poetics and Interpretation*, 20).

61. Berlin, *Poetics and Interpretation*, 17.

62. Todorov and Weinstein, "Structural Analysis of Narrative," 73.

of reading. Having explored both the elements that constitute the interludes' strangeness and how these elements inform their relation to the main ancestral narrative, this study can explore more closely the range of meanings that they might assume.

In particular, this study will propose that a hermeneutics of irony befits a reading of the interludes. Irony facilitates interpretation of the way that the interludes defamiliarize primary thematic material and suggests how the interludes might engage the narrative's principal focus on ancestral identity in subversive ways. To be sure, irony is not itself a final answer to the question of what the stories mean. It does, however, approach what they might mean. It narrows the range of meanings—irony at least indicates what is *not* meant—and therefore focuses the task of interpretation. It is to this task that the rest of the study will be devoted.

Close Ironic Readings of the Interludes

Chapters 3, 4, and 5 offer close ironic readings of the interludes of Hagar, Dinah, and Tamar. Each close reading will advance along a similar interpretive path. First, it will address the traditional interpretation of the interlude. It will explore how conventional readings naturalize the interlude, how they unify it with the main narrative and make sense of its strangeness in terms of the encompassing narrative's predominant interests. Second, it will offer an alternative reading, one that originates from an encounter in which the text resists the conventional reading, in which this study's reader finds himself stumbling over a distinct narratological peculiarity in the text. If the ancestral family tree is understood as the main interest of a conventional reading, then an unexpected root in the ground—a gnarled narratological protrusion—represents the singular starting point of each alternative reading. For this reason, the alternative readings will not share the same narratological focal point. What unites the close readings together are their results. The alternative readings each elicit an ironic interpretation that engages and develops a thematic aspect of ancestral identity: respectively, the ancestral family's relationship with God, its relationship with the land and its inhabitants, and its relationship with itself. The third and final segment of the close reading will therefore trace the irony of the interlude and the resultant thematic development.

A thumbnail overview of each close reading reflects the varied narratological foci and unified thematic interpretation of this study's story of reading. Chapter 3 illustrates the *mise en abyme* of Hagar's identity—she is a sojourner whose story mirrors the larger story of the ancestral sojourners—and explores how it ironizes the oft-presumed exclusivity of the ancestral–divine relationship. Chapter 4 detects an act of ventriloquy in the Dinah interlude and investigates how it ironizes Dinah's brothers' exclusivist mode of relations toward the land and its inhabitants. Chapter 5 probes the Tamar interlude's many allusions to ancestral birth narratives and considers how they ironize traditional formulations of ancestral self-identity, particularly in terms of matriarchal and patriarchal norms and the ideal of endogamous relations.

Summary

To recapitulate, this study asks the question: what are the strange stories of Hagar, Dinah, and Tamar doing in the ancestral narrative? Whereas traditional interpretation makes sense of them in terms of the surrounding ancestral narrative, this study privileges their strangeness and asks how they might defamiliarize a familiar narrative. To answer this question, this study embarks on a story of reading, a tale of text and reader that traverses interpretations both old and new. Its interpretive flexibility notwithstanding, this story of reading treads along a distinguishable path, one marked out by a poetics of the interlude and a hermeneutics of irony. This path suggests that the strange stories share in a common function, namely developing—more specifically, ironizing—themes of ancestral identity: the ancestral–divine relationship, ancestral relations to the land and its inhabitants, and ancestral self-identity. As this story of reading will demonstrate, the strange stories and the strangers within them decenter the ancestral family. They subvert conventional definitions of ancestral identity by exposing their permeable, provisional nature. Ancestral identity may be contained *in* the ancestral family, but it is not contained *by* it.

1

Poetics:
The Interlude as a Narrative Structure

READERS FREQUENTLY IDENTIFY THE Hagar, Dinah, and Tamar stories as interludes. This chapter seizes on this label as a point of entry for exploring the structure and function of the strange stories. The concept of interlude bears a range of connotations, particularly in the musical domain. Analogizing narratives identified as interludes to musical interludes, this chapter advances a poetics of the interlude. That is, it appropriates the musical concept of interlude as a way for understanding the structure and function of the strange stories within the ancestral narrative. Taking the sonata-rondo episode as a particular model for what interlude can mean in a fuller sense, it demonstrates how the Hagar, Dinah, and Tamar stories, which are normally read in a more limited way, can indeed constitute interludes of a more complete order.

A Poetics of the Interlude

A shift in interest point of view and a disjunctive relation to the surrounding plot distinguish the stories of Hagar, Dinah, and Tamar from the ancestral narrative. Less focused on the ancestral family and its concerns, the stories seem disconnected from and irrelevant to the ancestral narrative. Thus many readings situate them on the periphery. In this sense, these stories accord etymologically with their common tag "interlude." They happen "between" the "play,"[1] that is, between what

---

1. Dictionaries trace the word's etymology back to the medieval Latin *interludium*, to *inter* ("between") and *ludus* ("play").

really matters in the narrative. They are intermediately positioned and secondary in terms of significance. Surfacing between stories of ancestral patriarchs, matriarchs, and their march toward the fulfillment of the divine promises, the interludes furnish a perspective on marginal interests, on matters that distract from the main ancestral drama. Thus the Hagar "interludes" retard fulfillment of God's covenant, while simultaneously offering a glimpse of the "diselected."[2] The Dinah "interlude" diverts attention away from Jacob,[3] recounting instead a story of his daughter and sons—a story that again retards fulfillment of the covenant, as Jacob's holdings in the land prove short-lived. The Tamar "interlude" takes a brief detour from the Joseph story to focus instead on his brother Judah's foibles;[4] once more, the interlude delays progression of the main story,

---

2. For readers who refer to Gen 16:1-16 and/or Gen 21:8-21 as interludes, see Good, who identifies Ishmael's birth as "an interlude between promise and fulfillment" (*Irony in the Old Testament*, 92); Speiser, who describes Gen 16:1-16 as "an interlude of acute suspense" concerning the identity of Abram's heir (*Genesis*, 119); Hackett, who confers upon both stories the label "interlude" on account of the fact that either Hagar or Ishmael, rather than an ancestral character, is "at the center of things" ("Rehabilitating Hagar," 24). The term "diselected" alludes to the conceptualization of "diselection," outlined in Heard, *Dynamics of Diselection*. Heard conceptualizes "diselection" as the converse of election, the process by which characters are chosen for the special covenantal relationship with God. Diselection refers to the related process by which certain characters are separated from the characters who become the "elect."

3. For readers who refer to Gen 34 as an interlude, see Fishbane, who characterizes the chapter as an "interlude" that functions to "divert the pace of the Jacob cycle" (*Text and Texture*, 48); Rendsburg, who likewise identifies the chapter as an "interlude" that offsets the progression of the Jacob cycle (*The Redaction of Genesis*, 56–59); Kille, who appears to follow Fishbane's and Rendsburg's readings, and posits that the "interlude" "does not advance the story of Jacob so much as link the Jacob narrative with the events that will follow, when the focus turns to his sons" ("Jacob," 79); Turner, who acknowledges the general tendency to identify Gen 34 as "an interlude in the patriarchal story," although Turner himself disavows such an identification (*Genesis*, 151); Jeansonne, who labels the story as "the interlude at Shechem," presumably indicating the temporary nature of Jacob's stay near the city (*The Women of Genesis*, 91).

4. For readers who refer to Gen 38 as an interlude, see Good, who refers to Gen 38 as "a sort of 'meanwhile, back at the ranch' interlude while Joseph gets to Egypt" (*Irony in the Old Testament*, 107); Arnold, who explains, "In the literary flow of Genesis, this chapter is an interlude, building suspense about what will happen to Joseph in Egypt" (*Genesis*, 325); Rendsburg, who labels the chapter as an "interlude" because "Joseph [is] not present" (*The Redaction of Genesis*, 80); Kugler and Hartin, who labels the chapter as "interlude" on account of its departure from the Joseph story (*An Introduction to the Bible*, 62); Brodie, who characterizes the chapter as "an early interlude" that "allow[s] the story to develop," as it "intimates some of what follows, especially concerning Judah himself" (*Genesis as Dialogue*, 295).

which is said to concern Joseph's and his family's salvation from their respective predicaments.

Readers' common classification of the strange stories as "interludes" volunteers the concept as a guide for this study's project of poetics. Poetics, to recapitulate, consists in positing a theory of how texts mean, which is also to say, how readers can draw meaning from texts. It proposes structures of signification that outline possibilities for interpretation. As a musical concept, interlude is rich with suggestions for how one might understand the structures of signification that underlie a strange segment within a larger composition. For this reason, this study submits a poetics that analogizes narratives identified as interludes to musical interludes. If readers generally identify the strange stories as interludes, then it makes sense to subject interpretation of the stories to the full range of the concept's connotations. Put simply, the different ways that persons have understood and used the concept of interlude sketch out the different ways that readers can interpret narrative structures that are thus identified.

While analogies drawn between music and literature still meet with ambivalent responses from scholars in both fields, this study hopes to demonstrate that, the verbal/nonverbal distinction between music and texts notwithstanding, such analogies may prove instructive, particularly as both fields seek to understand the signification of their respective forms. In his essay "Brucknerian Transpositions," Hugh S. Pyper points one promising way forward for developing these sorts of analogies. He begins by citing an article by musicologist Derek B. Scott that draws an analogy from biblical narrative to illumine the puzzling structures of Bruckner's symphonies. Both works, Scott posits, are comprised of "non-culminative and fissured structures,"[5] or, as Pyper reformulates this insight, both "pose similar problems to their composers in maintaining coherence and clarity across attention spans and therefore similar problems to critics and audiences in coming to grips with the formal solutions that they propose."[6] Thus the structure and function of biblical narrative may help musicologists to account for Bruckner's symphonies, which fail "to fit the expected norm of cumulative and seamless musical argument."[7] Pyper then entertains the possibility of reversing the direction of analogy. "For biblical scholars, are there useful musical analogies which might

---

5. Scott, "Bruckner's Symphonies," 103–4, cited in Pyper, *The Unchained Bible*, 123.
6. Pyper, *The Unchained Bible*, 124.
7. Pyper, *The Unchained Bible*, 124.

open our eyes to the fact that our expectations and understanding of form and structure in biblical books could be expanded?" He specifically designates questions of musical form and the history of musical analysis as interrelated sources for fruitful music-to-Bible analogies. That is, how musical forms are received in the various "social and cultural dimensions" of history might inform how form and structure within the biblical text has been, or can be, understood.[8] Edward Said similarly suggests the benefit of analogies that address the relation between a work's formal structure and its possibilities of signification. In particular, he posits the merit of analogies between music and literature. The literary and musical, he explains, are similar in the way that they signify through the internal relations of their components. Just as literature operates according to a centripetal force, in which words find meaning in their relation to other words internal to a work, so too with music: its "sonorous material" is relatively unique to the ear and must be considered in its own internal relations.[9]

For the purposes of this study, Pyper's and Said's insights invite consideration of how the relation between musical forms and musicology's understanding of their signification can inform a poetics of comparable literary forms. How music historians and musicologists understand the form and function of interlude illumines a poetics of those narratives that receive the same label.

The Interlude as a Musical Concept

Scholarship traditionally understands the stories of Hagar, Dinah, and Tamar as interludes in the sense of their being intermediately positioned and thematically secondary to the ancestral narrative. A poetics of the interlude, however, extends beyond this sense of the concept. Interlude bears a range of connotations. The musical interlude, in particular, demonstrates not only positional and hierarchical implications, but also relational and functional aspects.

One secondary definition plainly states the interlude's contrastive relation to its surroundings: "a temporary amusement or diversion that contrasts with what goes before or after."[10] This aspect features in several

---

8. Pyper, *The Unchained Bible*, 125.
9. Barenboim and Said, *Parallels and Paradoxes*, 119–20.
10. "Interlude," *Oxford Dictionary of English*.

drama- and music-related uses of the word. For example, the operatic *intermezzo*, or interlude, refers to the "short, comic entertainment inserted between the acts of a serious opera, often including grotesque elements."[11] Although it is perhaps less commonly acknowledged than the interlude's connotation of contrastive relations, a functional connotation of development is also housed within the concept. As one dictionary of opera explains, the interlude sometimes "describ[es] or summariz[es] events between scenes," and in dramatic form can "take the form of a scene to some degree outside the main plot" that nonetheless develops or advances the plot (e.g., in *Moses und Aron*, the passing of forty days and the people's developing doubt regarding God and Moses).[12] Another mark of the interlude's developmental function can be found in the *intermedi*, or interludes, of Italian renaissance drama, a form that preceded the opera and its *intermezzo*. Intermedi "frequently had an allegorical connection with the substance of the main plot."[13] In this sense, they expanded on the main content of the work and contributed to a "continuous, if interrupted, story."[14]

The identification of the sonata form's development section and the sonata-rondo's episode as interludes highlights the idea that the interlude may function to develop primary thematic material. In particular, two German musicological terms synonymous with interlude, *Zwischensatz* and *Zwischenspiel*, invite the identification of the sonata's development and the sonata-rondo's episode as interludes. *Zwischensatz*—or "between units"—refers to "[t]he middle section in ternary form," or more specifically "the development section in sonata-form."[15] Corroborating the identification of the sonata's development as an interlude, musician and theorist Percy Goetschius explains that the development "gr[ew] out of the brief *interlude* of the sonatine-form."[16] Goetschius' comment flags the evolution of sonata form as a phenomenon worth remarking upon. The evolution of sonata form marks one way that the concept of interlude ripens into a fuller form. The sonata's development models those aspects

11. "Intermezzo," *The Concise Oxford Dictionary of Opera*, 244.
12. "Intermezzo," *The Concise Oxford Dictionary of Opera*, 244.
13. "Intermedio," *The Concise Oxford Dictionary of Opera*, 244.
14. "Intermedio," *The Concise Oxford Dictionary of Opera*, 244.
15. "Zwischensatz," *Harvard Dictionary of Music*, 933. Sonata form mirrors ternary form in its thematic progression
16. Goetschius, *Lessons in Music Form*, 154. My emphasis. Sonatine-form refers here to the binary form forerunner of sonata form.

that suggest what interlude might signify in a more robust, developed sense—not only intermediate and secondary, but also contrastive and developmental.

In view of the fact that *Zwischenspiel*, the etymological equivalent to interlude, can refer to episodes in rondo form, it will be further worth remarking upon the sonata form's continued evolution into sonata-rondo form. The episodes in sonata-rondo form, which resemble the development in sonata form, point to an even more enhanced sense of interlude—one that allows for a heightened function of development and the phenomenon of multiple interludes in a single work. A poetics of the interlude thus finds in the sonata-rondo episode a model for what an interlude approaching its maximum semantic capacity might signify. It remains, therefore, to trace the evolution of the sonata and sonata-rondo in order to appreciate how the concept of interlude has filled out, and how it has assumed the function of development as one of its most integral features.

The Sonata-Rondo Episode as a Model for Interlude

This study now embarks on a review of how the musical interlude evolved in the sonata and the sonata-rondo, how it fleshed out and acquired the sense of being not only intermediate and secondary, but also thematically contrastive and developmental. This evolution maps out a suggestive analogue for the interludes of the ancestral narrative. Although readers have traditionally conceived of these stories as interludes in the more limited sense of the word, the musical concept as exemplified by the sonata and the sonata-rondo invites consideration of how these stories might actually signify in a richer way.

While this overview of the sonata and sonata-rondo will delve into technical detail at points, the main points for the reader's consideration remain intelligible without a background in music and are flagged here for the reader to remember. They are that the sonata and sonata-rondo introduce a concept of interlude that means more than being intermediately positioned and secondary in terms of narrative significance; it also means providing a meaningful contrast to the main work and developing its thematic material.

Sonata form became a distinct, codified musical structure during the Classical era. It evolved primarily from binary form, which had prevailed as a popular means of structuring music in the Baroque period. Binary form consists of two main themes, each in a different key (often I and V, or i and III). The two themes (A and B) are typically repeated once and set in tension with one another—that is, something like AABB. Over time, binary form metamorphosed into a more nuanced arrangement that allowed for something different between an exposition of the two main themes and a recapitulation of those same themes—that is, ABABCAB. Although this "something different" contrasted with the main themes, it was not *completely* different. It often took fragmented motifs from the main themes and reintroduced them in new, shifting contexts. Sometimes it modified the motifs themselves, employing techniques such as contrapuntal inversion.[17] In sum, it comprised "unstable" music that re-introduced existent, if nuanced, thematic strains in unfamiliar contexts, creating "a sense of breakup and turmoil" amid the more structured exposition and recapitulation of the themes.[18] Gradually this "something different" became an established part of the evolving sonata form. It fittingly assumed the name "development."

To appreciate how the evolution of the sonata's development section marks a more complex conceptualization of interlude, it helps to trace the singularity of the development, the exceptional characteristics that define its interludal intrusion into binary form. This singularity consists primarily in the different character of the development's thematic tension. First, whereas binary form expresses thematic tension through an outright tonal-thematic opposition between two different themes (A in I/i and B in V/III), the thematic tension of the development inheres in a subtler, more interconnected *contrast*. The development borrows the main themes' motifs, tweaks them, and appropriates them in unexpected contexts, against a tonally unstable backdrop (that is, not only in V/III, but in other keys as well). It constitutes a meaningful contrast to the primary thematic material because it engages that material, thus making it comparable, but in a defamiliarized fashion, thus inviting inspection of its difference. The development is not extraneous material, irrelevant and incomparable. It is, rather, material whose contrast assumes significance

---

17. Rosen enumerates the "techniques of thematic transformation": "(1) fragmentation; 2) deformation; 3) use of themes (or fragments) in an imitative contrapuntal texture; 4) transposition and arrangement in a rapidly modulating sequence" (*Sonata Forms*, 250).

18. Kerman and Tomlinson, with Kerman, *Listen*, 181.

precisely because it engages meaningful primary themes but in different terms.

Second, the tension roused by the development defies the listener's expectation[19] and thus contributes to a genuine thematic *development*, one that is unscripted and independent of the piece's formal strictures. To be sure, the listener expects tension in both binary form and the sonata, as a measure of strain and friction inhere in the standard tonal-thematic opposition between the two main themes (A in I/i and B in V/III).[20] But binary form controls the conflict. It presents the conflict within structured bounds: there are two different themes, they will assume a predictable tonal relationship, and they will proceed according to an established sequence. Within this predetermined structure, there is little room for development. In the sonata form's development, these bounds fall away, and the difference spirals uncontrolled in a kaleidoscope of motifs mixed and distorted, defamiliarized in their new melodic relations and tonal contexts. Here the primary thematic material undergoes an authentic development. It submits to a dynamic, unprogrammed transformation and as a result realizes unexpected possibilities of signification. Therefore, as an interlude, a segment "between" the "play," the development nevertheless contributes significantly to the play. It plays with thematic material, subjecting it to unpredictable variation and alteration, molding it in new relations and against new backgrounds—in a word, showing how it can sound different.

To recapitulate, the thematic tension roused by the sonata's development distinguishes itself from binary form's structured thematic dichotomy by its *contrast*, which springs from the development's thematic integration and defamiliarization, and its function of *development*, which derives from the development's unprogrammed motivic play. In other words, unlike binary form's thematic dichotomy, the sonata's development does not introduce an altogether new theme; it blends together existent themes in a defamiliarized medley of motifs. And it does not present the thematic tension in a predictable sequence; it innovates various configurations of motifs and sets them against a volatile tonal backdrop.

---

19. Hepokoski and Darcy distinguish the development's texture as "more unpredictable" than that of the exposition or recapitulation (*Elements of Sonata Theory*, 19).

20. Stein, *Structure and Style*, 106. Stein posits that the principle of contrast in the Baroque forms of music that preceded sonata form inhered primarily in the tonal difference rather than in any marked thematic opposition.

What might be summarized as *motivic interchange*, then, is integral to the tension of the sonata's development. Whereas previous forms clearly demarcate themes and the motifs that comprise them, sonata form embraces motivic development across its different sections. So Charles Rosen observes of Joseph Haydn, one of the chief innovators of sonata form, that his sonatas allow "each motif" to "penetrate to every part of the work" to the effect that "his sonata forms are elucidated by the development of the motif."[21] Of course, the sonata form's recapitulation returns largely to the original expressions of the two main themes and their motifs (albeit now wholly in I); the development's inventive exploration of the motifs does not irreversibly change them. Nevertheless, it does "develop" them. It adjusts the frame within which the listener hears their restatement in the recapitulation. It activates particular potentialities of the motifs that, though engaged only for the duration of the development, remain in the memory of the listener and alter the listening context of those motifs' restatement in the recapitulation. To appropriate a sentimental but illustrative image from Henry Ward Beecher: "[W]hen one, walking the winter street, sees the door opened for some one to enter, and the red light streams a moment forth, and the forms of gay children are running to greet the comer, and genial music sounds, though the door shuts and leaves the night black, yet it cannot shut back again all that the eyes, the ear, the heart, and the imagination have seen."[22] Though the recapitulation figuratively "shuts" the door on the development, still it cannot "shut back again" all that has been heard.

At this stage, the sonata's development section shows the interlude to be capable of meaningful thematic contrast and development. The interlude not only sits in between the primary parts of the piece; it also engages primary themes in a way that contrasts them with their original expression and develops their possibilities of signification. The unpredictable motivic interchange of the sonata's development, which fosters this contrastive and developmental character, reaches even greater heights in sonata form's most complex offshoot, sonata-rondo form.[23] Sonata-rondo form seems to have derived from the sonata form's appropriation of elements of the rondo—or its predecessor, the French Baroque *rondeau*—which follows the general progression ABACA (in which the

21. Rosen, *Sonata Forms*, 181.

22. Beecher, *Life Thoughts*, 11.

23. Caplin characterizes the sonata-rondo structure as "perhaps the most complex of the classical forms" (*Classical Form*, 235).

episodes B and C are two distinct interludes among the refrains).[24] The progression of the sonata-rondo is theoretically ABACAB1A, although in practice it often undergoes further modification.[25] The sonata-rondo distinguishes itself from the rondo primarily by its developmental, rather than sequential, handling of themes[26] (which, one could surmise, derives from its roots in sonata form). Regardless of its exact thematic sequence, the sonata-rondo entails thematic integration across its refrain-episode structure. That is, thematic fragments, or motifs, from the refrain commonly feature in the episodes alongside their episodic counterparts. Below is an example, which outlines the main motifs in the Rondo of Mozart's Piano Sonata K. 309:

$a\,b$ (in I)	$c\,d\,e\,f$ (in V)	a (in I)	d (in I) g (in IV)	(Absent)	$c\,d\,e\,a\,f$ (in I)	$c\,b\,a$ (in I)
A (Refrain)	B (Episode)	A (Refrain)	C (Episode)	A (Refrain)	B¹ (Episode)	A (Refrain)

[27]

As per his custom, Mozart omits the third refrain. What is more noteworthy, however, is the thematic exchange: his incorporation of a motif (a) from the refrain in the third episode, and likewise his incorporation of an episodic fragment (c) in his final refrain, which functions here as a coda. This example demonstrates the motivic integration across refrain and episode common to the sonata-rondo form.[28] The episodes engage motifs from the refrain, and in turn their own motifs make their way into the refrain. Both exchanges contribute to the refrain's development.

---

24. "Rondo, Rondo Form, Rondo-Sonata Form," *Harvard Dictionary of Music*, 740.

25. Rosen, *Sonata Forms*, 118.

26. Schmidt-Beste, *The Sonata*, 98–99.

27. This is a modified representation of a model given in Rosen, *Sonata Forms*, 121.

28. It is true that the motivic integration and development typically transpires in the second episode, which is the rough equivalent of the sonata form's development. Nonetheless, it was not uncommon for motifs from the refrain to surface in the other episodes. E.g., the first episode of Mozart's Rondo in Piano Sonata K. 311 incorporates a thematic fragment from the preceding refrain—as observed by Schmidt-Beste, *The Sonata*, 98. Also, the third episode often serves as the rough equivalent of the sonata form's recapitulation and thus incorporates thematic elements from the initial refrain (as in the above example from Mozart's Piano Sonata K. 309).

A Conceptualization of the Interlude according to the Sonata-Rondo

Thus the episodes of sonata-rondo form go a step further than the development of sonata form and extend the interlude's conceptual capacity. Like the development, the episodic interludes appropriate, tweak, and transpose existent motifs and contribute to the development of the piece. But unlike most development sections, their own thematic elements can infiltrate the refrains, meaning that the piece's thematic development consists not only in the suggestive defamiliarization of primary thematic material but also in the way that outside thematic material can pass through into the piece's primary sections. In this way, the sonata-rondo episode exemplifies an evolved, enriched sense of interlude. *Not only intermediate and secondary, the interlude also contrasts meaningfully with the original expression of the primary themes and develops these themes through a dynamic process of motivic exchange.* It appropriates primary motifs and recontextualizes them, showing how they might sound in different settings, and in turn its own strains slip into the piece's primary material. The difference between the initial refrain and its restatements marks the episode's work of thematic development. The play of the interludes both confers on existent motifs new thematic overtones and introduces into subsequent refrains outside motifs, and so the later refrains reverberate with motifs—from without as well as from within—that are not the same as the ones heard in previous refrains. Here they sound different. Simply put, after the interlude, the primary thematic material will never sound the same.

As this study shall elucidate presently, the strange stories of Hagar, Dinah, and Tamar may be read as interludes in a fuller sense of the concept, one that takes its cues from the sonata-rondo episodes. That is, they may be read as interludes not only in their intermediate position and secondary status vis-à-vis the ancestral narrative, but also in their contrastive relation and developmental function. Like sonata-rondo episodes, these stories inhabit a continuous position within the overarching story[29] and yet at the same time complicate and transform that story's themes.

---

29. Hepokoski and Darcy emphasize the continuity of the development. It is, in other words, not an anomalous intruder into the piece. "Developments often refer back to (or take up as topics) one or more of the ideas from the exposition"; its "thematic choice and arrangement . . . derives its significance through a comparison with what had happened in the exposition" (*Elements of Sonata Theory*, 19).

Appropriating key motifs and defamiliarizing them against the context of strange characters' interests, they engage in a process of motivic exchange that invests primary themes with new possibilities of signification.

The Stories of Hagar, Dinah, and Tamar as Interludes

Traditional scholarship classifies the strange stories as "interludes" on account of their intermediate position and their secondary standing in terms of the ancestral narrative's interests. This study wishes, however, to approach the stories with an eye to their strangeness, to heed their alternate subjectivity and their respective peculiarities. Each story spotlights an outsider to the ancestral family: Hagar the Egyptian maidservant, Shechem and the Hivites, and the presumably Canaanite Tamar. By attending to these characters and the singularity of their stories, this study can explore how the stories function as interludes in the fuller sense of the word, as not only intermediate and secondary but also contrastive and developmental.

The alternate subjectivity of the stories of Hagar, Dinah, and Tamar accounts for more than the simple fact that these stories are about less central characters, that they are secondary in terms of the narrative's interests. It also explains the stories' contrastive relation to the surrounding narrative and their developmental function. Reading the interludes according to their alternate subjectivity, first, appreciates their positive content. It welcomes the way that the interludes engage primary thematic material in terms other than those of the primary narrative. Rather than dismissing the interludes by virtue of their distance from the main ancestral plot or naturalizing them by subjecting them to the primary narrative's interests, it celebrates the particularity of their non-ancestral characters, whose sight, speech, and action drive much of the story, and acknowledges a meaningful contrast between their stories and the ancestral story. The stories may still be secondary on account of their size, position, and interests, but they assume a significance of their own by which they stand in contrastive relation to the ancestral narrative.

The strength of these stories' contrastive relation derives from the considerable degree of separation that their alternate subjectivities achieve from ancestral subjectivity. Unlike other outsider subjectivities that the ancestral narrative briefly appropriates, Hagar, Shechem and the Hivites, and Tamar are not cleanly embedded within the overarching subjectivity of the ancestral family. Whereas other outsiders—such as Pharaoh, Abimelech, and the Hittites—enjoy narrative attention only inasmuch as their story entangles with the ancestral family's story, the outsider subjects of the interludes achieve a degree of independence from the ancestral family. To the extent of this independence, they each have *a story of their own*, as abridged and fleeting as it may be. Perhaps most illustrative of this independence is the narrative's intimate portrayal of the outsider subjects through its divulgence of imperceptible details (e.g., their thoughts and feelings), particularly when they are apart from the ancestral family. Both Hagar and Tamar, for instance, are expelled from the ancestral family, and yet the narrative follows them to their place of expulsion and mediates how they understand or feel about their circumstances. Similarly, the narrative depicts the torrent of Shechem's desire throughout the interlude of Dinah. And although Shechem and his people ultimately fall victim to the ancestral family, it is notable that they nonetheless enjoy a more personal and arguably sympathetic portrayal than do other outsider victims in Genesis, like Chedorlaomer and his allies or the Sodomites.

The outsider subjectivity descried in these stories not only identifies the stories as interludes in their contrastive sense, it also exposes their possible developmental function. Alternate subjectivity facilitates motivic exchange and evolution. Just as the sonata-rondo episodes transpose motifs from the refrain into new thematic and tonal contexts and contribute to their transformation, so these narrative interludes transpose motifs from the ancestral narrative into new keys—those involving an outsider's subjectivity—where they assume unfamiliar melodic and tonal relations, in such a way as to develop understanding of their significance. Themes that had previously sounded in unambiguously ancestral tones now acquire connotations that point outside the ancestral family. Maybe, the interludes suggest, the central aspects of ancestral identity are not as centered in the ancestral family as they had seemed.

A brief glance at each interlude will suffice to demonstrate how it can develop ancestral themes by transposing ancestral motifs to a story marked by an outsider's subjectivity.[30] Approached via alternate subjectivities, the conventional terms of ancestral identity—the ancestral family's privileged relationship with God, its status as future inheritors of the land and thus as opponents to the land's current inhabitants, and its pure,

---

30. The "Thematic Development" sections in chs. 3-5 provide a more detailed analysis of the developmental function of each interlude (pp. 118, 170, 230).

endogamous lineage—begin to unravel. The interludes of Hagar, Dinah, and Tamar engage these three thematic aspects of ancestral identity each in turn.

The Hagar interludes transpose the motifs of sojourn and divine promise to a story unsettled by Hagar's subjectivity. Several scholars have observed aspects of this transposition by noting how the stories of Hagar are an inverse realization of the divine prediction for the ancestral family in 15:13–14. That is, just as the ancestral family will be oppressed as sojourners and slaves in a strange land, and then subsequently delivered, so Hagar is a sojourner and slave who is oppressed at the hands of the ancestral family and then divinely delivered (on two separate occasions).[31] Furthermore, Hagar herself receives a promise of offspring quite reminiscent of the one that Abram[32] receives.[33] Hagar's interludes effectively turn the ancestral narrative inside out: they spotlight an outsider who shares the distinctly ancestral experience of sojourn and divine companionship at the same time as they cast the ancestral family in the unfamiliar role of an inhabitant of the land. Appropriating the ancestral narrative's motifs of sojourn and divine promise, which suggest various aspects of the ancestral–divine relationship, and reversing them in a transposition of subjectivity, Hagar's interludes momentarily throw the exclusivity attributed to the ancestral–divine relationship into doubt. Perhaps it is not

---

31. Turner, *Genesis*, 77; Brett, *Genesis*, 58; Frymer-Kensky, *Reading the Women of the Bible*, 232. Some studies, like Dozeman, "The Wilderness and Salvation History," 23–43, identify the realization of Gen 15:13–14 with Israel's experience of slavery and exodus, and thus read Hagar's experience as a curious reversal: here Egypt is enslaved by and liberated from the predecessor of Israel. A few scholars even go so far as to suggest a causal link between Abraham and Sarah's treatment of Hagar and the predicted events of Gen 15—that is, because Abraham and Sarah oppressed Hagar, their Egyptian slave, so their descendants will be oppressed as slaves under the Egyptians. See Reis, "Hagar Requited," 106; Zakovitch, *"And You Shall Tell Your Son—,"* 28; Rosenberg, *King and Kin*, 90.

32. With regard to characters whose names change in the course of the narrative (e.g., Abram/Abraham), this study will endeavor to remain true to the narrative sequence. Therefore when it refers to characters at moments before the name change, it will use the former name, and after the name change, the latter name. When it refers to characters in the abstract—that is, beyond their existence at one particular narrative moment—it will employ the latter name. The one exception to this approach will be the character of Jacob/Israel, to whom this study will refer to as Jacob in the abstract. This is for two reasons. First, the narrative itself regularly uses Jacob after the name change. Second, using Jacob discourages the tendency toward retrospective interpretation, that is, interpretation that retrofits an Israelite identity onto the ancestral family.

33. Humphreys, *The Character of God*, 102.

only the ancestral family who encounters God and enjoys a privileged place in his plan.[34]

The Dinah interlude transposes motifs of the promise of land, the promise of universal blessing, and intermarriage to a story haunted by the subjectivity of Shechem and the Hivites. This mix of motifs, all of which touch on the question of ancestral relations to the land and its inhabitants, makes for a volatile thematic medley that asks big questions: how is God's promise of other people's land consistent with God's blessing on these same people? And how does the ancestral practice of endogamy fit into the equation? The resolution to the story, in which Dinah's brothers reject interethnic union and massacre the town, offers answers in the form of one extreme. But the fact that the indignant discourse and acts of Dinah's brothers dominate the narrative to an excessive extent—their voice possibly even invading the narrative level in a series of evaluative remarks (vv. 2, 5, 7, 13, 27)—brings their justifiability under scrutiny. The brief narrative segments of Shechem and the Hivites' subjectivity further question the brothers' exclusivist mode of relations and introduce an alternative for consideration. Perhaps what Shechem proposes—union between the ancestral family and the Hivites—is indicative not of what is to be avoided but rather of what is a viable, and even necessary, way of living into the promises of land and universal blessing. Perhaps the inhabitants of the land are more than characters destined for dispossession.

The Tamar interlude transposes numerous motifs of generational transition and procreative struggle to a story disturbed by the subjectivity of a presumably Canaanite woman who works through unconventional means to secure ancestral progeny. Eliciting comparison to previous ancestral birth narratives, the motifs identify Tamar with the matriarchs in several ways. A procreative dilemma, matriarchal initiative and trickery, the birth of twins—these, among other parallels, suggest that Tamar's story is, in its own way, an ancestral birth narrative. Thus, even as the motifs deviate from the rigid pattern of previous ancestral birth narratives and are defamiliarized against an outsider's subjectivity, so they also include Tamar among the matriarchs. The motifs' coalition with Tamar's subjectivity stretches the conventional formulation of ancestral identity, in which endogamy is central. Perhaps the ancestral family's traditional

---

34. As this study exercises a narrative approach in its reading of the biblical text, it treats God's gender as the narrative text does. With regard to names, this study chooses to refer to the divine character simply as God unless an alternative usage is understood to convey special significance.

self-identity—as matriarchs and patriarchs of certain norms, especially that of endogamy—reflects a misguided ideal that is better left behind.

As this brief review has demonstrated, the interludes' capacity for thematic development consists in their alternate subjectivity and their appropriation of ancestral motifs. If the ancestral narrative showcases the ancestral family's story and defines ancestral identity, then the interludes of Hagar, Dinah, and Tamar develop ancestral identity by pioneering its frontier, by allowing common thematic elements to wander into undefined territory and assume new thematic relations. Mieke Bal's observation regarding definition and negativity elucidates this development: "[T]he logic of opposition has it that negativity is by definition vague, if not void. It cannot be defined, hence, not articulated, and as a result it remains unmanageable; indeed wild."[35] One difficulty with definition, this observation would suggest, is that it cannot guard completely against outside objects—what are undefined, or negative—to assume its meaning.[36] In the case of the Hagar and Tamar interludes, outsider characters—i.e., characters who stand in a negative relation to the ancestral family—assume features integral to ancestral identity, thus exposing the provisionality and permeability of ancestral identity. The interlude of Dinah operates along the lines of negativity as well, but in a different way: it counterposes the brothers' dominant ideological stance to the ultimately silenced subjectivity of Shechem and the Hivites. Unlike Hagar and Tamar, Shechem and the Hivites do not directly assume elements of ancestral identity. But in the brothers' very attempt to exclude Shechem and the Hivites from the ancestral family, they raise the question of their inclusion. They cannot eliminate their negativity; they cannot preclude the possibility that inhabitants of the land could yet find welcome into the ancestral fold.

Summary

The common identification of the strange stories as interludes invites a poetics based on the concept. Interlude as a musical concept is rich

---

35. Bal, *Narratology*, 129.

36. To illustrate this point, one might consider the situation of Walter in *The Muppets*, whose crisis of identity leads him to sing: "Am I a man, or am I a muppet? If I'm a muppet, then I'm a very manly muppet. Am I a muppet, or am I man? If I'm a man, that makes me a muppet of a man." Undefined, Walter sees in himself qualities that would allow him to assume different identities.

in connotations and sketches out several implications for such a poetics. The sonata-rondo episodes serve as a particularly suggestive model for interlude, proposing that it is not only intermediate and secondary but also contrastive and developmental. A reading of the strange stories corroborates this more robust sense of interlude. These stories differ significantly from their surroundings by their non-ancestral subjectivities. They, moreover, make an appreciable difference to key ancestral themes, repeating them but in strange, unfamiliar contexts where they assume new meanings. Thus they develop ancestral identity. In each case, the interlude prods suspiciously at assumptions of what is ancestral. Does the ancestral family retain the exclusive privilege of the presence and promises of God? How does its future claim to the land relate to the divine proclamation that all the families of the earth will be blessed by way of the ancestral family (Gen 12:3)? A corollary of which is: how should the family relate to the inhabitants of the land? And does the narrative share the ancestral predilection for endogamy, or is ancestral identity founded in more inclusive terms? The interludes, in other words, do not settle for a fixed formulation of ancestral identity. Instead, like the sonata-rondo episodes, they exchange and reshape motifs in unexplored contexts, thus contributing toward thematic development. They continually ask, each in their own way, "Just how 'ancestral' is ancestral identity?"

2

Hermeneutics: Irony

THIS CHAPTER ADVANCES ON the hermeneutical question that follows from reading the stories of Hagar, Dinah, and Tamar within a poetics of the interlude. What meaning results from the interludes' thematic development? That is, what do the interludes say about the themes that they engage? How do the interludes affect interpretation of the ancestral narrative as a whole?

How a reader answers these questions is determined in part by his or her perspective. So Adele Berlin observes: "A text read from one perspective might mean something different if read from another perspective."[1] Because this study reads within a poetics of the interlude, a perspective that anticipates development as a result of thematic appropriation and defamiliarization, this chapter seizes on irony as a hermeneutical lens. Irony interprets the critical appropriation of a discourse in a new, incongruous context. It offers a cogent explanation for situations in which narrative elements seem out of place—situations like the interludes. The thematic strains that twist and wind through the interludes sound distorted and strange in the context of an alternate subjectivity and different motifs, and irony volunteers a convincing way to make sense of this thematic trajectory.

This chapter accordingly begins with a consideration of irony as a hermeneutical concept. Drawing again on the correlation between the musical and the literary, it considers how musicological discourse on irony as a hermeneutical subject informs literary discourse. It then maps

---

1. Berlin, "Literary Approaches to Biblical Literature," 53.

out a history of irony, zeroing in on recent discussion of irony in literary and biblical discourse. Assimilating different aspects of recent conceptualizations, it approaches a working definition of its own for the purposes of this study. Lastly, as a final preliminary to the close ironic readings of the interludes, it attends to the common charge of anachronism—of reading a text according to a concept of which the text is unaware—and demonstrates that a hermeneutics of irony is well suited to the ancient text of Genesis.

Irony as a Hermeneutical Concept

The correlation between music and literature, which helped to establish the interlude as a poetical concept, corroborates the idea of irony as a hermeneutical concept. The debate in musicology over the conceptual significance of irony gestures toward its hermeneutical capacity. Whereas the sonata and sonata-rondo are obviously questions of form (poetics), irony is not. Irony, the musicological debate makes clear, is a matter of interpretation.

Theorists both within and without musicology have traditionally questioned the validity of discussing irony in music. D. C. Muecke, one of the pioneer theorists of irony in the field of literary criticism, asserts that music is primarily a formal phenomenon whereas irony involves representation:

> [T]o be ironical is to be ironical about something, and the non-representational arts do not even refer to anything. Their object is not to represent things, which would be to make appearances, but to make things, to construct "reality" in the shape of designs in space, lines, colours, stone, gold, musical sounds. These designs must have our undivided attention, if we are attending at all, since there is nothing else to attend to: that is to say, these designs are not meant to remind us of anything else. They are as unironical as mathematical theorems or scientific hypotheses.[2]

Muecke does concede that music retains the capacity for irony inasmuch as it can quote itself. But he appears to regard self-referencing music as less than pure music. When music quotes itself, "it does not efface itself" as, he would imply, it normally does.[3]

---

2. Muecke, *Irony*, 4.
3. Muecke, *Irony*, 5–6.

Lars Elleström cites similar arguments from the realm of musicology. While critical musical reviews do occasionally describe music as ironic, musicologists doubt the correctness of these analyses. Elleström observes that they hesitate to identify irony in music because they perceive no essential connection between musical form and meaning. In other words, music cannot accommodate what is essential to irony: incongruous meanings. Elleström explains, "Frits Noske's remark that 'in order to contradict, music must first adopt a meaning' is a representative of this view. The 'meaning' of music is not in the music itself, Noske believes, and hence musical irony is not really a musical phenomenon."[4]

Like Muecke, Noske and like-minded musicologists restrict music to the matter of form and bracket out questions of reference and meaning. That irony too is to be excluded from the discussion would indicate its hermeneutical nature.

Yet discussion of irony persists in musicological discourse, suggesting that the division between musical form and meaning is not as impassable as Muecke, Noske, and others think. Linda Hutcheon approaches one significant gap in the division. Music, she posits, can have "'semantic' associations."[5] She observes, however, that these often derive from certain "handy hermeneutic helpers"—that is, texts associated with the music.[6] At first glance, then, music's semantic associations would seem to confirm that meaning is separate from music. Any meaning that one might attribute to the music in these cases originates from the text. And yet, Elleström notes, musicologists regularly discuss how music *modifies* the meaning of its associated text. This begs the question: if music can engage and alter the meaning of a text, why bracket off meaning as a matter distinct from the music itself?[7] Why draw such a rigid distinction between form and meaning when form can affect an associated meaning?

While the particulars of the debate of musical meaning are beyond the scope of this study, it suffices to say that, as centuries of music criticism would attest, music and meaning are inextricable: music gives rise to contrasting moods, feelings, and thoughts. Music, in short, has effects

---

4. Elleström, *Divine Madness*, 201, quoting from Noske, *The Signifier and the Signified*, 102.
5. Hutcheon, *Irony's Edge*, 142.
6. Hutcheon, *Irony's Edge*, 141. Cf. Elleström, *Divine Madness*, 102.
7. Elleström explains, "As soon as one accepts that music has the capacity of 'modifying' the meaning of a literary text, one must also accept that it has the capacity of modifying its own meaning" (*Divine Madness*, 212).

that can signify—which is to say, it can have meaning.[8] For example, a reel, when brightly played, effects joy in Scottish listeners and suggests physical movement. Such signifying effects, or meanings, Elleström points out, spring primarily from the relation between musical form and listener expectation.[9] In other words, while music is not meaningful, or more specifically ironic, in and of itself, it is only heard in the context of a listener within a listening community, a context that necessarily confers meaning on the music. The fact that the conventions of interpretation are not communally codified nearly as strongly or uniformly in music as they are in language should not detract from their significance in determining musical meaning. How a listener determines the meaning of the musical forms that he hears depends on the conventions of interpretation that guide him. When musicologists speak of irony, then, they refer not to a formal quality of the music but rather to a specific signifying effect or meaning, one that makes sense only within a listening community whose interpretive conventions allow for irony. Certain forms may have more potential to achieve the effect identified as irony, but the effect is irreducible to any one configuration of forms, for neither communities nor conventions are uniform: they are always heterogeneous and changing.

Just as the debate over musical meaning demonstrates that the matter of musical irony belongs to the realm of hermeneutics rather than form (poetics), so it would suggest likewise for irony in literature. For although language communicates much more uniformly than does music, do they not ultimately share in the same phenomenon? Forms are not identical to signifying effects or meanings, such as irony, but give rise to them through the interpretive act.[10] The sonata-rondo is not itself ironic, but its formal characteristics may accommodate ironic effects. Irony results from a way of reading or listening that primes an audience to pick up on incongruities and their possible ironic effects. As this study will demonstrate, a hermeneutics of irony is especially illumining for the

---

8. Culler discusses the sense in which a work's meaning is inextricably bound with the work's "effect, the process [it] can provoke" (*Literary Theory*, 55–57). While Culler refers specifically to texts here, he is speaking within the broader context of the process of signification. The fact that music involves an audience, persons who come to be addressed by the music, suggests that music itself is a form of signification and thus might be included as a process of signification, a process that has effects, or meanings.

9. Elleström, *Divine Madness*, 214–17.

10. Hutcheon puts it succinctly: "[I]rony isn't irony until it is interpreted as such" (*Irony's Edge*, 6).

interludes, where familiar motifs resound against unfamiliar contexts and develop new—and sometimes contrasting—thematic associations.

Historical Review of Irony

To read with a hermeneutics of irony, to identify ironic effects, is no simple matter, for one must first determine what passes for irony. On this question there is little consensus. Throughout history, critics have applied the term to a wide variety of phenomena—from a single word to a person's entire life, from a rhetorical strategy to the essence of existence. To approach a working definition, this study will first embark on a brief historical review of the word before exploring its recent use in both literary and biblical criticism. Within this framework, this study will situate its own understanding of irony.

There is no shortage of historical accounts of irony. Some accounts chronicle the history of the word; others endeavor to trace a particular concept of irony in its use. The distinction between "irony" as a word and as a concept is important. In his introduction to one particular concept of irony, D. C. Muecke states, "[T]he phenomenon existed before it was named . . . and the word existed before it was applied to the phenomenon."[11] According to Muecke, the word "irony" has not always applied to the phenomenon of irony. Whether or not one accepts Muecke's definition of the phenomenon, his point illustrates the semantic variability of the word. The word "irony" has meant different things—has suggested different concepts—at different times. What follows is a sketch of the word's genealogy that attempts to make some basic, if reductive, classifications of what irony has meant in different eras. This timeline borrows considerably from the work of D. C. Muecke, Joseph A. Dane, and Claire Colebrook, all of whom offer more extensive histories of the term.[12] With their help, this study provides a serviceable backdrop against which it can explore the more recent formulations of irony, from which it derives its own understanding.

---

11. Muecke, *Irony*, 14.

12. Muecke, *Irony*, especially 13–24; Dane, *The Critical Mythology of Irony*; Colebrook, *Irony*.

Classical Greece

Most histories of the term begin with Plato, and with good reason: Plato's works contain some of the first recorded mentions of *eironeia*,[13] and one of his main characters, Socrates, has inspired definitions of irony from an early time. But even if Plato's mention of *eironeia* is accepted as inaugural, an originary concept of irony proves illusory. Plato's application of the term and its derivatives suggests a number of different conceptual possibilities and thus defies attempts at a unified definition. The *Symposium*, for instance, characterizes Socrates' response to Alcibiades' advances as ironic, and yet the sincere tenor of Socrates' response runs counter to the dissimulation so often associated with irony.[14] Later in the text, when Alcibiades' character describes Socrates' conduct as ironizing, he hints at one conceptual alternative to the typical view of irony as dissemblance. Instead of indicating a contradictory relation between what is said and meant, irony might refer to a way of relating to the world—specifically, devaluing what others value:

> You know that he does not care if anyone is beautiful, but despises it more than anyone could imagine, nor if a man is wealthy, or if he has any other honor valued by the many. He thinks that all such possessions are worth nothing and that we ourselves are nothing; I tell you, he spends his whole life ironizing and despising such things.[15]

Elsewhere in Plato, however, the term irony aligns with its more traditional conceptualization as pretense. In the *Apology*, Socrates responds to the proposition that he flee Athens: "For if I tell you that this would be to disobey the god, you would not be persuaded by me [whom you imagine to be] ironic."[16] Similarly in *Laws*, Socrates uses the word to refer to the hypocrisy of the atheist who feigns religious behavior.[17]

---

13. Muecke, *Irony*, 14.

14. Dane characterizes Socrates' response as truthful and straightforward. "Socrates' 'usual ironic manner' as conceived by Alcibiades seems to be a logical manner of denial and rejection: he rejects Alcibiades' sexual advances; he rejects the implications of those advances (he will not exchange his own beauty for Alcibiades'); and he denies the premise of Alcibiades' proposition (it is not true that Alcibiades judges value correctly)" (*The Critical Mythology of Irony*, 17–18).

15. *Symp.* 216d–e, cited and translated in Dane, *The Critical Mythology of Irony*, 19.

16. *Apol.* 38a, cited and translated in Dane, *The Critical Mythology of Irony*, 20.

17. *Leg.* 908e, cited in Dane, *The Critical Mythology of Irony*, 20.

The discrepancy of Plato's use of the word notwithstanding, its earliest manifestations in ancient Greek literature share in conceptualizing irony more as a mode of behavior or attitude than as a rhetorical tool. Thus Aristophanes describes one of his characters in *Clouds*, an aspirant member of Socrates' think tank, as "a slippery, oily knave, an *eiron*, a braggart."[18] This negative evaluative connotation resonates with much of the ancient Greek tradition. Muecke summarizes the term's use elsewhere: "For Demosthenes an 'eiron' was one who evaded his responsibilities as a citizen by pretending unfitness. For Theophrastus an 'eiron' was evasive and non-committal, concealing his enmities, pretending friendship, misrepresenting his acts, never giving a straight answer."[19]

In the *Rhetoric*, Aristotle also attributes a negative connotation to irony. He depicts irony as a kind of mockery, a way of belittling an opponent, and he attributes it to "wretches" who are more dangerous than sincere, straightforward speakers.[20] But his final references to irony in the *Rhetoric*, as Dane points out, take a turn toward neutralizing the negative connotation. Here Aristotle refers to irony as a manner of speaking—perhaps prefiguring the impending rhetorical conceptualizations of irony—by which a speaker may contrast his point with a rival's: "he said X, whereas I say Y."[21] In *Nicomachean Ethics*, Aristotle's neutralization of the word grows into a modest valorization. Aristotle contrasts the *eiron* and the *alazon* (boaster) as two social types and gives his recommendation to the *eiron*: "Those who use irony moderately, and those who are ironic openly and not excessive in their use of it seem gracious."[22]

Aristotle also associates the *eiron* with Socrates, a point which theorist Joseph A. Dane does not take lightly. Dane juxtaposes the presentation of *eiron* as a social type in the works of Aristotle, who invokes Socrates as an example, and Theophrastus, who makes no mention of Socrates. Theophrastus' description of irony, he argues, outlines one possible history of irony: irony as a negative social stereotype with little value

---

18. *Cloud*, line 449, cited and translated in Dane, *The Critical Mythology of Irony*, 20.

19. Muecke, *Irony*, 14–15. Muecke perceives these negative connotations of *eironeia* uniformly enough across ancient Greek writing to describe the term as having "abusive meanings."

20. *Rhet.* 1379b, 1382b, cited in Dane, *The Critical Mythology of Irony*, 45.

21. *Rhet.* 1420a, cited in Dane, *The Critical Mythology of Irony*, 45.

22. *Eth. Nic.* 1127b, cited in Dane, *The Critical Mythology of Irony*, 46.

in terms of rhetoric or otherwise.[23] Aristotle's portrayal of irony, which helps to fix the link between Socrates and irony, commands a greater influence on the word's development. Although the link lies latent for centuries, it flickers to life in Cicero and Quintilian and then blossoms more fully in the nineteenth century and beyond, when the character of Socrates is held up as an exemplar of irony—not just irony as a positive social type, but also as a rhetorical tool and even as a mode of existence.

The concept of irony shifts from a mode of behavior or attitude to a rhetorical implement as early as the fourth century BCE. In the *Letter to Alexander*, now attributed to Anaximenes, irony is a rhetorical technique of dissimulation: "Irony is to say something while pretending not to say it, or to propose some action in the opposite words."[24] The examples that Anaximenes offers for irony showcase praise as blame and vice versa: "On the one hand, those who do evil to our allies seem very worthy, while we, who are the cause of many benefits, seem to be wretches."[25] (In other words, Anaximenes suggests the irony of the statements: "The enemies of our allies are worthy," and, "We are wretches." The praise and blame that are stated are the opposite of what is implied.)

Ancient Rome into the Middle Ages

Roman treatment of the concept of irony, as exemplified in Cicero's and Quintilian's writing, further fastens the word to a rhetorical definition, albeit broadly conceived. For Cicero and Quintilian, irony can function not only in an isolated word or phrase but also in extended fashion—in an entire speech. The two also sustain the association between irony and Socrates. In *De Officiis*, Cicero briefly refers to irony, which he characterizes as a clever and refined way of speaking, by way of Socrates: "Among the Greeks, however, we take Socrates to be charming and witty, of pleasant speech, and in all speaking a simulator, which the Greeks called an *eiron*."[26] In *De Oratore*, he again associates irony, here an extended rhetorical tactic, with Socrates:

---

23. Dane, *The Critical Mythology of Irony*, 46–47.

24. Quoted in *Rhetores Graeci*, 1:57–58, cited and translated in Dane, *The Critical Mythology of Irony*, 47.

25. Quoted in *Rhetores Graeci*, 1:57–58, cited and translated in Dane, *The Critical Mythology of Irony*, 47.

26. *Off.* 1.30.108, cited and translated in Dane, *The Critical Mythology of Irony*, 48.

> Urbane dissimulation is when you understand something other than what is said; not in the way I spoke of earlier, when you say the contrary ... but when you are mocking when the entire speech itself is serious, when you understand and say diverse things .... I believe Socrates to have far surpassed all others in wit and humanity in this irony and dissimulation.[27]

Quintilian distinguishes more explicitly between concise instances of irony and their extended counterparts. Differentiating between the two in terms of trope and figure, he categorizes the trope as a shortened form of allegory in which "contraries are shown."[28] Extended use of irony is a figure. It is "the counterfeiting of the entire will .... Just as in the trope, where words are diverse from other words, here the sense opposes the speech and expression."[29] Quintilian's formulation of irony as a figure outstrips the idea that irony contains an "articulable" meaning (that is, the idea that irony can be decoded by simple semantic inversion: "it's a glorious day" meaning "it's a miserable day") and outlines the possibility that irony may characterize not only a speech but even a person's life.[30] Thus he is able to entertain the possibility that "an entire life [might] have irony, as seemed to be the case of Socrates. For he was called an *eiron* because he pretended to be ignorant and an admirer of others as if they were wise. And just as a continuous metaphor results in allegory, so does the development of the trope result in this schema."[31]

Several of the possibilities for irony that Cicero and Quintilian indicate—particularly irony as a contrast that moves beyond simple communicable meanings, a concept which draws strength from its embodiment in Socrates—lie fallow for a succession of centuries. In the medieval era the word finds meaning mainly in the definitions drawn up by rhetoricians, who like Quintilian consider irony as a subset of allegory. The *Etymologiae* of Isidore of Seville, which Dane cites as illustrative of the medieval understanding, limits irony to tropes and expressible figures

---

27. *De or.* 2.67.269–70, cited and translated in Dane, *The Critical Mythology of Irony*, 49.

28. Quoted in *M. Fabi Quintiliani Institutionis*, 8.6.44–54, cited and translated in Dane, *The Critical Mythology of Irony*, 49.

29. Quoted in *M. Fabi Quintiliani Institutionis*, 9.2.46, cited and translated in Dane, *The Critical Mythology of Irony*, 50.

30. Dane, *The Critical Mythology of Irony*, 51.

31. Quoted in *M. Fabi Quintiliani Institutionis*, 9.2.46, cited and translated in Dane, *The Critical Mythology of Irony*, 51.

of thought. "Irony is a statement that has a contrary meaning because of its pronunciation," and, "Irony is when the speaker, through simulation, wishes something diverse from what is said to be understood. It occurs when we praise someone we wish to vituperate, or vituperate someone we wish to praise."[32]

Romanticism and New Criticism

Although isolated mentions of irony in the seventeenth and eighteenth centuries indicate that the rhetorical stronghold on the word is loosening, it is not until the nineteenth and twentieth centuries that the potential for the word irony sketched out by Cicero and Quintilian is realized. The Romantics and the New Critics are the inheritors of the expanded sense of the word. Within their discourse, the term moves beyond a simple rhetorical figure to incorporate situational and dramatic irony. Indeed, now irony may characterize an entire literary work, a person's life, or even universal existence. Friedrich Schlegel's formulation offers an instructive summary of the Romantic concept of irony. As Claire Colebrook explains with recourse to Schlegel's words, "Irony was not just signalling the opposite of what was said; it was the expression of *both sides or viewpoints at once* in the form of contradiction or paradox. 'Irony is the form of paradox. Paradox is everything simultaneously good and great.'"[33] This inclusive contrast, which Schlegel roots in the discursive practice of Socrates,[34] could inhere not only in a quip or short speech but also in the fundamental incongruities perceived to characterize existence. This broadened understanding would come to colonize concepts that previously went by other names under the expansive conceptual contours of irony. Bishop and historian Connop Thirlwall, for instance, in 1833 published an essay titled "On the Irony of Sophocles" that delineates irony along the lines of a contradiction between intent and consequence. To preface his elucidation of this phenomenon, which he calls "practical irony" (and which today is often called situational irony), he invites his readers early on "to reflect how little the good and ill of their lot has

---

32. Orig. 1.37.22–23, 2.21.41, cited and translated in Dane, *The Critical Mythology of Irony*, 53.
33. Colebrook, *Irony*, 53–54, quoting from Schlegel, *Philosophical Fragments*, 6.
34. Colebrook, *Irony*, 54.

corresponded with their hopes and fears."[35] What had previously gone by the name *peripeteia*—the opposition of intention and consequence of action[36]—now falls under the umbrella of irony.

The broadening of irony's definition in the Romantic era helped to lay the foundation for its conceptualization within New Criticism, in which it retains its comprehensive semantic range. Cleanth Brooks' numerous references to irony mark him as an appropriate representative for New Criticism's reception of the word. As Dane summarizes, Brooks distinguishes between two sorts of irony: irony in its traditional rhetorical guise and a more genuine irony, fundamental to poetry. The former represents verbal irony, a matter of rhetoric and the intellect, while the latter consists in "the pressures of the context."[37] This latter irony is the condition of wholeness. It encompasses the necessary contradictions within a literary work. It derives from the way a work's particular context necessarily modifies the meaning of the elements within. Whereas the traditional understanding of irony posits a vertical hierarchy between meaning and statement, Brooks and the New Critics present irony as the horizontal strain that inheres in a complete literary work.[38] New Critic I. A. Richards exemplifies the typical valorization of this horizontal tension in his definition of irony as "the bringing in of the opposite, the complementary impulses" to effect "a balanced poise."[39] As for the Romantics, so for the New Critics: irony means the inclusive relation between opposite meanings rather than the emigration from one discarded meaning to a new, better one.

Irony in Literary Discourse

Briefly put, the history of the word "irony" is this: referring in its ancient Greek context to a mode of behavior or attitude, irony evolves to acquire rhetorical connotations. Although Cicero and Quintilian's conceptualization of irony allows for extended rhetorical forms—indeed as a mode of

---

35. Thirlwall, "On the Irony of Sophocles," 2:486.

36. For a helpful discussion of *peripeteia* as conceived by Aristotle, see Belfiore, "περιπέτεια as Discontinuous Action."

37. Brooks, *The Well-Wrought Urn*, 732, quoted in Dane, *The Critical Mythology of Irony*, 151–54.

38. Dane, *The Critical Mythology of Irony*, 149.

39. Richards, *Principles of Literary Criticism*, 250, quoted in Muecke, *Irony*, 19.

discourse or even existence—the medieval reception of the word largely limits it to simple rhetorical tropes that operate by articulable semantic inversions. Only by the nineteenth century does irony expand again, here under the guidance of the Romantics who, often reassociating irony with the figure of Socrates, formulate its concept philosophically to include not only verbal instances (simple or extended) but also situational and existential instances. Irony becomes a fact of life—maybe *the* fact of life. The New Critics inherit this perspective in the twentieth century, and they transpose it from life to text.

Thus in the twentieth century irony becomes an object of literary discourse. It becomes, in particular, part of the enthusiastic debate over where meaning resides. Does it—meaning, or more specifically irony—derive from the author's intention, exist independently in the text, or originate in the reader's interpretation? As this study will show in the following literature review, irony enters this debate not only as an interested party awaiting its fate, but as a contributor. That is, irony has something to say about the play of meaning, because it accentuates the relation between text and reader; it highlights the contours of the process whereby meaning is born. By attending to irony, the critic attends to the interchange that begets meaning.

Carolyn J. Sharp frankly acknowledges the overwhelming volume of scholarly work on the concept of irony: "The literature is so vast that reviewing it comprehensively would be impossible."[40] Recognizing its own limits from the start, this review humbly undertakes its task to explore and assimilate various theories on irony—particularly theories that deal with irony as a literary phenomenon. Neither an exhaustive review of literary and biblical studies' "ironologists"[41] (theorists of irony) nor an exhaustive review of the selected theorists' work, this literature review singles out scholars who might serve as mouthpieces for the main theories of irony and outlines their key contributions, especially with regard to the question of the locus of ironic meaning.

---

40. Sharp, *Irony and Meaning in the Hebrew Bible*, 11.
41. Muecke, *Irony*, 18.

Text-Centered Conceptualizations: Muecke and Booth

Interest in irony as a literary concept swelled in the 1960s and 70s.[42] Seminal works in the theory of irony such as D. C. Muecke's *Irony* and Wayne C. Booth's *A Rhetoric of Irony* appeared on the scene, and shifts in theory notwithstanding, they have yet to take their final bow five decades later. Muecke and Booth share similar approaches to theorizing irony, particularly in their tendency to formalize the concept. Muecke, for instance, identifies irony's constitutive elements and catalogues different ways of being ironical. Booth famously attempts to stabilize irony—to define irony according to unambiguous, rhetorical forms through which the author intentionally flags its presence and subtly steers the reader toward its correct interpretation. Because both have been pioneers, and their works catalysts, in the developing conversation on irony, attending to their formulations of irony facilitates an understanding of recent theoretical discussion on the concept.

In the introduction to his aptly titled *Irony*, Muecke laments the confusion surrounding the term: "Some kinds of irony have as yet no recognized name, and among those that have there is a good deal of duplication and overlapping."[43] Thus he sets the stage for his own project of cleaning up the concept of irony. Muecke goes about his task systematically. First he provides a history of the word. As noted before, he marks a distinction between the word and concept. Indeed, he asserts that the phenomenon "existed before it was named."[44] Thus he betrays a relatively ahistorical, essentialist understanding of the concept. Regardless of its designation (or lack thereof) throughout history, irony is a single, determinate phenomenon. Consequently, after the terminological history, he defines irony's constituent elements and enumerates the definitive modes of being ironical.

While shifts in theory have led to less formalized conceptions of irony, Muecke's historical account and his own classifications of irony remain helpful in keeping one abreast of its various basic conceptualizations. Tracing accounts of irony from ancient Greece to contemporary literature, Muecke identifies two simple categories of irony: verbal and situational (of which dramatic irony is a subcategory).[45] Muecke then

---

42. Sharp, *Irony and Meaning in the Hebrew Bible*, 11.
43. Muecke, *Irony*, 12.
44. Muecke, *Irony*, 14.
45. Muecke, *Irony*, 25.

outlines the elements that are "basic to all forms of irony": the element of "innocence" or "confident unawareness," the contrast between reality and appearance, the comic element, and the element of detachment.[46] Many theorists continue to highlight select elements from Muecke's list. While the focus invariably differs for each theorist, most continue to agree that the element of unawareness and the contrast between reality and appearance are constitutive of irony. On Muecke's latter two elements, however, disagreement persists. The sometimes-tragic quality of irony challenges the universality of its comic element, and the notion that irony invites commitment nuances its alleged element of detachment.[47]

Like Muecke, Booth exhibits an inclination toward formalizing in his work *A Rhetoric of Irony*. His project launches from a familiar starting point: concern over the lack of definition for the term irony. "[I]rony has come to stand for so many things that we are in danger of losing it as a useful term altogether."[48] Unlike Muecke, however, Booth eschews a history of irony—he seems more than satisfied with Muecke's own "ranging over the meanings of the word" irony[49]—in favor of "an exclusively rhetorical focus" on how irony works as a persuasive act of communication.[50] If Muecke's conceptualization of irony aligns more closely with the ancient Greek emphasis on a mode of behavior or attitude, then Booth's inclines more toward its later conceptualization as a figure of rhetoric. For Booth, definition is to be found just as much in irony's function as in its form. Indeed, he works from the premise that "some statements cannot be understood without rejecting what they seem to say."[51] In other words, irony functions to engender a confrontation of meaning in which the listener must reject the surface meaning and seek out another.

Booth offers four basic characteristics of irony: it is intended, covert, fixed (i.e., it points away from the surface meaning toward an alternate meaning), and finite (i.e., it does not lead to an infinite series of semantic

---

46. Muecke, *Irony*, 25–40.

47. Hutcheon offers a chart that reviews "irony's many functions" as catalogued by other scholars and endeavors "to articulate and order some of the ways critics over the years have voiced their approval or disapproval of what is often presented as a single thing—irony—operating in single way" (*Irony's Edge*, 46–47). It corroborates the variance of opinion on these two elements.

48. Booth, *A Rhetoric of Irony*, 2.
49. Booth, *A Rhetoric of Irony*, viii.
50. Booth, *A Rhetoric of Irony*, viii.
51. Booth, *A Rhetoric of Irony*, 1.

negations).⁵² The second and third characteristics resonate notably with Muecke's first two. Even more notable, however, are the first and last characteristics, which reflect Booth's agenda in limiting his discourse to "stable irony." Booth seeks to ground the theory of irony in determinate terms—in a "literary fixity"⁵³—based on authorial intention and definite meaning.

Postmodern currents have since capsized Booth's more essentialist assertions. Nonetheless his overview of irony's rhetoric continues to prove salutary in its exploration of the purpose of irony. While Booth's endeavor to disambiguate irony may suggest a simplified conceptualization, his theorizing in fact marks the profundity of irony's implications. He looks beyond irony's basic semantic exchange to the wider perspectives that underlie the meanings in competition. Irony, according to Booth, engages worldviews. It calls for a rejection not only of surface meanings, but of the "whole structures of meaning" that support them.⁵⁴ Booth's assertion here perhaps portends later theorists' interest in the political dimensions of irony, in the way irony pits conflicting ideologies against one another. Booth himself, however, neglects this interest in favor of more formal matters. Irony, if it is to succeed in its revolution of worldviews, must first be recognized, and so Booth pays considerable attention to the forms through which an author might flag her intention. He suggests a variety of ways that an author might invite the rejection of one meaning in favor of another, from the outright proclamation of a "known error" or the "conflict of facts within the work," to "clashes of style."⁵⁵

Reader-Centered Conceptualizations: Fish and Dane

It is worth noting here that a counterargument to Booth's project of fixing irony in authorial intention lies within his own argument—specifically in his lament that we might lose irony "as a useful term altogether." Irony "as a useful term" implies irony as a fundamentally critical tool, an instrument of the reader. Stanley Fish develops just this sort of readerly understanding of irony. Indeed, if Booth represents the champion of irony as rhetorically intended and definitely marked, then Stanley Fish stands

---

52. Booth, *A Rhetoric of Irony*, 5–6.
53. Booth, *A Rhetoric of Irony*, 3.
54. Booth, *A Rhetoric of Irony*, 36.
55. Booth, *A Rhetoric of Irony*, 53–76.

as his challenger. One can hardly consider Booth's work today without hearing Fish's critical voice whispering at its edges. Fish's protest against Booth's project derives from his simple observation that not everyone perceives the same ironies: "Irony is a risky business because one cannot at all be certain that readers will be directed to the ironic meanings one intends."[56] The title of Fish's essay—"Short People Got No Reason to Live: Reading Irony"—alludes to Fish's case in point: some listeners have interpreted the gibe in Randy Newman's song "Short People" as ironic while others have not.[57]

For Fish, readerly perspective, community, and convention all factor heavily into the act of interpretation. The position from which one reads and the conventions of interpretation that one's community prescribes determine in large part how one understands a text. Fish problematizes Booth's argument by stripping the text of its alleged objectivity. There is no fundamental "what" that underlies a text, Fish argues. *How* one reads determines *what* one reads.[58] Interpretation is always prior to the text. Even the text's "literal meaning" is a "product of perspective."[59] Thus, for Fish, Booth's project is doomed from the very start. The "perspicuity and independence of literal meaning" that grounds Booth's understanding of irony's semantic exchange—in which the reader rejects the literal meaning in favor of the ironic one—is itself an illusion.[60]

To illustrate his point, Fish turns to the example of Jonathan Swift's "Verses on the Death of Dr. Swift."[61] Fish points out that before Barry Slepian introduced an ironic reading of the poem, critics had read it unironically.[62] Slepian effectively persuaded others of his reading, Fish contends, by appealing to one of the conventions of reading that regulated their perspective: the question of the author's intention.[63] Slepian hypothesized a different intention; he "replaced their [the community's] Swift with another."[64] (A silly exercise to help illustrate: say "milk" five times fast.

---

56. Fish, *Doing What Comes Naturally*, 181.
57. Fish, *Doing What Comes Naturally*, 180.
58. Fish, *Doing What Comes Naturally*, 181–83.
59. Fish, *Doing What Comes Naturally*, 185.
60. Fish, *Doing What Comes Naturally*, 184.
61. See "Verses on the Death of Dr. Swift" in *Jonathan Swift*, 126–36.
62. Fish, *Doing What Comes Naturally*, 186–187. See Slepian, "The Ironic Intention," 249–56.
63. Fish, *Doing What Comes Naturally*, 191.
64. Fish, *Doing What Comes Naturally*, 188–89.

Now answer the question, "What do cows drink?" If you answered "milk," it is likely because your repeating it predisposed you to think of it first. Similarly, the image of the author that the reader has in mind might predispose him to see certain aspects of that image in the text.) In addition to invoking the matter of authorial intention, Slepian also played to the not uncommon critical tendency to venerate past greats. As Fish claims, "If Slepian can come up with a reading that improves the poem's reputation, the probability of its being accepted as a true reading will be very high."[65] Slepian's suggestion that Swift's intention, hitherto misunderstood, was dissimulation and that the ironic reading better reflects Swift's literary prowess thus met with an affirmative reception. By changing *how* the text was read within the confines of the interpretive community's perspective and conventions, Slepian changed *what* was read.[66]

Fish's stance on irony deviates significantly from the stance of Muecke and Booth. Irony, according to Fish, is not so much an object of the author's intention that the competent reader discerns as it is simply a "way of reading": "an interpretive strategy that produces the object of its attention, an object that will be perspicuous to those who share or have been persuaded to share the same strategy."[67] In contemporary scholarship on irony, Fish perhaps most visibly reflects the shift of focus from authorial intention to reader response. Several other scholars, however, have echoed his emphasis on the reader's determinant role in producing irony. Joseph A. Dane is one notable example. He advances a "mythology of irony." Irony, he explains, points not so much to a phenomenon as it does to an understanding, a set of "assumptions and accepted beliefs ... that control our reception of irony."[68] Whereas Fish contends that *how* a reader reads determines what a reader will read as irony, Dane takes a slightly different angle. Focusing on the conceptual variability of irony, he asserts that *what* a reader considers to be irony determines what a reader will read as irony. He reads irony "not as the referent of criticism but as

---

65. Fish, *Doing What Comes Naturally*, 189.

66. As Fish summarizes, Slepian "succeeds neither because he alone is uniquely in touch with the work itself nor because he has created the work out of whole cloth, but because, in accordance with procedures authorized by the institution, he has altered the conditions of seeing—the conditions under which one might take a 'close look'— in such a way as to cause many to see a work other than the work they would have seen before he wrote" (*Doing What Comes Naturally*, 191).

67. Fish, *Doing What Comes Naturally*, 194.

68. Dane, *The Critical Mythology of Irony*, 5.

the discourse of criticism itself," a discourse that is endlessly changing.[69] In direct opposition to Muecke, who posits that the phenomenon of irony "existed before it was named,"[70] Dane argues that the phenomenon of irony has never existed in and of itself, but rather has been (re)created as it has been named. Thus he outlines various understandings of irony, spotlighting the possibilities of meaning in its historical definitions and contemplating how at various historical junctures one semantic route was privileged over another. He shows, in other words, that irony may just as well have ended up with a very different meaning—a more limited, more negative one, for instance, if Theophrastus' definition had prevailed over Aristotle's and precluded the term's all-important association with Socrates.[71]

Dane concludes that irony ultimately means whatever the reader wants it to mean, and that, at least within the discourse on irony, no understanding is better than another: "There is no correct understanding of the word irony, no historically valid reading of irony; and to claim that irony has been consistently misread does not seem to me any different from assuming that every reading of irony, every invocation of irony, is legitimate."[72] While from one perspective Dane's negative thesis seems antagonistic toward the aims of ironic readings of texts, from another perspective it is salutary as a reminder of two things. First, irony is ultimately a critic's concept. Second, and a corollary of the first: it is one thing to argue pointlessly over what exactly irony is; it is another thing, however, to define a particular concept of irony and to read along such lines. Irony, as defined one way or another, may yet be, as Booth puts it, a "useful term."

"Double-Logic" Conceptualizations: Colebrook, Hutcheon, and Sperber and Wilson

If Booth and Fish's scholarly debate reflects recent theory's interest in the locus of ironic meaning, then Colebrook's *Irony*, the latest book devoted entirely to a literary-philosophical treatment of the concept, calls attention to another key issue: the politics of irony. Even so, she does not

---

69. Dane, *The Critical Mythology of Irony*, 191.
70. Muecke, *Irony*, 14.
71. Dane, *The Critical Mythology of Irony*, 46–47.
72. Dane, *The Critical Mythology of Irony*, 191.

abandon the question that embroiled her predecessors in debate. In fact, she astutely links the two concerns together, observing that how a concept of irony engages politics depends upon how that concept figures the relation between irony and meaning: "Those who emphasise the stability of irony value, or assume the value of, a politics directed towards community and unity. Those who celebrate the destabilising force of irony, by contrast, insist that politics is the rejection, contestation or disruption of shared norms."[73] In other words, the concept of a coherent, defined irony—the meaning of which is intended by an author and perceived by a competent audience—corresponds with the expectation of a coherent, defined community. Conversely, the concept of an uncertain, unbounded irony—the meaning of which is dynamic and changing according to ever-shifting contexts and readerly conventions—encourages the idea of an uncertain, unbounded community.

Colebrook's final conclusion merits particular attention here. After having traversed a wide spectrum of thought on irony, she proposes something of a middle way between the idea that irony has a determinate meaning and the idea that it ultimately devolves into meaninglessness. "Reading literature ironically requires that we think beyond the traditional philosophical commitment to propositional, translatable and non-contradictory thinking, recognising that truth is not simply there to be referred to by an innocent language,"[74] and yet at the same time:

> We can only read texts ironically, seeing the tensions and relations between what is said and not-said, what is and is not the case, if we commit ourselves to a sense and truth towards which speech and language strive. There cannot, then, be a simple abandoning of the structures of truth and reason or the difference of irony in favour of a postmodern world of textuality, where signs coexist without conflict, hierarchy or tension.[75]

Reading irony, Colebrook suggests, entails the rejection of both a simplistic understanding of linguistic intelligibility and the opposite notion of complete linguistic instability. Irony paradoxically renders unintelligible while encouraging the push for intelligibility. It operates by the same double logic of Culler's joke analogy, in which text and reader are, paradoxically, mutually determinative. Irony might be said simultaneously to

---

73. Colebrook, *Irony*, 45.
74. Colebrook, *Irony*, 177.
75. Colebrook, *Irony*, 177.

act upon the reader, whose involuntary reflex is an other-than-straightforward reading, and to be acted upon by the reader, whose response determines the contours of the irony's intelligible meanings.

Theorist Linda Hutcheon shares with Colebrook both this double-logic understanding of irony and an interest in the politics of irony. Defining irony as relational, inclusive, and differential, she explains irony in terms of process: "irony 'happens'—and that is the verb I think best describes the process. It happens in the space *between* (and including) the said and the unsaid; it needs both to happen."[76] Hutcheon's definition echoes the Romantic and New Critical perspective of irony as horizontal tension, as a comprehension of opposing forces. Unlike the more determinate formulations of Muecke and Booth, which might be said to envision irony as a move from mistaken perception to truth, her definition asserts that the "truth" of irony, if one may speak of such a thing, is constituted by its semantic friction. Irony entails "a kind of simultaneous perception of more than one meaning . . . in order to create a third composite (ironic) one."[77] Her definition, furthermore, implies the mutual necessity of text and reader. The said derives primarily from the text, and the unsaid primarily from the reader. The process of irony happens only in the push-and-pull between text and reader, as the said gestures toward the unsaid while the reader resolves the text. Hutcheon deftly sidesteps the notion that authorial intention necessarily plays a role in determining meaning by insinuating the interchangeability of intention and interpretation. She claims, "[I]nterpreters 'mean' as much as *ironists* do."[78] That is, "To call something ironic is to frame or contextualize it in such a way that, in fact, an intentionalist statement has already been made—either by the ironist *or* by the interpreter (or by both)."[79] Here one might hear a resonance with Cicero's articulation of irony—"when you understand something other than what is said."[80] Cicero later clarifies that the person understanding is also the person saying, but his initial formulation betrays the two-sided nature of intention, or understanding. To summarize Hutcheon's stand on the locus of ironic meaning, then, one might say that the text is essential inasmuch as it is the placeholder for irony, but who

76. Hutcheon, *Irony's Edge*, 12.
77. Hutcheon, *Irony's Edge*, 59–60.
78. Hutcheon, *Irony's Edge*, 12.
79. Hutcheon, *Irony's Edge*, 117–18.
80. *De or.* 2.67.269–70, cited and translated in Dane, *The Critical Mythology of Irony*, 49.

intends or understands the irony remains an open question. Both the addressee and the author are, in a sense, readers, interpreters.

As the title of her work suggests, Hutcheon extends her theory of irony into the realm of politics by exploring irony's evaluative dimension. For her, irony not only means but means with a marked evaluative "edge."[81] Tracing a wide variety of views on irony's affective dimension, Hutcheon demonstrates that irony is fundamentally neither negative nor positive, destructive nor constructive, detached nor committed, exclusionary nor inclusionary; rather its potential consists in the multiplicity of these affective charges and their political implications. Her discussion of discursive communities sheds light on the process by which various evaluations may be attributed. Contending against the conventional understanding that "competence" determines a hierarchy of listeners—in which those who are competent understand the irony and those who are not do not—she posits instead: "*[I]t is discursive communities that are simultaneously inclusive and exclusive—not ironies*," and, furthermore, "*everyone* has different knowledges and belongs to (many) different discursive communities."[82] In other words, the evaluative edge of irony depends more on the framework of evaluations and judgments that structures a reader's (or writer's) discursive communities and knowledges than on anything within the ironic text itself. To reformulate from Hutcheon's words, it is discursive communities that are fundamentally evaluative (and political), not irony. Irony only heightens the evaluative aspect of discourse by suggestively rubbing together meanings that are already fraught with evaluation.

Dan Sperber and Deirdre Wilson, the founders of relevance theory, also devote much of their attention to irony's evaluative aspect. If Hutcheon's work can be conceived to ask the question, "How does irony operate as an evaluative force?" then Sperber and Wilson's theorizing might be understood to inquire, "What exactly does irony evaluate?" As theorists aiming to offer an explanatory pragmatics, Sperber and Wilson make a distinction between their study of irony and "rhetorical and literary studies," which entertain "a broad range of loosely related phenomena" as irony.[83] Sperber and Wilson are interested in "overt communication and comprehension," in the measurable aspects of the communicative

---

81. Hutcheon, *Irony's Edge*, 37–56.
82. Hutcheon, *Irony's Edge*, 97.
83. Wilson and Sperber, *Meaning and Relevance*, 126.

act. While their interests do not coincide completely with the interests of theorists discussed here, this study finds their discussion to be relevant inasmuch as it offers a persuasive way of understanding irony—not as a measurable communicative act but rather as a tool of interpretation.

Sperber and Wilson define irony as the communication of an attitude rather than a proposition. Opposing the traditional rhetorical definition, which holds that irony can be reduced to a process of semantic inversion, they point out that pragmatically there would be no reason to revert to irony when one could simply state an ironic comment's semantic inversion outright.[84] (Furthermore, within the framework of the traditional definition, there is an unnecessary potential for confusion in the more semantically complex statements, which allow for a variety of different inversions. Even the example "What a glorious day!" allows for the possibility that "day" is the ironic variable, yielding the intended meaning "What a glorious night!" rather than "What a miserable day!")[85] Rather than locating the meaning of an ironic statement in the content of its words, they look instead to the attitude expressed toward the content. For them, ironical statements express "a belief *about* [the] utterance, rather than *by means of it*."[86] Irony does not make a proposition; it evaluates a prior one. Therefore they define irony as a type of "echoic use" in which the speaker expresses a dissociative attitude toward the echoed proposition,[87] which need not be an exact quote from any single person, but could be a proposition attributable to a group of people or even to society in general (e.g., a social norm or widely held hope or expectation).[88] An innovative formulation of irony within the field of pragmatics, Sperber and Wilson's definition might nonetheless be said to find its roots in a much older conceptualization, at least inasmuch as Aristotle's traditional description of the ironic statement—"he said X, whereas I say Y"[89]—im-

---

84. Wilson and Sperber, "On Verbal Irony," 56–57.

85. Wilson and Sperber, "On Verbal Irony," 54. Wilson and Sperber hint at this confusion. Cf. Yamanashi, "Some Issues in the Treatment of Irony," 272–73. Yamanashi, who treats irony within the theoretical framework advanced by Wilson and Sperber, addresses it more directly.

86. Sperber and Wilson, "Irony and the Use-Mention Distinction," 302. Italics in place of original's all caps.

87. Wilson and Sperber, *Meaning and Relevance*, 128.

88. Wilson and Sperber, *Meaning and Relevance*, 125.

89. *Rhet.* 1420a, cited in Dane, *The Critical Mythology of Irony*, 45.

plies the speaker's quotation of and concomitant dissociation from the quoted X.

Although Sperber and Wilson do not explicitly theorize a double-logic understanding of the locus of ironic meaning like Colebrook and Hutcheon do, their conceptualization nonetheless harmonizes with it, for they implicitly acknowledge the mutual determinacy of text and reader. Language contains the tissue of quotation from which an ironic proposition emerges. The body of prior discourse thus charges the text with the independent potential of provoking an ironic reading. But even as a quoted proposition surfaces in a text and triggers an ironic reading, so a reader identifies the original proposition and attributes an attitude toward it.

Irony in Biblical Discourse

Thus far this review has examined theorists of irony in the general field of literary theory. It remains now to consider those scholars who limit their focus to irony in biblical texts. Edwin M. Good, Carolyn J. Sharp, Lillian R. Klein, and Glenn Holland have plied their scholarly trade in hopes of elucidating irony in the biblical texts, and each offers helpful tools and considerations for reading irony in biblical texts. While others also have presented ironic readings of biblical texts, this study restricts its review to Good and Sharp because of their treatment of the Hebrew Bible as a whole, Lillian R. Klein because of her work's exemplification of Sharp's recommended hermeneutics, and Holland because of his specific attention to divine irony—a concept that proves pertinent to the entire biblical text, in which God is a central character.

From Local to Pervasive Irony

Robert Alter accredits Edwin M. Good's *Irony in the Old Testament* with being the first "book-length study in English by a professional Bible scholar that made a sustained effort to use a literary perspective."[90] While appreciative of Good's efforts, Alter finds fault with his work, especially in its "elastic" concept of irony and its lack of a "clearly defined critical method."[91] Of course, muses Alter, these problems might be "almost

---

90. Alter, *The Art of Biblical Narrative*, 15.
91. Alter, *The Art of Biblical Narrative*, 15.

equally perceptible in the work of many literary critics who discuss irony."[92] Here he echoes the common frustration that irony has come to mean many things and is, as Mieke Bal puts it, "not exclusive enough to be a useful tool."[93]

It is worth an interjection here to flag the coincidence of the literary and ironical hermeneutics in the first biblical studies English monograph that consistently applied either, and to consider what it might mean. The correspondence suggests that a literary consideration of the biblical text and an appreciation for irony are especially complementary. Without a clear definition of irony, it is difficult to specify the relation between a literary reading of the biblical text and an ironic reading. But even so, one might at least entertain with curiosity the notion that the Bible accommodates incongruities, across its corpus as well as across its individual books, to such an extent that it practically demands what might broadly be designated ironic readings from any who would wish to read the text, or one of its constituent parts, as an integral whole. Indeed, as the forthcoming definition of irony will indicate, the case of the ancestral narrative and its interludes invite just such a reading.

Alter's review of Good's study rightly observes that Good does not provide a systematic overview of irony in the Hebrew Bible but only catalogues a number of local ironies. Perhaps this represents a shortcoming. But it may equally prove a strength, in the sense that Good does not fall prey to generalizing from among the Bible's local ironies a single form or type of irony. Instead he offers close readings of different sorts of ironies in different texts, supplying subsequent scholars of biblical irony with food for thought. Not beholden to the constraints of a rigid definition, Good's inclusive approach to irony allows him to consider its different types. He can, for instance, appreciate the comedic irony of Jonah equally as well as the tragic irony of Saul. The flexibility of Good's hermeneutic of irony extends beyond questions of form to the matter of authorial intention: "What [the author] says may have an ironic effect on us, whether or not he worked for that effect. This effect is not invalid. The work stands before us, not as an antiquated object to which we apply analysis as to a cadaver, but as a living voice whose accents we hear and with which we enter conversation."[94] The contrast between Good and his contem-

---

92. Alter, *The Art of Biblical Narrative*, 15.
93. Bal, *Lethal Love*, 23.
94. Good, *Irony in the Old Testament*, 32.

poraries Muecke and Booth is notable. Rather than restricting irony to certain forms and an author's intention, he advances an understanding that appreciates the diversity of ironic effects.

Good's ranging work sparked interest in irony in the Bible and supplied a springboard for further studies. A number of biblical scholars have since tipped their hat to ironies in the biblical text, and a few have even devoted extended study to irony in a particular text. But it was not until Sharp that another scholar devoted a book-length study to irony in the Hebrew Bible. Published nearly half a century later, Sharp's *Irony and Meaning in the Hebrew Bible* sharpens the focus of Good's good work, defining and confronting the issues that attend reading irony in the Bible. On a theoretical level, Sharp enters the debate on the locus of meaning, and she—not unlike Colebrook and Hutcheon—offers irony as a way forward for understanding the hermeneutical tension among author, text, and reader. In addition, she complicates a simplistic understanding of the rhetoric of irony in the Old Testament, showing how the sorts of local ironies that Good identifies often extend beyond themselves to problematize larger themes, such as Israelite identity, gender roles, Israel's relationship with other peoples, and the character of God.

To outline the theoretical underpinnings of her work, Sharp begins by reviewing a selection of modern conceptualizations of irony. She opens with a consideration of Kierkegaard's idea of irony. That she focuses here on "the dynamic force of irony"[95]—as manifest in what Kierkegaard calls "the elusive and ineffable moment of understanding immediately displaced by the anxiety of misunderstanding"[96]—suggests her own understanding of irony as something neither here nor there, a process always in motion, not unlike the Romantics' and New Critics' concept of a horizontal tension inhering between multiple meanings. She rehearses Fish's debate with Booth on whether meaning lies with the author or reader, and ultimately rejects both Booth's and Fish's viewpoints. Indeed, throughout her work, Sharp continually draws attention to the way that irony challenges the hegemony of author, text, or reader. She explains: "Irony demands attention to cues and clues that originate from the text, yet its very presence deconstructs any simplistic construal of intent."[97] In

---

95. Sharp, *Irony and Meaning in the Hebrew Bible*, 12.

96. Kierkegaard, *The Concept of Irony*, 340, quoted in Sharp, *Irony and Meaning in the Hebrew Bible*, 12.

97. Sharp, *Irony and Meaning in the Hebrew Bible*, 88.

other words, irony highlights "the elusive nature of communication"[98] by highlighting the disjunction between signifier (what is said) and signified (what is meant). That the signifier alone is obviously insufficient to communicate meaning evidences a sort of textual intention. The text, it feels like, directs the reader away from the apparent meaning(s) that the signifier would suggest. But the fact that the signified does not proceed unambiguously from the signifier and thus must result from the reader's interpretation, indicates that the reader simultaneously determines meaning. On this point, Sharp echoes the double-logic understanding of theorists like Colebrook and Hutcheon, which formulates irony in terms of a process that privileges both text and reader.[99]

Sharp expands on this understanding with a reflection inspired by Barthes' idea about the quotational nature of texts—which, he contends, are constituted by "traces in displacement."[100] She explains that what is true of texts is "acutely" so of irony, for irony highlights the ironist's control of another discourse while, precisely by doing so, it suggests the impossibility that a discourse might be fixed and controlled.[101] The fact that the ironist appropriates another's discourse reveals the vulnerability of discourse to infinite (re)adoption. Thus she concludes: "Perhaps we need not choose between those two views, namely that irony constitutes a sort of dogmatic master discourse or else that irony is constitutive of the postmodern fragmentation of the coherent signifying subject. Both may be true."[102] In other words, irony exemplifies the paradoxical interplay between text and reader. To acknowledge irony is to acknowledge the ironist's claim to control, that is, the text's autonomy; but such an acknowledgment is precisely, at the same time, an appreciation for the reader's autonomy, for it implies that, just as the text ironically appropriates a

---

98. Sharp, *Irony and Meaning in the Hebrew Bible*, 4.

99. Sharp invokes the idea of "textual voicing" to stress the manner in which ironic meaning doubles back from readerly interpretation (or conversely textual/authorial intention): "The heuristic category of irony suggests that there is such a thing as textual voicing and that some sort of 'unspoken' presses upon the constraints of language in meaningful ways. Yet textual voicing can never be fully defined or domesticated, whether by the original author or by readers, whether according to the rubrics of naïve historicist reconstruction or those of a hypertextualized literary formalism" (*Irony and Meaning in the Hebrew Bible*, 18).

100. Barthes, *The Semiotic Challenge*, 259, quoted in Sharp, *Irony and Meaning*, 44.

101. Sharp, *Irony and Meaning*, 44.

102. Sharp, *Irony and Meaning*, 44.

prior proposition, so the reader may confer new meanings upon the text he reads.

Like Good, Sharp examines a number of biblical texts for local ironies. But in contrast to Good, Sharp offers a more structured analysis of irony, in both its particular expressions and its broader rhetorical implications. She continually stresses irony's capacity to transcend its immediate boundaries and change the complexion of an entire work. Indeed, she asserts that "the presence of irony subverts the act of communication itself" to the effect that its "impact may be felt throughout the entire system of the biblical text and throughout the reader's hermeneutics."[103] In this sense, there is no such thing as a merely local irony. One instance of irony destabilizes the entire text. It invites the reader's suspicion about other potential ironies.

Sharp's attention to the subversive rhetoric of irony leads her to explore four biblical subjects: the foreign ruler character, the prostitute character, prophecy, and the biblical wisdom tradition. In her treatment of each subject, she connects local ironies to their rhetorical implications for themes of identity, gender roles, otherness, and theology. Instead of summarizing her general findings, this study draws attention to Sharp's first exercise of ironic reading, which both demonstrates and undergirds her hermeneutics of irony. She observes in the creation story the power of God's word and particularly the unity that it asserts.[104] God's continual proclamation that the different articles of creation are "good," for instance, suggests their harmony over against their differences. In the creation of humanity, too, there is unity, for humanity is created in God's image. Furthermore, the narrator's wordplay suggests a connection among man, woman, and the earth: "The *'adam* is named as being of the ground (*'adama*), and the woman (*'issa*) is named as being of the man (*'is*)."[105] But ultimately the unity that these connections indicate masks their underlying differences and particularly the otherness that finds expression in the desire for that which is different. When this desire leads to transgression against God's constraints—that is, when the first humans desire to become like God—the differences become markedly clear: "As it turns out, humans are not the same as God, and man is not the same

---

103. Sharp, *Irony and Meaning*, 11.
104. Sharp, *Irony and Meaning*, 36.
105. Sharp, *Irony and Meaning*, 36.

as the ground, and woman is not the same as man."[106] Thus God's and the narrator's words are powerful "and yet unreliable."[107] Power inheres in the words of God and the narrator, words that establish the reality of a unity among God, humanity, and creation; and yet power also inheres in the undermining unspoken of these words, in the gaps that allow for the realization of a different actuality. For from the unspoken, the "seamless unity" of God's creation unravels into difference and alienation.[108] From the very start of the biblical narrative, then, the rhetoric of irony establishes its foothold and the reader witnesses the unreliable, unpredictable nature of both divine and narratorial discourse. So Sharp concludes, "Irony itself must, then, be seen as a fundamental texture of human existence outside the Garden, which is to say, out in the real world that Scripture 'reads' through its stories and genealogies, its songs and prayers, its laws and speeches."[109]

The hermeneutic of irony that Sharp proposes, one that appreciates how an irony outstrips its local confines and has rhetorical implications for the whole of a work, finds illustrative expression in Klein's reading of Judges. Klein's *The Triumph of Irony in the Book of Judges* does not merely catalogue a number of ironies in Judges. It points to an underlying structure for irony and reads the entirety of the text in light of this structure. According to Klein, the introductory material in Judges outlines the "ironic configuration of the book"[110] through "motifs and/or paradigms" that frame the forthcoming ironic contrast:[111] "the divergence of human and divine perceptions in the exposition alerts the reader to the ironic opposition of two 'voices' of the book: Yahweh's knowing voice and humanity's ignorant one."[112] In Sperber and Wilson's echoic terms of irony, the exposition of Judges introduces two basic propositions as well as the apparent preference for one over the other; therefore when the discredited proposition is echoed in the subsequent narrative, a measure of dissociation clearly accompanies it. In her exploration of the rest of Judges, Klein hearkens to the contrast between these two propositions,

---

106. Sharp, *Irony and Meaning*, 36.
107. Sharp, *Irony and Meaning*, 36.
108. Sharp, *Irony and Meaning*, 36.
109. Sharp, *Irony and Meaning*, 42.
110. Klein, *The Triumph of Irony*, 23.
111. Klein, *The Triumph of Irony*, 13.
112. Klein, *The Triumph of Irony*, 35.

or perspectives: the Yahwistic viewpoint, focused on covenant integrity, and the dominant viewpoint of the Israelites, focused on occupation and warfare. One marked example of this ironic contrast is the character of Jephthah. In his discourse with the Ammonites, Jephthah identifies Yahweh as the real judge and thus seems to be "a long-awaited exemplar, a Yahwist judge, a man who will surely avert the decline of Israel into short-ranged, merely human perspectives."[113] Yet his practice of "human sacrifice and internecine war"—"two anti-Yahwist actions"—ironizes this suggestion and exposes Jephthah's and Israel's continual decline.[114] Klein summarizes the cumulative effect of this and many other ironies in Judges: even where there is no explicit judgment, "the reader is invited to share Yahweh's [implicit] judgment of Israel.... The ironic structure dramatizes the interaction of human will, free but naïve, and Yahweh's will and knowledge."[115]

Divine Irony

Unlike Sharp, Good, and Klein, Holland focuses his reading of irony primarily on one specific biblical passage, 2 Cor 10–13. That he does not begin his treatment of that text until roughly two thirds of the way through his study reveals his dedication toward theorizing irony, particularly what he calls "divine irony." Holland concedes that the concept of irony today includes forms of irony that would not have been recognized as such in antiquity. But reading irony into an ancient text remains a legitimate endeavor for him "because 'irony' is a critic's term, not an author's term."[116] Thus Holland concerns himself not with ancient conceptualizations of irony but rather with ancient conceptualizations of what readers today might readily identify as irony. Primary among his assertions is that the modern concept of irony comes into view in ancient texts particularly in the clash between divine and human perspectives (an assertion with which Klein would no doubt agree).[117] The classic case of Greek tragedy illustrates this well.[118] The original audience did not identify the disparity

---

113. Klein, *The Triumph of Irony*, 89.
114. Klein, *The Triumph of Irony*, 98.
115. Klein, *The Triumph of Irony*, 191.
116. Holland, *Divine Irony*, 59.
117. Holland, *Divine Irony*, 60.
118. Holland, *Divine Irony*, 69.

between human intention and divine fate as "irony" (dramatic, tragic, or otherwise), but they appreciated the interplay nonetheless. To buttress his claim with examples outside of Greek tragedy, Holland points to stories from the Hebrew Bible, including the examples of Pharaoh and Job. Holland concludes that irony, when translated into the context of antiquity, is about the juxtaposition of appearance, "what humanity seems to see," and reality, "what the gods see."[119]

To flesh out his concept of divine irony, Holland turns to Socrates, who (in Plato's work) evaded the label *eiron* but whose behavior is nevertheless characterized as that of *eironeia*.[120] Holland locates the essence of Socratic irony neither in its effectiveness as a rhetorical trope or figure, nor in its characterization of Socrates' behavior, but rather in its divine origin. Having received the oracle that no one is wiser than himself, Socrates seeks wise men in order to refute the oracle, but finding no one who seemed genuinely wise, Socrates concludes that it is his duty to reveal to others their ignorance. As Holland explains, the irony in Socrates' encounters with others

> arises from the contrast between human expectations and the truth the god reveals. Human expectation is that wisdom consists of knowledge tempered by experience and contemplation. The god's revealed truth is that wisdom consists of being aware that one is ignorant. Plato's Socrates appropriates that irony and makes it his own, but in its origins it is undeniably divine irony.[121]

For Holland, divine irony does not yield truth in the sense of knowledge and certainty. It reveals the truth of humanity's ignorance, which is a truth committed to the (impossible) divine perspective.

There are obvious differences between Paul and Socrates, but even so Holland attempts to draw a parallel between the divine encounters that "led them to adopt the divine perspective"—a perspective that "in the context of the common beliefs and practices of their times, was most often expressed as irony."[122] Like Socrates, Paul (in 2 Cor 10–13) seeks to complicate his audience's perception of reality and advocate a divine perspective that recognizes the hollowness of humanity's assumed knowledge or status: "Socrates reckoned no one was wiser than he only because

---

119. Holland, *Divine Irony*, 79.
120. Holland, *Divine Irony*, 83–84.
121. Holland, *Divine Irony*, 94.
122. Holland, *Divine Irony*, 120.

he knew he knew nothing; Paul is nothing, but this is because God has chosen him to be nothing. To be nothing is an honor, a divinely sanctioned status. Paul can claim to be a better apostle precisely because he is more completely a nothing."[123] Importantly for both Paul and Socrates, their irony points toward truth, though that truth itself is more of an absence or void of human "truth" and an awareness of something more than it is a determinate alternative.

Definition of Irony

As Dane rightly observes, irony's variable definition means that "[i]t can be made to cover almost any literary topic imaginable."[124] Other theorists concur. Irony has enjoyed such a variety of conceptualizations that it risks losing its value as an interpretive tool.[125] Any attempt to read with a hermeneutics of irony must therefore define irony. In what follows, this study situates its definition of irony among the vast complex of irony's different formulations. Because "neither here nor there" characterizes this study's concept of irony in several ways, it will serve as a continual reference point for the definition.

Indicative of Text-Reader Double Logic

First, irony is neither here nor there in terms of the locus of meaning. As "double-logic" theorists like Hutcheon, Colebrook, and Sharp have demonstrated, irony resists exclusive association with either textual intention or readerly interpretation because it simultaneously requires both. Like a joke, irony both determines and is determined by the audience's response. The text determines the sense of irony, as it complicates meaning beyond the plain sense such that the reader feels compelled to reject what is said and locate meaning instead in what is unsaid. But the text's "act" of complication betrays an equal and opposite "act" of the reader, namely the reader's confrontation and requisite interpretation of the textual indeterminacy. The reflexive determinations—of text and reader—are incommensurate. Each asserts its priority, and yet each requires the priority

---

123. Holland, *Divine Irony*, 147–48.
124. Dane, *The Critical Mythology of Irony*, 10.
125. Bal remarks that irony is "not exclusive enough to be a useful tool" (*Lethal Love*, 23).

of the other. This phenomenon may be understood as an instance of the paradox of cause and effect: a cause can only be posited on the basis of an effect, and yet an effect can only be felt because of some cause. Neither can assume exclusive priority.[126] One might, of course, point out that this phenomenon extends beyond irony to the more general literary question of meaning's locus. The distinction to be made here is that irony heightens the sense of this phenomenon, accentuating both the textual and readerly forces at play. Readers invariably posit irony not as the result of a contrived reading but as a natural result of the text. And yet the disputes over the presence or nature of irony in a text—as in the debate between Booth and Fish—demonstrate the necessity of the reader's interpretive agency to the reading of irony.

Quotational, Evaluatively Dissociative, and Dialogic

Second, irony is neither here nor there in terms of an ironic proposition, that is, a final determinate statement of ironic meaning. The traditional rhetorical formulation of irony would suggest that ironic meaning is articulable, that it is simply the semantic inversion of an ironic statement. This formulation, however, crumbles when one considers the multiple variables involved in an ironic statement and the significance of the communicative context. Statements that contain multiple potential objects of inversion can yield a variety of different ironic meanings. And contrary to the assumption that a purposefully false statement entails irony—that it requires semantic inversion—there are some intentionally false statements that function in their communicative context to convey not their opposite but rather a broader sense of absurdity or senselessness.[127] As Sperber and Wilson's echoic account of irony points out, what the traditional definition of irony as semantic inversion overlooks is the crucial ingredient of expectation. Expectation, in other words, is the element that determines which semantic variables are engaged by irony, the element that transforms what would otherwise be an absurdity into irony. To adapt an illustrative example introduced by H. P. Grice and later developed by Sperber and Wilson:[128] Margaret and Pauline walk by a car

---

126. Culler, *On Deconstruction*, 86–88.

127. Wilson, "The Pragmatics of Verbal Irony," 1727.

128. Wilson and Sperber, "On Verbal Irony," 56, 61. This adaptation abridges Wilson and Sperber's example and substitutes two characters, Margaret and Pauline, for the first and second person (i.e., I and you).

that has had its windows smashed. Margaret exclaims, "That car's windows are intact." By itself, the statement is not ironic; it is simply absurd. But if Margaret had earlier complained that the street was being used as a dumping-ground for broken-down cars, and Pauline had responded incredulously that Margaret must be imagining things, then the statement would qualify firmly as ironic. Margaret's statement would not be pointless; it would be a purposeful quotation of Pauline's idea that the cars on the street are not broken-down. This illustration, incidentally, elucidates the two commonly recognized formal elements of irony—unawareness and contrast—that Muecke's and Booth's definitions advance. A prior proposition is voiced in such a way as to suggest that it remains a sincere, unsuspecting expectation, that it is unaware of its new, incongruous context. This unawareness draws out the contrast between its original meaning and the suggested reevaluation.

Irony thus operates not by making a proposition but by quoting one. Whether the quoted proposition has found expression previously in another person's utterance or instead in a more general idea, such as a cultural standard, it serves in the ironic statement to refer to an expectation. As Sperber and Wilson contend, and Hutcheon is at pains to point out, the result is that irony is principally not propositional but evaluative. Irony communicates neither a proposition nor its opposite, but rather a dissociative attitude toward the quoted proposition, spanning "from amused tolerance through various shades of resignation or disappointment to contempt, disgust, outrage or scorn."[129] A long-cited literary example of irony, Mark Antony's famous "Brutus is an honorable man" speech (in Shakespeare's *Julius Caesar*), exemplifies the spectrum of dissociative evaluation that irony encompasses. The refrain, an echo of a proposition that Mark Antony most vehemently opposes, proceeds from a seemingly straightforward declaration of Brutus' integrity to expressions of uncertainty, doubt, and finally outright rejection:

> No doubt it is not his own most personal opinion, but he is prepared to put it forward in a spirit of appeasement, echoing the sentiments of Brutus's supporters. Then, each time he repeats it, he mentions it in the context of further facts which make it clear that he is dissociating himself from it, more strongly each time: The irony is first hinted at, then strengthened, then forced home. Mark Antony carries his audience with him, through a

---

129. Sperber and Wilson, *Meaning and Relevance*, 130.

series of successively more hostile attitudes to a proposition
which itself remains unchanged from start to finish.[130]

Irony, as this example demonstrates, is much more than a simple semantic inversion. To be sure, it does express a negative evaluation of the plain sense of an utterance or idea, but this evaluation inhabits a wide range of dissociative attitudes, thus complicating the question of an irony's ultimate meaning. What attitude an instance of irony expresses, and what sorts of meaning this attitude might connote are open questions. It might be helpful, therefore, to prioritize the effects of irony in this order: evaluation and then meaning. That is, irony expresses first and foremost a dissociative attitude. This attitude in turn invites an alternative meaning.

Irony's invitation of an alternative meaning, however, does not result in a finalized meaning, a proposition with which one can definitively replace the original quoted one. Rather, irony's quotationality entails an irresolvable dialogue. M. M. Bakhtin's "dialogic approach" to language illumines this aspect of irony.[131] Bakhtin explains that a person may "make use of someone else's discourse for his own purposes, by inserting a new semantic intention into a discourse which already has, and which retains, an intention of its own . . . . In one discourse, two semantic intentions appear, two voices."[132] The two voices, furthermore, might engage in a confrontational dialogue; indeed, Bakhtin asserts, one "very often literally repeats the statement of the other speaker, investing it with new value and accenting it in his own way—with expressions of doubt, indignation, irony, mockery, ridicule, and the like."[133] (It is in this sense that Bakhtin affirms irony as a paradigm for all utterance, as a special case that accentuates the play of meaning in any discourse.[134] Irony derives from a prior

130. Sperber and Wilson, "Irony and the Use-Mention Distinction," 315.

131. Bakhtin explains, "[A] dialogic approach is possible toward any signifying part of an utterance, even toward an individual word, if that word is perceived not as the impersonal word of language but as a sign of someone else's semantic position, as the representative of another person's utterance; that is, if we hear in it someone else's voice" (*Problems of Dostoevsky's Poetics*, 181–85).

132. Bakhtin, *Problems of Dostoevsky's Poetics*, 189.

133. Bakhtin, *Problems of Dostoevsky's Poetics*, 194.

134. Clark and Holquist make note of Bakhtin's comparison of utterance to ventriloquy and his enshrinement of irony as a supreme example of the utterance's ventriloquial character. Discourse derives only from prior discourse, and yet is made ever anew by the new attitudes adopted toward that discourse: "Bakhtin argues that in such local instances as the English comic novel, what is often written off as mere irony actually constitutes a paradigm for all utterance: I can appropriate meaning to my own purposes only by ventriloquizing" (*Mikhail Bakhtin*, 15).

discourse and therefore textuality precedes the reader; but it assumes its meaning only when the reader identifies the prior proposition and interprets a dissociative attitude toward it, and therefore the reader precedes the text.) The unfinalizable dialogue between the two conflicting voices exemplifies the comprehensive meaning of irony, a meaning that aligns with the Romantics and New Critics' conceptualization as well as with Hutcheon's emphasis on irony's semantic inclusivity, its frictionality. Irony is not a simple hierarchy of meaning but rather a horizontal tension between two (or more) voices, a contest of meaning. It embraces not a single propositional meaning but the entire dialogic conflict. That this is so is most evident in the fact that an ironic statement necessarily voices the proposition against which it is poised. Inscribed within an ironic statement is the proposition that it challenges. For the ironic "voice" to be heard, the voice that it contests must also be heard.

This inclusivity, by the way, flags a distinction between irony and other tropes (e.g., metaphor, metonymy, and synecdoche). Whereas other tropes relate meanings in mercantile fashion, employing one sign provisionally as a means of exchange for another sign, irony employs a sign that remains in tension with that to which it is interpreted to point.[135] The said and the unsaid each assume "meaning only in relation to the other."[136]

Rhetorically Pervasive

Third, as a consequence of irony's dialogical aspect, irony is neither here nor there in terms of having identifiable limits. As Sharp is so keen to point out, irony is necessarily rhetorically subversive because its mistrust of the said and valorization of the unsaid undermines an entire discourse, suggesting that any said is vulnerable to the unsaid. Any part of the text, in other words, is liable to explode in dialogue between what is said and what lurks behind as unsaid. This, then, is to say that irony is never local, that its effect is always pervasive. The effect of a single "instance" of irony radiates throughout the text, exposing it to the possibility of further irony.

---

135. Hutcheon, *Irony's Edge*, 58–66. Hutcheon acknowledges that other tropes are semantically plural like irony but argues that, whereas in other tropes the vehicle acts more as a means to a separate end, irony's vehicle (i.e., what is said) is itself a fundamental part of the ironic meaning.

136. Hutcheon, *Irony's Edge*, 59.

Furthermore, as Colebrook's reading of irony's political ramifications would suggest, this formulation of irony as unbounded, as infinitely capable of disturbing its surroundings, has the political effect of unbinding communities, of questioning their boundaries and making them susceptible to redefinition. Or as Hutcheon points out, irony engages the structures of knowledge and value that constitute communities, and through its suggestion of preference it reorders the terms by which communities are constructed. Identity is therefore always implicated in the process of irony. Challenging the ideologies that structure a community's identity, irony calls into question that identity. It initiates a dialogue that cannot be finalized, complicating identity beyond a simple definition. It is no coincidence that irony in the ancestral narrative problematizes ancestral identity. Dealing with thematic structures around which ancestral identity is formed, it necessarily calls into question the knowledge and values that constitute ancestral identity.

Semantically Excessive

Fourth, and as a corollary of irony's indeterminacy and unboundedness, irony might be conceived of as neither here nor there in the sense that its meaning is ultimately unknowable. Holland's articulation of divine irony in the characters of Socrates and Paul sketches the outlines of irony's unknowability. Both characters employ irony as a sort of known unknown. That is, their irony knowingly points toward an unknown—beyond the realm of humanity to a divine worldview that cannot be attained. Irony resides in each character's self-effacing commitment to a truth that is acknowledged to be ungraspable by human word or deed. To be sure, Genesis does not explicitly gesture toward this sort of irony. But the oblique motivations underlying the divine character's involvement in the story does accord with a sense of divine irony. Harold Bloom's colorful reading of Yahweh's character in selected texts from Genesis points out the narrative's "elliptical style"—particularly with regard to Yahweh's character—and posits that it "derives from a shrewd sense that a reader's preconceived responses need to be evaded, or provoked into freshness by dissociative means."[137] The dissociative echoes throughout Genesis, whether or not attributed to a disjunction between its characters' worldview and the divine perspective, lend themselves to a sense that the

---

137. Bloom, *The Book of J*, 26.

narrative does not render a coherent worldview, that truth is somehow just outside its grasp. As this study will demonstrate in its close readings, the interludes of Hagar, Dinah, and Tamar problematize the unity of ancestral identity and suggest that any such identity is neither here nor there, that it is not what the ancestral family thinks it to be, not what the reader may think it to be, but rather something more. Sharp's conclusion with regard to irony's surplus meaning gives voice to this sense of divine—or otherwise ungraspable—irony: irony signifies "more than."[138]

Having traced irony's flitting dynamic—its neither-here-nor-there-ness—this study hazards a working definition that will recapitulate the description of irony traced here and inform the use of irony as a hermeneutical tool: accentuating the paradoxical determinations of text and reader, irony is a quotational, evaluatively dissociative, dialogical, rhetorically pervasive, and semantically excessive mode of discourse.

Why Read Irony in Genesis? Against the Charge of Anachronism

Before proceeding to the close ironic readings of the interludes, one final matter requires attention: the legitimacy of reading irony in Genesis. It is not uncommon for ironic readings of ancient texts to meet with accusations of anachronism. The charge, so it goes, is that it is anachronistic to apply the term "irony" to texts that have no such word. According to this study's understanding of irony as a critic's term, as a tool for discussing and analyzing a text, irony qualifies for the study of any text. But in the endeavor to take a text on its own terms, the question of anachronism remains: is it legitimate to read according to a concept of which the text may be unaware? Does a hermeneutic of irony not apply excessive readerly force on the text? As this question poses a valid concern, the query must be made: does the text of Genesis understand the sort of irony postulated by this study? Any answer in the affirmative must show that the poetics of biblical narrative (and Genesis in particular) suits ironic readings; it must identify features of the text that foster such readings. It must demonstrate—to analogize to the phenomenon of spoken irony—an ironic "tone" in the text. What elements in the text betray the ironic tone of voice?

---

138. Sharp, *Irony and Meaning*, 21.

That the Old Testament lacks an equivalent for the word "irony" does not necessarily signal its ignorance of the idea. Lexicalization—"the existence of a word for a concept"[139]—need not limit a person's appreciation of a phenomenon. Much of the Old Testament, for instance, demonstrates a keen grasp of narrative, of how to tell a story, and yet it lacks a direct synonym for "story" or "narrative."[140] Its familiarity with narrative finds expression not in a single term synonymous with "story" or "narrative" but rather more broadly in the poetical significance it confers upon words. Words create and order the world (Gen 1), and, as Alter observes, the words of characters do much the same, so much so that "many pieces of third-person narration prove on inspection to be dialogue-bound, verbally mirroring elements of dialogue which precede them or which they introduce."[141] The determining force of words reflects what one might call a literary impulse, a commitment to constructing a meaningful, coherent narrative. The priority is not simply to record events but to tell a story—to weave meaning through events, characters, spaces, and other narrative elements by the centripetal force of words.[142]

Although the Old Testament lacks a word synonymous with irony, it exhibits its appreciation for the concept—much as it does for the idea of story—through its general poetics, through the ways it might be said to structure meaning. Three elements, in particular, register its grasp of irony: repetition, *peripeteia*, and frugal narration. A penchant for repetition suggests the text's awareness of the potential ironic effect that attends quoting an old element in a new context; the text's illustrations of *peripeteia* demonstrates its mastery of a particularly salient sort of ironic reversal, the expression of contrast between the intention and consequence of an action; and the sparing narrative style attests to the power that the text confers upon the unsaid, the space that is necessary for irony to blossom.

---

139. Fowler, *Linguistic Criticism*, 215.

140. Berlin muses, "It is ironic that, although telling is so important in the biblical tradition, there is no word for story" (*Poetics and Interpretation*, 11).

141. Alter, *The Art of Biblical Narrative*, 65.

142. Centripetal refers here to the interrelating force of words, the way that they operate as part of a linguistic order that structures meaning according to their relations. This centripetal force opposes the centrifugal force that is sought in the attempt to use words to refer to extralinguistic phenomena. Cf. Frye, *The Great Code*, 57–60.

Repetition

The prevalence of repetition within biblical narrative furnishes an instructive starting point from which to explore Genesis' appreciation of irony. Repetition is a short step away from irony, for repetition, if it is read to be intentional, is quotation, and quotation, if it is read to express a negative evaluation of the original proposition, is ironic. A repeated proposition, in other words, might be ironic if the new context into which it is transposed suggests a negative evaluation of the proposition's previous voicing. To illustrate with a straightforward biblical example: in Mark 9:22–23, a father pleading for his son's health says to Jesus, "If you are able to do anything, have pity on us and help us"—to which Jesus replies, "If you are able!—All things can be done for the one who believes" (NRSV).[143] Jesus revoices the father's question of his ability, "If you are able . . ." in the frame of his declaration of ability, recontextualizing the phrase in order to introduce an element of incongruity—in order to challenge the original proposition.

In *The Art of Biblical Narrative* Robert Alter catalogues types of repetition in the Old Testament: repetitions of *Leitworter* ("leading words"), motifs, themes, sequences of action, and type-scenes.[144] Although he does not always articulate his analyses of these repetitions in terms of irony, he nonetheless makes the case that repetition often serves the function of allusion, purposefully eliciting comparison between different instances of a repeated element in order to highlight not only similarities but also points of distinction. Comparisons that spotlight difference naturally engage what we call irony; the echo of an instance stands in an incongruous relation with its precedent, critically divergent of expectations established by the repetition. Rehearsing a few different cases of repetition in Genesis that transpire on the levels of *Leitworter*, motif, theme, and type-scene will suffice to demonstrate the text's awareness and appreciation of just this sort of repetition—what this study calls irony.

The Joseph narrative (Gen 37–50) is home to a number of repetitions, several of which illustrate well the text's apprehension of irony. The first case explored here turns on the repetition of the *Leitworter* הכר נא and their attendant theme of deception.[145] In Gen 37:32–33,

---

143. All biblical quotations will be my own translation unless parenthetically indicated otherwise.

144. See Alter, *The Art of Biblical Narrative*, 95–96.

145. This study will adhere to the following policy on the citation of Hebrew. If

Judah and his brothers present Jacob with Joseph's bloody coat, inviting him to recognize it—הכר נא. He does, and presumes Joseph dead. In Gen 38:25–26, Tamar—whom Judah had unwittingly slept with after buying her as he would a prostitute—presents Judah with the items he gave as surety for payment and demands, "Recognize [them] please (הכר נא)." Judah does, and countermands the death sentence that he had decreed previously, when he had judged his daughter-in-law's pregnancy as a sign of her harlotry. These *Leitworter* attract interpretive attention in the early rabbinic midrash, *Genesis Rabbah*—which, incidentally, would appear to corroborate the historical reach of their ironic effect. Rabbi Johanan speculates on the sense of divine justice that transpires between Judah's participation in deception—namely, when he and his brothers deceive Jacob into believing that Joseph has died—and his victimization by deception: "The Holy One Blessed be He said to Judah, 'You said to your father "Recognize! (הכר נא)" (37:32). By your life, Tamar will say to you, "Recognize! (הכר נא)" (38:23).'"[146] The repetition of dialogue suggests for Johanan an ironic equivalence between the deception that Judah perpetrates against Jacob and the deception that Tamar perpetrates against Judah, and his interpretation points to an irony that might be fleshed out further. The expectations attendant on the *Leitworter* meet with contradiction in Tamar's story. Recognition here functions to deceive not unjustly but justly. Thus the echoed dialogue highlights an incongruity—the reversal of Judah's roles—and encourages judgment of his character: from cunning perpetrator of a rather unjustifiable crime to unwitting victim of a scheme that he himself justifies (38:26), Judah is the unjust deceiver justly deceived.

Another case of ironic repetition concerns not only Judah but also his brothers. The story establishes early on the motif of Joseph's dreams and the corresponding prediction that his family will one day bow (חוה) before him (37:7, 9). His brothers, however, set out to wreck Joseph's dreams. As they make plans to do him harm, they voice their expectation that his dreams will amount to nothing: "We will see what becomes of his dreams" (37:20). The motif then lies dormant until Joseph and his brothers meet again. At this point, the motif echoes ironically as the brothers

---

quoted, the Hebrew is represented according to the consonantal text of the *BHS*. If cited parenthetically outside a quotation or if referred to in the abstract (i.e., outside a specific usage), the Hebrew is represented according to its lexical entry (typically its verbal root or its absolute singular form).

146. *Gen. Rab.* 85.11–12.

unsuspectingly bow down (חוה) to Joseph (42:6), acting contrary to their expectations. As if to confirm this irony, the narrative recounts that, upon their second trip to Egypt, the brothers bow down (חוה) to Joseph twice more (43:26, 28). The thrifty motivic repetition showcases the text's consciousness of irony. Repeated only in the contexts of the brothers' expectation and its opposite reality, the motif of Joseph's dreams of worship marks the incongruity between what the brothers anticipate and what transpires, underlining the brothers' ignorance and Joseph's unexpected triumph.

A third case of ironic repetition might be found in the type-scene that Gen 38 appropriates. Because this case will receive extensive treatment later in the close reading of the Tamar interlude, it will be enough here to trace the basic outline of irony. At first glance, the story of Gen 38 resembles no type-scene. Only at its end does an explicit parallel emerge. Tamar's birth of twins bears resemblance to Rebekah's twin birth of Jacob and Esau. Besides an exact match of narration—והנה ת(א)ומ(י)ם בבטנה (25:24; 38:27) [147]—both stories describe a physical struggle between the twins. Taking its cue from this parallel, a retrospective reading of Gen 38 discovers that, while Tamar does not experience the conventional barren matriarch type-scene—that is, the initial problem of barrenness that is then overcome through divine aid—her experience mirrors the matriarchs in several defamiliarized ways. She too encounters an obstacle in acquiring offspring. But her problem is not barrenness; rather, she struggles to find a mate who remains alive and willing. And just as Rebekah and Rachel meet their husband by a body of water, so too Tamar meets a man by water.[148] But Tamar meets and conceives by her father-in-law instead of her husband. Lastly, Tamar's eventual achievement of conception and birth parallels the matriarchs' experience as well. But whereas God plays the decisive role in the matriarchs' conceptions and births, he is absent from the resolution to Tamar's tale. Indeed, the resolution to her tale is not so straightforward. Even after conception, Tamar must contend with another threat—not to the child, but to her own life. These strange echoes of the barren matriarch type-scene in Tamar's story invite a comparison between Tamar's circumstances and the matriarchs', but the failure of the motifs to inhabit the expectations engendered by previous scenes ultimately seems to ironize the suggestion that Tamar too is a

---

147. Gen 25:24 uses תומם, while Gen 38:27 uses the lengthened form תאומים.

148. Assuming that Enaim (עינים) means something like "two springs" or "two wells."

matriarch. This mother is, in a sense, a pseudo-matriarch. Or more strongly put, she is an anti-matriarch. Her experience diverges from the matriarchs' in certain key aspects: she is a non-ancestral woman who, without the help of God, secures offspring, not from a husband but from her own father-in-law.

Peripeteia

In addition to its propensity for repetition, the biblical narrative demonstrates an appreciable grasp of *peripeteia*, a narrative device that enjoyed use and recognition in Greco-Roman antiquity. A distinguishing ingredient of what Aristotle calls the complex narrative,[149] *peripeteia* is "the change to the opposite of the things done"[150]—meaning that the character's action effects the opposite of its intended result[151]—and it frequently results from a character's ignorance. Aristotle offers the example of the messenger in Sophocles' *Oedipus the King*: his first revelation—that Polybus is dead—is meant to cheer Oedipus but instead evokes in him the fear of incest, and his second revelation—that Polybus is not Oedipus' father—is meant to remove that fear but instead heightens it.[152] Interestingly, as Muecke has observed, some translations of Aristotle's *Poetics* render *peripeteia* as irony[153]—and not without reason, one may presume. A character's intention, whether echoed explicitly or invoked by a reader's memory, resounds ironically in the context of its opposite consequence.

The Joseph narrative includes two archetypal instances of *peripeteia*, both of which illustrate a comic turn of events. The antagonistic party intends to subject the protagonist to exile and inefficacy, but the planned action ultimately meets with the opposite consequence: the protagonist

---

149. Belfiore, "περιπέτεια as Discontinuous Action," 183–94. Belfiore explains that Aristotle explicitly associates simple plots with continuous action. Belfiore contends that, as a corollary of this relation, complex plots are comprised of discontinuous action. This would seemingly accord with Aristotle's understanding of complex plots, as he identifies *peripeteia* and *anagnorisis* as its two distinguishing elements. Both *peripeteia* ("a change to the opposite of the things done," that is, action that accomplishes the opposite of its intention) and *anagnorisis* (which refers to a recognition scene) entail discontinuity: they alter the direction of a plot's movement.

150. *Poet.* 1452a22–29.

151. Belfiore, "περιπέτεια as Discontinuous Action," 189.

152. Belfiore, "περιπέτεια as Discontinuous Action," 191.

153. Muecke, *Irony*, 14.

achieves his/her goal, while at the same time effecting a familial reunion. In the first case, Joseph's brothers sell him off to traders, intending to shatter his dreams. In the end, however, his dreams are realized, and his brothers do precisely that which they had hoped to avoid: they bow down before him. Similarly, in Gen 38, Judah desires to keep Tamar at a safe distance from his family, and so he sends her away; but then he unwittingly sleeps with her. In both cases the biblical narrative allows the antagonistic party to voice its intention, and in both cases it suggests through lexical equivalence an ironic parallel between the intention and its opposite consequence. Joseph's brothers do the very thing that Joseph had dreamt (חוה, "bow down"; 37:7, 9; 42:6; 43:26, 28)—which they thought they had preempted (37:20). And after Judah directs Tamar to remain (ישׁי) at her father's house as a widow (אלמנה) in order to prevent another fatal union between her and his family (38:11), she defies him by situating herself (ישׁב) in a place other than her father's home and changing out of the clothes of her widowhood (אלמנה) (38:14), which leads ultimately to the intimacy that Judah had sought to preclude. In both instances, the lexical equivalence draws attention to the echo of intention in its incongruous context, thereby highlighting the ironic *peripeteia*.

Frugal Narration

Whereas one might consider repetition to constitute an essential *ingredient* of irony, *peripeteia* might be considered a pronounced *example* of the ironic process. Juxtaposing an intention and its reverse consequence, *peripeteia* showcases the incongruity of irony—its contending voices. The hospitable narrative conditions for both ironic repetition and the specific case of *peripeteia* derive from the third piece of evidence for the Old Testament's appreciation of irony, namely, its thrifty narrative style. Its sparing narration serves as a sort of enzyme for irony. Blanketing much of the story in silence and leaving only the "decisive points" articulated,[154] the narrative accentuates the relation between said and unsaid that is so decisive for irony. The narrative's empty spaces and mutely drawn equivalences allow for previous "saids" to echo, to reverberate in cavernous spaces, inviting the question: are these reverberations merely a confirmation

---

154. Auerbach, *Mimesis*, 11.

of what has gone before, or do they ring ironically? As Carolyn Sharp asks, "What . . . if the unspoken is at odds with the articulated?"[155]

Genesis supplies numerous cases of the unsaid's ability to nuance the plain sense of the said. The first Hagar interlude offers one particularly salient example, which is well worth a brief exploration here, before it receives a more extensive analysis in the first close reading. In Gen 16, the narrative recounts how Sarai oppresses her maidservant, Hagar, and how Hagar then receives a divine promise. On the surface, the narrative moves along a tersely narrated psychological axis: first detailing Sarai's plan, that she be built up by having a son, and then relating its opposite consequence, that she is less esteemed in Hagar's eyes—another example of *peripeteia*, incidentally—the narrative provides an account of why Sarai oppresses Hagar and why Hagar runs away to the wilderness, where she encounters God and receives a promise of multiplied offspring not unlike that given previously to Abram. A powerful tale in its own right that outlines the divine relation with an outsider, the story gains in significance when what is said rubs against what remains unsaid. A string of equivalences with the preceding story, in which God makes a covenant with Abram, summons up echoes in the unsaid space. God had explained to Abram that his descendants would be sojourners (גר) in a land not theirs, where they would work as slaves (עבד) for a people who would subjugate them (ענה) (15:13);[156] later God would judge their oppressors and they would come out with great possessions (15:14). The divine forecast reverberates soon thereafter—but in a rather unexpected manner. Hagar, whose name (הגר) resembles the designation for a sojourner, is a maidservant (שפחה; commonly collocated with עבד)[157] whom Sarai humbles (ענה) (16:1, 6). Hagar then runs away from her mistress and receives a divine promise of descendants, numerous and independent. The parallels between Hagar's experience and that which God foretells of Abram's descendants echo in the unsaid space of Gen 16, and the echoes chafe against a story that on the surface concerns Sarai's (and perhaps synecdochically, the ancestral) quest for offspring—a story that makes no explicit reference to the previous story. The echoes tease out an ironic reversal of the picture outlined by God's promise to Abram in the preceding story. Hagar's resemblance to the ancestral descendants may in fact

155. Sharp, *Irony and Meaning*, 7.

156. For an explanation of this uncommon translation, see the discussion of Gen 15:13–14 in the section "The Concept of Sojourn (גור)" in ch. 3 (p. 99).

157. E.g., Gen 12:16; 20:14; 24:35; 30:43; 32:6.

indicate that a non-ancestral character is capable of relating to God just as intimately as the ancestral family does. Conversely, the resemblance between Sarai and the future oppressors of the ancestral family may insinuate that, far from enjoying an inviolably privileged relationship with God, the ancestral family is judged by God here just as its future oppressors will be later.[158]

Another case of friction between said and unsaid, this one a bit more playful, is found in Gen 21:1–7, which narrates the birth of Isaac to Sarah and Abraham. The episode concludes with Sarah asking, "Who would have said (מלל) to/of Abraham that Sarah would nurse children? For I have borne a son in his old age" (21:7). Sarah's question remains unanswered. Its rhetoric would seem designed to express surprise and incredulity at a rather unlikely turn of events. This surface meaning, however, gains in significance when considered against the unsaid; that is, in remaining unanswered, the question carries a semantic potential that might be exploited by entertaining a response. Preceding Sarah's question, the narrator four times attributes an event to what God had previously "said" (loosely construing a variety of biblical Hebrew verbs of articulation as "say"): God visits Sarah as he "said" he would (אמר; 21:1) God does with Sarah what he "said" he would (דבר; 21:1) Sarah bears a son at the appointed time that God had "said" (דבר; 21:2) and Abraham circumcises Isaac eight days after his birth as God had "said" he should do (צוה; 21:4). The narrative's insistence that every detail of Isaac's birth has proceeded according to God's word reverberates in the hollow space that follows Sarah's question. Regardless of whether Sarah has God in mind at all (and perhaps she does; cf. v. 6), an attentive reader certainly may. A gentle irony ignites in the juxtaposition of an unanswered question, which seemingly expresses incredulity above all else, and its empty space, in which echoes an answer that exchanges providential purpose for fortuity.

The Interlude

It is no coincidence that several of the examples of these poetical features—repetition, *peripeteia*, and a frugal narrative style—come from

---

158. Cf. Reis, "Hagar Requited," 87–88, 106; Zakovitch, *"And You Shall Tell Your Son—,"* 28; Rosenberg, *King and Kin*, 90; all of which suggest that the affliction endured by Abram's descendants is a consequence of the affliction first endured by Hagar.

the interludes. The interludes hum with an ironic charge. They harbor themes from the ancestral narrative (repetition), alternative subjectivities that sometimes reverse ancestral intentions (*peripeteia*), and little to no commentary on their significance to the ancestral narrative (frugal narrative style).

Indeed, the concept of interlude itself might be understood as a poetical structure that accommodates the potential for ironic effects. It harmonizes notably on several points with this study's definition of irony. The motivic interchange of an interlude necessarily involves quotation: thematic fragments from the main body are purposefully repeated in the interlude. The thematic appropriation places the fragments in an unfamiliar context where their defamiliarized form suggests that they are being quoted to a different, potentially evaluatively dissociative, effect. This effect, moreover, is pervasive. Even as the interlude gives way to the primary content (refrain, recapitulation), the memory of its difference alters the hearing of the thematic restatements. Simply put, after the interludes, the themes will never be the same. It is in this sense that the interlude might be said to be dialogic: it encourages a dialogue between the effects or meanings attributed to the thematic elements as they occur in the main body and as they occur in the interludes. This dialogue, in turn, renders the interlude semantically excessive: its meaning is not to be found in one voice or another—one instance of a theme or another—but rather in the unfinalizable interplay between thematic statements.

While the correspondence between interlude and irony does not itself signal a necessary connection, it does demonstrate that the interlude as a form charges the text with the potential for ironic effects. The idea raised by Good's joint expedition into the literary and ironical dimensions of the biblical text here finds confirmation, at least in the context of the book of Genesis. A literary reading of Genesis demands an appreciation of its ironic capacity, for the narrative suggestively counterposes the ancestral narrative against the interludes within it. It mixes primary thematic material in the strange new contexts of the interludes, where the incongruous relations of the motivic iterations invite reevaluation of the thematic material. The hermeneutical lens of irony is necessary to hold the motifs in the tension between their original voicing and their revoicing, to understand how they can mean one thing in their original setting and something different against the backdrop of the interludes.

Summary

The debate over irony in musical discourse suggests that irony is fundamentally a hermeneutical matter, that it is a question not of form but of interpretation of form. As such, irony characterizes not the interludes themselves but rather a lens through which one might read the interludes, a way to interpret the effects of their recitation of ancestral motifs in unfamiliar contexts. Surveying the history of irony as a concept, and particularly its conceptualization in recent literary and biblical discourse, this study arrives at its own working definition of irony as a quotational, evaluatively dissociative, dialogical, rhetorically pervasive, and semantically excessive mode of discourse. As a final preliminary to reading the interludes with a hermeneutics of irony, this study demonstrates that the text of Genesis appreciates irony, that several of its narrative features—repetition, *peripeteia*, a frugal narrative style, and the interludes themselves—charge the text with significant ironic potential.

3

The Hagar Interludes

Traditional Interpretation

THE CLOSE READING OF the Hagar interludes begins in a familiar place. Like the Introduction, it commences with an acknowledgment of the traditional reading of Gen 12–50. To recapitulate, the Introduction establishes the general identification of Gen 12–50 as the ancestral narrative, as a story about the ancestral family's budding relationship with God, the land and its inhabitants, and itself. It observes that the conventional reading construes ancestral identity—the family's relationship with God, the land and its inhabitants, and itself—in exclusive terms. By flagging this traditional interpretive trajectory, it foregrounds the strangeness of the strange stories, stories whose disjunctive relation to the ancestral plot and alternate subjectivity defamiliarize ancestral identity.

This close reading also appreciates the classification of Gen 12–50 as the ancestral narrative. Its focus, however, rests not on the general exclusivity attributed to ancestral identity but rather on the specific exclusivity attributed to the ancestral–divine relationship, for this relationship serves as the primary pivot around which conventional readings naturalize the strangeness of the Hagar interludes. This close reading therefore begins by addressing the effect that an ancestor-centered reading has on understanding the ancestral family's relationship with God. It explores how conventional readings take the divine program as the narrative program and then confer narrative priority on the ancestral family, and how this yields a reading of an exclusive ancestral–divine relationship. It then examines how the reading of an exclusive ancestral–divine relationship precipitates the interpretation that the Hagar interludes are a narrative foil that illustrates one aspect or another of this relationship.

The Divine Program as the Ancestral Prerogative

Readings of the ancestral narrative customarily treat the divine agenda outlined in Gen 12:1-3, 7 as the unifying thread that holds the various stories together. God's announcement is "programmatic."[1] It functions not only as a promise from God to Abram, but also as an "announcement of plot" from the narrator to the reader.[2] The narrative will be about the ancestral family's journey toward descendants, blessing, and inheritance of the promised land. As von Rad puts it, the words of "the great promise . . . overarch the story" of the ancestral narrative.[3]

Furthermore, this traditional line of reading observes that the divine announcement does not merely introduce and anticipate the plot. It recurs regularly, continually structuring the interests of the ancestral family's story. Abraham, Isaac, and Jacob each receive one or more announcements that descendants, blessing, and land await the family.[4] The placement of these announcements—one appears near the start of each narrative cycle[5]—suggests their function as interpretive frames that confirm the significance of the divine program for each generation of the ancestral family.[6] Thus the divine program is "the constant element in

---

1. Turner, *Announcements of Plot*, 55, and von Rad, *Genesis*, 169. While Turner and von Rad interpret the divine announcement as programmatic specifically for the Abraham story, others apply it more broadly to the ancestral narrative. See, e.g., Clines, *The Theme of the Pentateuch*, 48.

2. The application of the phrase "announcement of plot" to the Genesis narrative has been popularized by Turner's *Announcements of Plot*, which considers Gen 12:1-3 as an announcement of plot for the Abraham story.

3. Von Rad, *Genesis*, 169.

4. E.g., for Abraham, Gen 12:1-3, 7; for Isaac, 26:3-4; for Jacob, 28:13-14.

5. Gen 12:1-3, 7 in the Abraham Cycle (12:1—25:18), 26:3-4 in the Jacob Cycle (25:19—37:1), and 35:11-12 just before the Joseph Cycle (37:2—50:26).

6. Turner summarizes the significance of the repeated announcements: they are confirmations that God's plan continues with the family's next-in-line and reminders that the plan has not yet reached fruition. Regarding the announcement in Gen 35:11-12, he explains: "Such echoes of the patriarchal promises affirm Jacob as continuing not only the family line, but also maintaining God's favour. However, they also underline that nothing promised to Abraham in ch. 17 has come to fruition, nor yet to Jacob. The stuttering progress towards fulfilment continues" (*Genesis*, 153).

the midst of all the changing situations of this very chequered history."[7] Its prominence throughout the narrative attracts such interpretive attention that, as Victor P. Hamilton summarizes, "Almost everybody who has written on the subject agrees that the theme of divine promise unites the patriarchal cycles."[8]

A natural tension, however, arises as a result of this line of reading. On the one hand, the interpretive focus rests on the divine character, whose programmatic announcements thematically structure the narrative. On the other hand, attention centers on the ancestral family as the first and continued recipients of the divine promises, as the regular beneficiaries of the divine program. This thematic friction elicits the question: whose story is this—God's or the ancestral family's? In other words, if the divine program becomes the narrative program, who stands at the center of the narrative program? Although few readings capitulate to this simplistic binary,[9] most do exhibit the tendency to concentrate on one party more than the other. As the label "ancestral narrative" indicates, it is typically the ancestral family who assumes the ultimate emphasis.[10] Although the divine program precipitates the ancestral narrative, the ancestral narrative is read to subsume, or predominate over, the divine program. The ancestral family is read to circumscribe the outworking of the divine promises. The narrative drama, then, centers not merely on the divine program but more specifically on the ancestral family that lies at heart of it. So John C. L. Gibson explains:

---

7. Childs, *Introduction to the Old Testament*, 151. Cf. Goldingay, "The Patriarchs in Scripture and History," 11–12.

8. Hamilton, *The Book of Genesis: Chapters 1–17*, 39. See also Fretheim, who observes, "Genesis 12:1–3 are *universally* considered to provide the key, not only for the story of Abraham, but for the rest of Genesis" (*Abraham*, 32; emphasis mine).

9. Most commentators do not explicitly address the question of whose story the narrative is. It is, however, often implicitly acknowledged and resolved by the observation that the ancestral family's story and the divine purpose seem mutually determinative of one another: to speak of one, in other words, is necessarily to speak of the other. Westermann sums up this interconnectedness in his claim that the ancestral story is narrated "theologically." The story of the ancestral family "cannot be spoken of without at the same time speaking of God" (*Genesis 12–36*, 24).

10. This is not to suggest that the divine character or his program is neglected. Even as the ancestral family assumes interpretive priority, readers commonly acknowledge "the consistent hidden presence and purpose of God" as foundational to the plot. See, e.g., Moberly, who also identifies God as "the most important" character in Genesis (*Genesis 12–50*, 19).

> Everything he [Abraham] does following his call and everything that happens to him are either directly related to them [the promises] in the narratives or may be brought into connection with them by the exercise of a little imagination. Will he be able to settle in Canaan? Will he have a son? How will his contacts with the peoples already in the land turn out? If we keep these questions in our minds as we read through the chapters 12–25, we will see how the working out of the promises supplies both the main element of tension in the plot of the stories and the primary key to their interpretation.[11]

Note, in particular, the absence of mention of the divine character. The divine program contributes to "the main element of tension" in the plot and is "key" to the stories' interpretation, but the ancestral family retains the reader's attention as the primary subject of the story. The divine program becomes, effectively, the ancestral program. That is, it is not God's promise of descendants, blessing, and land that structures the plot, but rather the ancestral family's anticipation and pursuit of descendants, blessing, and land.

There are exceptions to the tendency to privilege the ancestral family, most notable among them the readings offered by W. Lee Humphreys in *The Character of God* and Jack Miles in *God: A Biography*, both of which take God as the primary subject of the story. Even among readings such as these, however, the ancestral characters typically retain the spotlight as God's unique associates. There is thus little critical difference between ancestor-centered readings and God-centered readings inasmuch as the latter take the ancestors as the center of the divine program. In fact, the difference is nearly indistinguishable once the concept of ancestral election is unveiled. Whether God or the ancestral family is taken as the narrative's primary subject, the ancestral family assumes the determinative role. It is the central cog on which the story turns. So Hamilton explains:

> The election of Abraham is not designed to isolate this family from the other families of the earth. On the contrary, this family is to become the vehicle by which all families of the earth may be reconciled to God . . . . Thus the selection of Abraham's family is a means to an end in God's overall plan for his world . . . . How will this blessing come about? Gen. 12:1ff. makes it clear that reconciliation with God is possible only when there

---

11. Gibson, *Genesis*, 2:12. This is not to suggest that ancestor-centered readings completely disregard the role of the divine character, but rather to illustrate their tendency to shift the focus from him to the ancestral family.

is reconciliation with Abraham, or at least the absence of strife. *One cannot be reconciled with God and be at odds with Abraham.*[12]

The reason for the interpretive predilection for the ancestral family often remains unstated, but one might surmise a few plausible causes. First, the ancestral family is the main subject of the story. Who acts, sees, and speaks most in the ancestral narrative?[13] In a word, the ancestral family: Abraham, Isaac, Jacob, Joseph, and their close relations. God occasionally appears, but he is not a consistent presence.[14] Indeed, his presence wanes as the story progresses.[15] His appearance, furthermore, is characterized more by speech than by action,[16] to such an extent that one might almost consider him more of a stage director than active participant. Although his stage directions trigger the ancestral drama, the ancestral drama dominates the story and in a sense absorbs the directions. In other words, what seems to matter in the narrative is not the success of God's plan but the ancestral family's fate. The narrative drama, by and large, revolves around the ancestral family and its struggles—with itself, with the land and its inhabitants, and with God—for preservation and growth in the land.[17]

---

12. Hamilton, *The Book of Genesis: Chapters 1–17*, 52. Emphasis mine. Cf. Marshall, who gives voice to the common label of Abram (and implicitly the ancestral family) as "a funnel" that directs the outworking of the divine will (*Genesis*, 41).

13. Bal, *Lethal Love*, 21, identifies these three questions as guides to identifying whom the story represents as the subject(s).

14. It is noteworthy that Moberly, who asserts God's regular presence in the narrative, qualifies this assertion in terms of visibility: God is a "consistent *hidden* presence" (*Genesis 12–50*, 19; my emphasis).

15. Cf. Fox, who observes that "as the book [of Genesis] progresses, there is notably less and less human contact with the deity" ("Can Genesis Be Read as a Book?" 34). For further discussion of God's diminishing presence in the narrative, see the section "The Dynamic of Agency in the Ancestral Narrative" in ch. 5 (p. 178).

16. Humphreys observes, "Most frequently God's appearances in the narrative of Genesis involve speech," and "it is speech that makes him meaningfully present for other characters and for readers" (*The Character of God*, 9).

17. Clines summarizes this interest in the ancestral family's survival in the land: "In thematic terms, Genesis 12–50 is primarily concerned with the fulfilment (or, perhaps, the non-fulfilment) of the posterity-element in the divine promises to the patriarchs.... In this question about the fulfilment or otherwise of the promise lies the significance of the triple narrative of the 'ancestress in danger' (chs. 12; 20; 26), the significance of the barrenness of the wives of the patriarchs (Sarah, Rebekah, Rachel), the significance of the fraternal rivalries that endanger the life of one or more of the heirs of the promise (Ishmael; Jacob; Joseph; Benjamin), and the significance of the famines in the land of Canaan (Gen. 12.12; 26.1; 41.54) that threaten the survival of the patriarchal family as a whole" (*The Theme of the Pentateuch*, 48).

Second, interpreters may retrojectively transpose the Primary History's center of attention, the people of Israel, onto the narrative in Genesis.[18] Eager to trace the origin of Israel, interpreters overlook the divine character, perhaps taking him for granted as a natural accompaniment to the people of Israel, and focus on the family. The label of Gen 12–50 as "ancestral" or "patriarchal" hints at this possibility inasmuch as it suggests that the significance of the narrative rests primarily in the family as the ancestors or forefathers of a particular people, namely Israel. This possibility is further corroborated by the fact that readings of the ancestral narrative often become readings of Israelite identity. From this perspective, the story world of Genesis is "a story world focused on Israelite ancestry"[19] and how it came to stand distinct from other ancestries: "One of the central concerns of the *patriarchal* stories is the issue of *Israel's* identity: who belongs to the 'chosen people' and who does not? Israel alone receives the special promises of God, while its relatives—the Ishmaelites, the Edomites, the Ammonites, the Moabites, the Midianites, the Arameans—are excluded."[20]

A third reason for the interpretive focus on the ancestral family is the tendency to read according to theological preconceptions that equate the divine character's word with narrative ontological reality. Lisa Zunshine's explanation of the cognitive psychological concepts metarepresentation and representation assists in illumining this tendency. A metarepresentation consists of two components: the source and the content of a representation.[21] "The 'meta' part of the representation, that little 'tag' that specifies the source of the information ... is what prevents the representation from circulating freely within our cognitive system."[22] With regard to the information that Abram will bring forth a great nation (12:1–2), the metarepresentation would consist of the

---

18. Primary History refers to the narrative that spans the Pentateuch, Joshua, Judges, 1–2 Samuel, and 1–2 Kings.

19. Ngan, "Neither Here Nor There," 73.

20. Exum, "The Accusing Look," 144. My emphasis. Cf. Okoye, who shares the similar view that the narrative subordinates stories that point away from Israelite identity: "[S]ome peoples are included in [the narrative] only by having their history and their interests either wiped out or subordinated to those of Israel" ("Sarah and Hagar," 164). For a comprehensive look at how the ancestral narrative may define Israelite identity (through the divine process of election and "diselection"), see Heard, *Dynamics of Diselection*.

21. Zunshine, *Why We Read Fiction*, 47.

22. Zunshine, *Why We Read Fiction*, 50.

source of information—"The LORD said"—and the proposition itself—"I will make you into a great nation." Metarepresentation is significant in the reading process—as well as in day-to-day life—because it allows the reader to receive information under different "degrees of advisement."[23] Metarepresentation, in other words, makes information conditional. It may or may not be dependable; it may apply only in certain contexts. Zunshine distinguishes representation from metarepresentation in terms of this conditionality: while metarepresentational information is only as dependable as its source, representation is processed without a source tag and thus as "architecturally true."[24] Theological readings of Genesis that treat God's words as indicative of the story world's reality process them as representation; the source tag "God said" becomes redundant.[25] In other words, God is as reliable as the narrator. (Is this any surprise? The common label for the traditional narrator, "omniscient," would suggest that readers naturally identify both agents as equally reliable.) The divine program thus is identical to the narrative program, and so attention shifts from questions of the divine character—what are his motives? is he reliable?—to questions of the ancestral family—how will they live into this promised reality? From the start, the narrative drama consists not in what the divine character says but in how the ancestral family will respond.

The interpretive preference for the ancestral family is subtle but important. It attunes readings to the ancestral family who receives the divine promise, rather than to the divine character who makes promises. The ancestral family thus becomes not just one of many among whom God may mediate his purposes. It is *the* family. The divine program is read solipsistically through the interests of the ancestral family. As a result, the ancestral relationship with God is read in exclusive terms, in terms that treat the divine program as consisting exclusively in the ancestral family.[26] The divine program is the ancestral family's privilege; the ancestral

---

23. Zunshine, *Why We Read Fiction*, 60, 129.

24. Zunshine, *Why We Read Fiction*, 62.

25. Cf. Cosmides and Tooby: "Once [information] is established to a sufficient degree of certainty, source . . . tags are lost . . . e.g., most people cannot remember who told them that apples are edible or that plants photosynthesize" ("Consider the Source," 70, quoted in Zunshine, *Why We Read Fiction*, 51).

26. E.g., Humphreys says, "God, who earlier engaged humanity directly, will now engage all other humans through Abram: As they engage Abram, so they engage him, and he them" (*The Character of God*, 83). Humphreys' reading is significant because it, unlike most, privileges the divine character. This hermeneutic would seem to be

family "alone receives the special promises of God."[27] It is therefore no coincidence that interpreters commonly identify the ancestral family as "the elect," as specially chosen to carry out God's will in the world.[28] God may engage and indeed bless other characters, but the ancestral family remains his chosen instrument.[29] The "fact of separateness by divine design" marks their story.[30]

The Hagar Interludes as a Foil

The exclusive relationship that the ancestral family enjoys with God is constructed not only on the basis of its apparent funneling of the divine program but also on the support of outsider characters whose experience is seen to accentuate the special nature of the ancestral family's divine relationship. The Hagar interludes are a case in point. Turning attention away from the ancestral family and focalizing the story briefly through an Egyptian maidservant, the interludes resist immediate unification with the thematic trajectory of the ancestral narrative. They are strangers in the narrative. They do not naturally accord with the ancestral family's interests in offspring, land, and blessing. Interpreters therefore rationalize their inclusion, or "naturalize" them,[31] in terms of how they throw into relief aspects of the ancestral drama, particularly the ancestral–divine relationship and the realization of the divine promises.

Conventional readings generally interpret the Hagar interludes as a narrative foil in one or more of the three following ways: (1) they exhibit a partial fulfillment of the divine promise of offspring that accentuates

---

more flexible to reading various mediations of the divine program. Treating God as the subject rather than the ancestral family, Humphreys would not be as beholden to reading the ancestral family as the sole mediator of the divine will. Thus it is all the more striking that Humphreys zeros in on the ancestral family and attributes to it an exclusive role in the divine program.

27. Exum, "The Accusing Look," 144.

28. Barth gives classic articulation to the ancestral family's special selection: "As God elects Abraham, so among his sons He elects Isaac, and among Isaac's sons Jacob" (*Church Dogmatics*, II:2: 218-19).

29. Kaminsky, *Yet I Loved Jacob*, 34. Kaminsky clarifies that divine election is not equivalent to blessing (or in theological terms, salvation). It has simply to do with being chosen. For a broader discussion of how election plays out in Genesis, see the rest of Kaminsky, *Yet I Loved Jacob*, and Heard, *Dynamics of Diselection*.

30. Heard, *Dynamics of Diselection*, 183.

31. See fn. 21 in the Introduction (p. 6).

the later, richer fulfillment; (2) they dramatize the event of "diselection," which again foregrounds the realization of God's promise in Isaac;[32] and (3) they illustrate a case of ancestral doubt that complements and enriches the eventual fulfillment of God's promise and the subsequent show of ancestral faith. In each case, the ancestral family remains the narrative focus. Hagar's stories serve to illustrate, in one way or another, the nature of the family's special relationship with God.

The first reading trajectory regards the Hagar interludes as evidence that the divine promise of offspring has reached fruition, albeit partially. Just prior to the Hagar interludes, Abram airs his doubts regarding the promise, and God responds with reassurance and the specification that Abram's heir will be his own biological offspring (15:4). Thus the first interlude, in which Abram has a son through Hagar, would seem to represent the fulfillment of God's promise. Bill T. Arnold states that the pregnancy of an Egyptian slavewoman, "a surprising turn of events," indicates "how deeply Yahweh is committed to the covenant promises to Abram's offspring."[33] Similarly, John Goldingay considers the first interlude to be about "the promise of offspring": "The birth of Ishmael is a step towards one aspect of this undertaking."[34] Westermann, who appreciates the multivocal nature of the Hagar interludes—"It was clearly the narrator's intention to allow many voices to speak which do not echo the main theme"[35]—also perceives in them the unifying thread of promise. He highlights in particular the inclusive reach of God's promise, the way God's promise of offspring retains its relevance for Ishmael even after Isaac is born: "Both in his saving action and in his blessing the God of Abraham remains with Ishmael, now driven from his family. God's grace is not restricted to Isaac's line."[36] The comments of Arnold, Goldingay, and Westermann register one way that the Hagar interludes are read as a foil. Demonstrating a fulfillment of the divine promise, the interludes nonetheless portray only a shadow of the promise. They represent "a step towards one aspect" of it. Or they are a supplement to the story of the promise: God's commitment or "grace" is so deep that it reaches even to

32. For an explanation of the concept of "diselection," see fn. 2 in ch. 1 (p. 22).
33. Arnold, *Genesis*, 164.
34. Goldingay, "The Patriarchs in Scripture and History," 14.
35. Westermann, *Genesis 12–36*, 249, speaks specifically here of Gen 16, but his observation may be extended to include the second interlude, as he notes that there are varying narrative interests there as well.
36. Westermann, *Genesis 12–36*, 343.

Ishmael—which is really to say that the main focus of God's commitment or grace lies elsewhere, with Isaac. The Hagar interludes may depict a fulfillment of the promise, but this depiction ultimately does little more than underscore the grander fulfillment that succeeds it.

The second foil-reading of the Hagar interludes begins on the same path as the first. It appreciates the divine promise's seeming fulfillment in Ishmael. It is ultimately, however, a less generous reading, as it differentiates between Ishmael and Isaac on the basis of the covenant and finds Ishmael wanting. Whereas the first reading traces through Hagar's story a movement from non-fulfillment to fulfillment, this second reading hesitates and eventually reverses from fulfillment to non-fulfillment. When Hagar bears Ishmael (16:15–16), he initially appears to qualify as the son of the divine promise. Turner reflects, "This seems confirmed by the command [from the divine messenger to Hagar] to return to her mistress Sarai, and thereby to Abram's household."[37] But even so, Ishmael's place in the promise is not assured. Gordon J. Wenham detects negative evaluative tones at the start of the first Hagar interlude that cause him to regard the promise's apparent fulfillment with suspicion: "At the end Abram has a son. But is he the son of promise (15:4) or not? . . . The unhappy circumstances surrounding the conception of Ishmael leave question marks: only time will tell whether he is the child of promise."[38] And indeed, time does tell: what initially may have looked like fulfillment becomes non-fulfillment in view of the covenant in Gen 17 and the birth of Isaac in Gen 21:1–7. The interludes of Hagar and her son Ishmael become little more than a "diversion,"[39] or "cul-de-sac,"[40] in the divine plan. Hagar and Ishmael are "branches" pruned from the ancestral tree.[41] "This process," says Arnold, "is part of the inexorable movement of Genesis, as it traces Israel's ancestry in a straight line through a process of divergence, in which each generation has only one son continuing the line."[42] Whereas the first approach treats the Hagar interludes as a foil by rendering them as stories that show shadows of the promise,

---

37. Turner, *Genesis*, 78.

38. Wenham, *Genesis 16–50*, 12–13. Wenham cites Sarai's blaming God for her infertility and Abram's obedience to his wife (which echoes the first man's obedience to the woman in the garden) as unpromising indicators of Ishmael's status.

39. Wenham, *Genesis 16–50*, 13.

40. Von Rad, *Genesis*, 196.

41. Heard, *Dynamics of Diselection*, 2.

42. Arnold, *Genesis*, 195.

the second approach takes a step beyond the shadows into the light of the promise, where the silhouette of fulfillment in Ishmael recedes into non-fulfillment. Von Rad explains, "Ishmael is not the heir of promise but a secondary descendant who retires from the line of promise."[43] Thus in this second reading the significance of the interludes is not that of a partial fulfillment that points to its completion, but of a non-fulfillment that highlights its opposite. Ishmael is the "not-elected one" whose story foregrounds the story of "the one *elected*."[44]

In contrast to the first two lines of reading, which ask the question, "What do Hagar's stories mean for the divine promise of offspring?" the third asks, "What do these stories tell us about the ancestral family?" It psychologizes the ancestral characters and locates the narrative drama in the question of their faith. R. W. L. Moberly models this sort of reading in both the framework he establishes for reading the Abraham cycle and his specific interpretation of the Hagar interludes. "Probably the overarching concern of the Abraham cycle is God's promise to Abraham of a land and a son (12.1–3), a promise whose fulfilment is delayed, so that *Abraham has to live in hopeful faith*."[45] In light of this, "Sarah's action of giving Hagar to Abraham may reasonably be read as showing impatience with the lack of fulfilment of the promise."[46] Von Rad reads along similar lines, though he (like others) does not restrict the show of impatience, or lack of faith, to Sarai alone: "[T]he story of Hagar shows us . . . a fainthearted faith that cannot leave things to God and believes it necessary to help things along."[47]

Perhaps the most interesting aspect of this third approach is that, in its emphasis on divine promise and the ancestral response, it reads against the grain of the particular narrative details. The first Hagar interlude begins with Sarai, who is barren—but who has a plan. As she says to Abram, "Come, please, to my maidservant. Perhaps I will be built up through her" (16:2). The first six verses of the interlude are very much Sarai's—her words, sight, and action determine the plot—and her concern ostensibly rests with her own status, rather than on the divine covenant and promises (of which, furthermore, there is no indication that she has

43. Von Rad, *Genesis*, 196.
44. Brueggemann, *Genesis*, 183.
45. Moberly, *Genesis 12–50*, 23. Emphasis mine.
46. Moberly, *Genesis 12–50*, 23.
47. Von Rad, *Genesis*, 196. Cf. Brueggemann, *Genesis*, 151.

heard).⁴⁸ Nonetheless, readings of this third approach neglect, or look beyond, Sarai's personal concern and posit the hypothetical interests of Abram. Turner summarizes this conflict of perspectives, textually explicit versus readerly supplied: "Her [Sarai's] words underline the differing perspectives of the characters and the reader. For Sarai, Hagar's pregnancy will herald the end to her years of childlessness. For Abram and the reader, it ushers on to the scene Abram's heir and the fulfilment of Yahweh's promise."⁴⁹ As Turner's words suggest, this approach entails that the reader psychologize and read according to Abram's interests, which are of course the divine covenant and promises. Hagar and Ishmael become bit part characters, only significant inasmuch as they expose the ancestral lack of faith in the divine promise.⁵⁰ The Hagar interludes are thus once again a foil to the ancestral narrative, this time foregrounding ancestral doubt or impatience and its consequences⁵¹ in order to highlight the promise's eventual fulfillment and the succeeding show of ancestral faith.⁵² It is little coincidence, according to this line of reading, that the story that follows the interludes is the story of the binding of Isaac. Juxtaposed to this tale of ancestral faith par excellence, the Hagar interludes throw into even deeper relief the sureness of God's covenant and the great stride that Abraham makes in trusting God's promise.⁵³

48. Turner, *Genesis*, 77.

49. Turner, *Genesis*, 77.

50. E.g., Brueggemann, who sees Ishmael's birth as "a temptation for Abraham to trust in the fruit of his own work rather than in the promise" (*Genesis*, 152). See also Schneider, *Sarah*, 102. Schneider perceives Abraham's lack of faith in God's promise in the second interlude as well as the first. His apparent reluctance to let Ishmael go raises the question of how deeply he trusts God. Several other commentators follow similar interpretive possibilities. See, e.g., Heard, *Dynamics of Diselection*, 92–94; Gunn and Fewell, *Narrative in the Hebrew Bible*, 94–97; Amos, "Genesis," 12.

51. E.g., Wenham: "Sarai's anxiety to have a child seems to have delayed the promise's fulfillment some fourteen years. Hasty action springing from unbelief does not forward the divine purpose" (*Genesis 16–50*, 13).

52. Provan, Long, and Longman III model this interpretive trajectory in their summary of the latter portion of the Abraham cycle. They read a drama that moves from the depths of Abraham's doubt to the heights of his faith. First "Abraham grows weary of waiting for God to act" on his promises. But then, "[i]n the culminating moment of Abraham's life, he shows his utter trust in God" (*A Biblical History of Israel*, 110).

53. Schneider, *Sarah*, 102. Schneider thinks that Hagar's interludes invite the question of Abraham's faith and thus are meaningfully juxtaposed to the story of Isaac's binding, which appears to provide an answer. See also Heard, *Dynamics of Diselection*, 92–94; Gunn and Fewell, *Narrative in the Hebrew Bible*, 94–97; Amos, "Genesis," 12. It is also worth noting that several readers perceive parallels between the second Hagar

In addition to these three reading trajectories, there is an alternative approach. Many feminist readings look beyond Abraham and the divine promise in order to attend to the particularity of Hagar and Sarah, characters whose interests do not necessarily align with the main narrative.[54] A brief survey of these readings will help to flesh out this alternative line of interpretation and show how, despite its different angle, it still ultimately reads the interludes as a narrative foil.

While Sarah and Hagar may assume less importance than the patriarchs in the grand scheme of the ancestral narrative, for these interludes they take center stage. Sarah's speech, sight, and action determine the early segments of plot in each interlude, and the latter segments feature Hagar as an independent subject in relation to the divine character. Close readings can therefore mine each character for a wealth of detail that, although seemingly unrelated to the main narrative, nonetheless piques the attentive reader's curiosity. Phyllis Trible's interpretation exemplifies this practice of close reading. For her, the female characters exhibit characteristics comparable to their male counterpart, Abraham. She compares, for instance, Sarai in the first interlude to Abram in the first flight to Egypt:

> In that story, Abram's first words ever addressed Sarai; now Sarai's first words ever address Abram. As Abram schemed to save himself by manipulating Sarai and Pharaoh, so Sarai schemes to promote herself by manipulating Abram and Hagar. As Abram tricked Pharaoh into manhandling Sarai, so Sarai would persuade Abram to manhandle Hagar. Like husband, like wife.[55]

She also catalogues numerous facets of Hagar's singularity. She is "the first person whom a messenger of God visits; the first woman to receive an annunciation; the only woman to receive a divine promise of descendants; the only person to name God; the first woman in the ancestor stories to bear a child . . . and the first person to weep."[56] Several of Hagar's distinc-

---

interlude and the binding of Isaac—parallels that, one might speculate, invite comparison between the two stories. See, e.g., Wenham, *Genesis 16–50*, 99–100; Hamilton, *The Book of Genesis: Chapters 18–50*, 99–100; Turner, *Genesis*, 98–99.

54. Although traditional readings often posit that Sarai's motive for a child is to fulfill the divine promise, there is no indication in the narrative that she is initially aware of the promise. Her desire for a child appears to originate not in expectation of the divine promise's fulfillment but rather more simply in her wish to "be built up" (16:2).

55. Trible, "Ominous Beginnings," 38.

56. Trible, "Ominous Beginnings," 61.

tions place her alongside Abraham; she like him enjoys divine attention and promise.

Although feminist interpretations of the Hagar interludes generally accord primacy of interpretive attention to Sarah and Hagar, they nevertheless acknowledge that these characters' significance derives from Abraham and the promise of an heir. Tammi J. Schneider justifies her treatment of Sarai as a consequential character by noting how the promise of offspring implicitly hinges on her bearing a child (even before God designates her as the mother): "[W]hile Sarai may not always be a major player in the story, from the very beginning of the focus on Abram, her status as his wife and as barren is a major factor of the plot, whether it is stated explicitly or not."[57] Sarai's character, in other words, is important not as a "player" but as a "factor," as a means to an end. In their book, *Gender, Power, and Promise: The Subject of the Bible's First Story*, Danna Nolan Fewell and D. M. Gunn explain the logic of attending to secondary characters by pointing out that secondary characters are, in a sense, constitutive of the primary characters. A primary subject presupposes a secondary subject from which it is different, a dominant voice can only make its case by acknowledging the presence of other voices[58]—the implication being that, even though the biblical text exhibits a patriarchal proclivity, there are nonetheless meaningful secondary perspectives and voices, such as Hagar's and Sarah's, to be found within it. So Trible muses with regard to the Hagar interludes: "[T]he text follows its bias, but not without nuances and nods in other directions."[59] When all is said and done, however, the alternative approach that reads against the narrative's primary interests ends where it began—on the fringes of the narrative. It follows the non-ancestral interests of Sarah and Hagar as far as it can, before surrendering to the narrative's principal interest in Abraham and the divine promise. In this sense, the Hagar interludes once again stand as a foil in the primary narrative. The alternative approach's magnified focus on the peculiarities of Sarah and Hagar ultimately accentuates their negativity in relation to the story of Abraham and the divine promise. As Fewell and Gunn note of Hagar and Ishmael, "Banished to the wilderness, expelled from the garden of Canaan, they inhabit only the margins of the text."[60] Similarly Sarah's self-interest capitulates to the nar-

---

57. Schneider, *Sarah*, 28.
58. Fewell and Gunn, *Gender, Power, and Promise*, 16.
59. Trible, "Ominous Beginnings," 57.
60. Fewell and Gunn, *Gender, Power, and Promise*, 52.

rative's overriding concern in the covenant, and she too is pushed to the margins.⁶¹ Against the difference of these characters, against their narrative marginality, the centrality of Abraham and the son of the promise, Isaac, is made manifest.

The Hagar Interludes as *Mise en Abyme*

The conventional reading that the divine program is a prerogative of the ancestral family, that the ancestral family enjoys a privileged relationship with God, turns the strange stories of Hagar into a foil. The alternate subjectivity and deviation from the main plot are treated as contrasts that accentuate the ancestral family's special connection to God. This study proposes an alternative approach, one that reads the significance of Hagar's interludes to extend beyond the ancestral family and its relationship with God. Attending to the particularity of Hagar and her story, it uncovers a way of reading the interludes as stories that contest the main thrust of the ancestral narrative, as stories that rupture the priority of the ancestral family's relationship with God. This way of reading stems from a knotty narratological complication, namely, the deep resonance between Hagar's sojourning identity and the ancestral family's.

The Concept of Sojourn (גור)

"Now Sarai, the wife of Abram, had not borne [children] to him. And she had an Egyptian maidservant, and her name was Hagar" (16:1). So begins the first Hagar interlude. This narrative introduction provides the seeds from which the readings surveyed above emerge. Following upon the divine reassurance of offspring (e.g., 15:4), the reminder of Sarai's childlessness structures anticipation of an attempted resolution.⁶² The ancestor-centered readings thus have something to chew on hermeneutically: what follows will concern the fulfillment of the divine promise to Abram. The alternative approach, likewise, finds sufficient food for thought. The apparent shift in subjectivity—it is Sarai who is lacking a child, and her

---

61. After Sarah defends her son's claim to the inheritance, calling Abraham to cast out Hagar and Ishmael (21:10), she disappears from the narrative until her death (23:1–2). Cf. Trible, who posits that the patriarchal inclinations of the narrative, which are focused on covenant, lead it to "abandon through silence" Sarah as well as Hagar ("Ominous Beginnings," 53–54).

62. Sarai's barrenness is first suggested in Gen 11:30.

maidservant Hagar who later captures the narrative gaze—affirms its examination of the women. In either case, the resulting interpretation renders the interludes as a narrative foil and maintains the centrality of the ancestral family as special participants in the divine program.

Within the same introduction, however, lies a thematic echo that frustrates the narrative priority of the ancestral family, fracturing the coherence of its identity as privileged partner of the divine. An essential fiber of ancestral identity and the ancestral-divine relationship emerges in an unexpected place—in an outsider living in the family's midst.

Hagar's name is the echo. It is the faint crack from which grows the much larger fissure in the ancestral family's identity as partners of the divine. Yet for many it passes by unnoticed. Clare Amos explains: "In Genesis names and their meanings matter and too little attention has been paid to Hagar's name. Hagar reminds us of *ha-ger*, a Hebrew word that means something like 'sojourner,' 'stranger,' or 'resident alien.'"[63] Hagar (הגר), in other words, is suggestive of the root גור, "to sojourn." This latent resonance invites speculation into how Hagar's character might engage a concept that saturates Genesis. Sojourn, or what Norman C. Habel identifies as a "distinctive immigrant ideology,"[64] characterizes the ancestral family's way of life from the start of the narrative to its finish.[65] And indeed, the concept of sojourn is peculiarly *ancestral*, as it attaches itself exclusively to the ancestral family: every mention of sojourn (גור) in Genesis features an ancestral character as its subject.[66] The ancestral family's travels and residence in the narrative landscape of Genesis receives identification as sojourn consistently enough—Abraham, Isaac, and Jacob are each associated with sojourn on more than one occasion—that sojourning might reasonably be considered a trait[67] central to ancestral

---

63. Amos, "Genesis," 10–11. See also Jeansonne, *The Women of Genesis*, 44; Hughes, "Seeing Hagar Seeing God," 50; and, for an earlier acknowledgment of this lexical similitude, Clarke, *The Holy Bible*, 7:lxi. Many commentators interestingly either overlook or ignore the suggestive lexical resemblance, choosing instead to treat Hagar's name as solely a personal name, a tribal designation, or a name connoting flight or expulsion. For a catalogue of these views, see Gordon J. Wenham, *Genesis 16–50*, 6.

64. Habel, *The Land Is Mine*, 115. Habel identifies this ideology specifically within the Abraham cycle.

65. The first and last explicit mentions of ancestral sojourn are Gen 12:10 and 49:9.

66. Gen 12:10; 15:13; 17:8; 19:9; 20:1; 21:23; 21:34; 23:4; 26:3; 28:4; 32:4; 35:27; 36:7; 37:1; 47:4; 47:9; 49:9.

67. Cf. Chatman, *Story and Discourse*, 121–38. Chatman describes a trait as a

identity.[68] Particularly illustrative of this fact is Jacob's exchange with Pharaoh near the end of Genesis. Asked by Pharaoh what the years of his life are, Jacob responds, "The years of my sojourn are one hundred thirty" (47:9). If Jacob's words to Pharaoh are representative of the ancestral family's experience, then for it life has been indistinguishable from sojourn. The two are one and the same.

The concept of sojourn, furthermore, is deeply rooted in the context of the divine-ancestral relationship. God is a nearly ubiquitous character in the mentions of sojourn: he talks about sojourn,[69] intervenes in ancestral sojourn experiences,[70] and is acknowledged by characters as a key player in the sojourner's life.[71] The divine and ancestral associations with sojourn intersect most saliently in the fact that ancestral sojourn is divinely prescribed. Not only does God's initial call to Abram mandate that the ancestral family uproot itself and move to a land that is not its own, but God also stipulates that sojourning will be a necessary experience of the ancestral family before it enjoys the realization of the divine promises. The ancestral family will be sojourners both physically and temporally displaced from the land (15:13–14; 17:8) before they inherit it.[72] Thus Elisabeth Robertson Kennedy, whose work *Seeking a Homeland* offers a comprehensive review of the concept of sojourn in Genesis, concludes that sojourn "is intimately related to [the] central theme" of the divine promises.[73] To speak of one is to speak of the other.

Sojourn's close association with the divine promises points, in turn, to its association with the expectation of ancestral landedness. The promise of land hovers about the ancestral experience of sojourn so closely that, while sojourn may abstractly mean being a stranger in the land, in the ancestral narrative it paradoxically points to inhabiting land. The first

---

character quality that is consistent throughout a portion of the story and is more generalized than a habit.

68. While the correspondence of interest in sojourn between the ancestral narratives and the rest of the Pentateuch invites comparison, the law's disregard for the ancestors' first sojourns—it focuses instead on Israel's sojourn in Egypt—suggests an important distinction. In other words, the stories of Abraham, Isaac, and Jacob may lead to the story of Israel, but they are not themselves the story of Israel. Theirs are different sojourns.

69. E.g., Gen 15:13; 17:8.

70. E.g., Gen 12:17; 19:10–11; 20:3–7.

71. E.g., Gen 21:22; 23:6; 26:28.

72. Kennedy, *Seeking a Homeland*, 92.

73. Kennedy, *Seeking a Homeland*, 2.

three mentions of sojourn serve well to index its close association with land: the ancestral sojourn in Egypt immediately follows the first divine promise of land (12:7–10), and the next two mentions of sojourn appear in the divine covenants with Abraham—in announcements that indicate that the ancestral offspring will be sojourners but will eventually inherit the promised land (15:13–14; 17:8). Sojourn for the ancestral family therefore expresses not only a negative relation to the land—a sojourner is *not* an inhabitant—but also a positive relation: it anticipates the ancestral family's preservation and eventual landedness.[74]

Sojourn in Genesis thus joins the three elements together: the ancestral family, God, and the promised land. A definition of sojourn true to the narrative context, then, is not merely anyone living in a land that is not one's own. Sojourn is a distinctively ancestral activity, and one that is essentially connected to the divine character and his promise of land. It is the ancestral state of "divinely blessed waiting."[75]

Or is it? Accepting the invitation extended by Hagar's name to explore how her character engages the concept, this study finds that echoes of the ancestral sojourn experience reach far beyond her name. Her experience strikingly mirrors many aspects of the ancestral family's sojourn experiences. Both interludes, Gen 16:1–16 and 21:8–21, follow upon stories that detail the ancestral family's sojourns and, inasmuch as Hagar's name clues the reader in to the concept of sojourn, elicit a comparison between the family's sojourn experiences and Hagar's. The concept of sojourn, this comparison would suggest, may extend beyond the limits of the ancestral family.

There are five neighboring stories of ancestral sojourn—each marked by a word derived from the root גור—which invite immediate comparison with the Hagar interludes.[76] The ancestral sojourn in Egypt (12:10–20) offers a basic narrative representation of the sojourn experience, particularly in Sarai's experience. The divine prediction regarding

74. Kennedy, *Seeking a Homeland*, 69.

75. Kennedy, *Seeking a Homeland*, 235. To my knowledge, Kennedy never articulates the concept as exclusively related to the ancestral experience; her study, however, would suggest such a conceptualization, as she explores sojourn only in relation to the ancestral family's story.

76. The sojourn stories selected for comparison with the Hagar interludes have been chosen on the basis that they precede one of the interludes and are therefore part of the readerly memory in the context of which Hagar's sojourn experiences are read and understood. The forthcoming reading experiment imagines a reader whose attentiveness to the concept of sojourn yields a close analysis of how Hagar's sojourn experience compares with prior ancestral experiences.

the ancestral offspring (15:13–14) provides the clearest definition of sojourn, outlining its connotations for the sojourner's relations to the land, the land's inhabitants, and God. The divine covenant with Abraham (17:1–8) underlines the thematic intimacy between sojourn and the divine promises of land, nationhood, and divine partnership. Lot's experience of sojourn in Sodom (19:1–11) adds detail to the basic representation of Gen 12:10–20; it dramatizes the sociopolitical dynamics of sojourn,[77] particularly through its vivid illustration of the encounter between sojourner and inhabitant. And the first ancestral sojourn in Gerar (20:1–18) offers a second basic narrative representation of the sojourner experience, again most notably in Sarah's experience. This study will compare these stories with the Hagar interludes by reading them retrospectively in the order of their proximity to the Hagar interlude that they precede. That is, the echoes of sojourn in the first Hagar interlude will call forth first a reading of Gen 15:13–14 and then Gen 12:10–20. Similarly, the echoes of sojourn in the second interlude will call forth readings of Gen 20:1–18, 19:1–11, and 17:1–8.

The comparison begins between Hagar's first interlude and the preceding mention of sojourn, which is found in the divine prediction of Gen 15:13–14. There God informs Abram: "You shall surely know that your offspring will be sojourners (גר) in a land that is not theirs. And they will serve (ועבדום) them [the inhabitants?], and they [the inhabitants?] will subjugate (וענו) them for four hundred years. Moreover, the nation that they serve I am going to judge (דן אנכי). And afterward they will come out with great possessions."[78] Here the concept of sojourn receives its clearest formulation in Genesis—being in a land that is not one's own (v. 13). The rest of the prediction fleshes out this definition. Sojourn for the ancestral offspring will mean serving another people—presumably the inhabitants

---

77. Whereas Sarah's sojourn experiences in Gen 12:10–20 and 20:1–18 are considered by this study to be basic narrative representations of sojourn, Lot's is distinguished by its level of detail. Sarah's realization of the sojourn experience generally involves being an object of straightforward discourse, sight, and simple transactions (e.g., לקח and שלח). Lot's sojourn experience, on the other hand, offers the particular drama of a sojourner's resistance, which accentuates the power dynamics at play between sojourner and inhabitant. The inhabitants make threats and act violently, making palpable the sojourner's vulnerability and helplessness at their hands.

78. The Hebrew is ambiguous here as the subject and object of "serve" (עבד) and "subjugate" (ענה) are the same third masculine plural pronoun, the antecedent of which is indeterminate. The most natural translation is that the ancestral offspring serve and the inhabitants of the land subjugate.

of the land—who will subjugate them. It will, furthermore, find resolution when God brings judgment on the nation they serve.

Although the two recognized biblical Hebrew homonyms of גור are not directly related to sojourn and do not appear in Genesis, it is worth remarking on the semantic overlap between them and the connotations of sojourn in Gen 15:13–14. The homonyms' respective meanings center on conflict and fear.[79] This bundle of homonyms is not unlike the various meanings associated with a modern synonym for sojourner, "alien." Alien may indicate a resident who was born elsewhere. But it may also refer adjectivally to a thing that is "unfamiliar and disturbing," as well as nominally to an extraterrestrial being,[80] whose appearance in narrative more often than not strikes fear into the hearts of the earthly characters. Alien in modern usage, like גור in the biblical context, may refer to a sojourner, but it may also connote a potentially conflictive relationship or a fearful phenomenon. Sojourn (גור), as anticipated by God in Gen 15:13–14, envisions an experience that would likely be characterized by elements of its homonyms, conflict and fear. The asymmetry of power between inhabitant and sojourner, and particularly the vulnerability that it entails on the sojourner's part, suggest both the potential for confrontation between sojourner and inhabitant and the prospect of the sojourner's fear of the inhabitant. As will become evident, these elements indeed typify several of the ancestral sojourn experiences.

The definition and model of sojourn in Gen 15:13–14 is conspicuously embodied by Hagar's first sojourn experience.[81] Before she is even named, Hagar is introduced as שפחה מצרית, an Egyptian maidservant (16:1). Her ethnic designation marks her as a sojourner in the strictest of senses: with the ancestral family presumably still in Hebron (cf. 13:18), she is in a land that is not hers. Her identification as a maidservant, furthermore, aligns her with the position of servitude that the ancestral

---

79. Brown, Driver, and Briggs define the first homonym as "stir up strife" and the second as "dread" (*A Hebrew and English Lexicon*, 158–59).

80. "Alien," *Oxford Dictionary of English*.

81. Many studies note a connection between the divine prediction in Gen 15 and Hagar's experience in Gen 16. E.g., Turner, *Genesis*, 77, which remarks upon the basic correspondence between the divine prediction of Abram's offspring as oppressed aliens and the story of Hagar, an Egyptian who is also an oppressed alien. A few even go so far as to suggest a causal link between Abraham and Sarah's oppression of the Egyptian slave Hagar and the predicted events of Gen 15—Israel's slavery and oppression in a foreign land. See Reis, "Hagar Requited," 106; Zakovitch, *"And You Shall Tell Your Son—,"* 28; Rosenberg, *King and Kin*, 90.

offspring assume in the divine prediction. Although the specific term here (שפחה) is of a different root than that used in Gen 15:13 (עבד), it comes from the same semantic paradigm: שפחה appears to be a feminine equivalent of עבד, servant (cf. 12:16). Hagar's position as one of servitude finds confirmation at the end of the first scene in a direct lexical equivalence. Sarai, unhappy that she has become less in Hagar's eyes (16:5), does what the inhabitants of Gen 15:13 do: she subjugates (ענה) the sojourner, Hagar (16:6). It should be noted that "subjugate" is an uncommon translation for the root ענה, which is more commonly translated as "oppress" or "deal harshly with" (see NRSV 15:13; 16:6). This study has decided upon this translation because of the contexts of the divine prediction and Hagar's situation, both of which illustrate the basic social hierarchy between servant and master and suggest that the word refers more to the general act of social relegation, of making subservient, than to a particular act of violence.[82] In Gen 15:13, the stark collocation and contrast of ענה with עבד—ועבדום וענה אתם—suggests that they describe the same event from opposite perspectives: to serve (עבד) is to be on the opposite side of one who subjugates (ענה). In the case of Hagar, Sarai's act of ענה appears to be a response to a loss in status: first, she has given Hagar to Abram "as a wife (לאשה)" (16:3), suggesting that Hagar is no longer merely a servant, and then as a result of Hagar's conception Sarai has become less (קלל) in Hagar's eyes (16:4). These circumstances, coupled with Sarai's complaint to Abram that she has lost esteem in Hagar's eyes (16:5), invite the interpretation that Sarai is trying to rectify the balance of power, that her act (ענה) is meant to put Hagar back in her place.[83]

At this point in the story, Hagar is a sojourner who serves and is subjugated, just as God has predicted the ancestral offspring will be. Sarai's complaint to Abram points to another equivalence. When she blames him

---

82. See Bechtel, "What If Dinah Is Not Raped?" 19–36, for further biblical support for this sort of translation of ענה.

83. Cf. Trible, who reads in Sarai's diminished status (קלל; v. 4) "a reordering of the relationship" between mistress and servant. "The exalted mistress decreases; the lowly slave increases." Thus Sarai's motivation in reproaching Abram is "status": she "wants returned the superior status that she unwittingly relinquished in using Hagar" ("Ominous Beginnings," 39). See also Gossai, who states, "Challenge of power becomes the crux at this point in the narrative" (*Power and Marginality*, 9). Unlike many translations, including Trible's, this study's translation of ענה as "subjugate" does not explicitly include the idea of oppression or abuse or humiliation. Each of these, however, is an imaginable realization of the act of subjugation and thus remains a possibility for interpretation.

for her loss of esteem in Hagar's eyes, she invokes God's judgment—"May the LORD judge (ישפט) between you and me" (16:5)—and thereby recalls, by a different but synonymous verbal root,[84] God's statement that he will judge (דין) the nation that subjugates the ancestral offspring (15:14). Although there is no explicit indication of God's judgment subsequent to Sarai's appeal, the locus of divine attention is suggestive. As the divine messenger explains to Hagar: "The LORD has paid heed (שמע) to your subjugation (עניך)" (16:11). In the case of Sarai, Hagar, and Abram, God has listened first and foremost to Hagar.

The divine judgment in Hagar's favor is further registered by the contrast between the intimacy of her divine encounter and the lack of any such divine encounter in Sarai's (or Abram's) case. Names, in particular, betray the intimacy of Hagar's relationship with God. The divine messenger addresses Hagar by name, something that neither Sarai nor Abram do. He also indicates that God has been attending to her plight even before she fled to the wilderness: God heard her subjugation under Sarai (note the lexical equivalence of ענה in vv. 6, 11). And, if Hagar's words are to be believed—when she names him, "You are El Roi [God who sees me]," and then asks, "Have I truly here seen him who looks after me?" (v. 13)—both God and Hagar see one another.[85] God's concern for Hagar and Hagar's personal encounter with God stand in stark contrast to the ancestral experience in this story. Sarai twice invokes God's name, once attributing her barrenness to him and once appealing to his judgment, but her words find no corroboration in narrative reality. In fact, the narrative reality appears to exceed Sarai's imaginative capacity inasmuch as her call for divine judgment envisions the divine purview to be limited to her and Abram. The intimacy of the ancestral–divine relationship to which Sarai's words lay claim meets with contradiction in these cases. God is attending neither to Sarai's womb nor to the dispute between her and Abram, but instead to Hagar.[86] One last subtle narrative detail drives

---

84. Liedke, "דין." E.g., 1 Sam 24:15, where דין and שפט are used synonymously to refer to the same act of divine judgment.

85. The name that Hagar gives God and her subsequent question are ambiguous in the Hebrew. This study has based its translation on that suggested by Wenham, *Genesis 16–50*, 2. For a basic summary of the various translations, see Wenham, *Genesis 16–50*, 3. Despite the differences among the translations, they generally agree that Hagar's words indicate that God has seen her and she has seen God.

86. Humphreys observes much of this contrast between Hagar's experience of God and Sarai's (and Abram's) and articulates its significance in terms of the "distinct authority structure shaped by gender and class and ethnicity": "Yahweh on one level

this point home. The notice that Sarai is lessened (קלל) in Hagar's eyes recalls the original divine promise to Abram that the one who curses (קלל) him will be cursed (12:3),[87] and might therefore heighten anticipation of Hagar's demise. Instead, it serves to accentuate the surprise of God's seeming alliance with Hagar. She is not cursed; on the contrary, she receives the promise of offspring.

In the divine prediction of Gen 15:13–14, divine judgment precipitates the ancestral offspring's liberation and reception of great possessions. In the case of the first Hagar interlude, divine judgment does not function so auspiciously—in fact, it entails that Hagar return and be subjugated under Sarai—but it does nonetheless involve the promise of liberation. The divine messenger announces that Ishmael will be a "wild ass of a human (פרא אדם)," that his hand will be with/against (-ב) everyone's, and that he will dwell before/against (על פני) all his kin (16:12)—all of which likely connote his independence.[88] The divine messenger also announces that the LORD will multiply Hagar's offspring beyond counting, recalling the similar promise to Abram in 15:5. Inasmuch as the divine prediction of ancestral sojourn in 15:13–14 presumes the preceding promise of multiplied offspring, Hagar's experience corresponds further to the concept of ancestral sojourn: her sojourn too is associated with the

---

seems at home with the hierarchy and its underlying values that position characters in relation to each other in terms of sex, class, and ethnicity.... Yet on another level the meeting of the male God and the female Egyptian handmaid—of the extremes of the social hierarchy in the world of this story—is striking. He appears to Hagar and not to Sarai. He appears to see her and maybe to be seen by her. He gives her a promise that recalls the promise he gave Abraham and thereby links her to the man Yahweh called and blessed in Genesis 12. She alone names God. This is the only encounter between God and a woman that results in a commemorative place name (compare Jacob and God in Genesis 32:23–33). All this is in painful contrast to the continued irony and agony of Sarai in her situation" (*The Character of God*, 101–5).

87. Turner, *Genesis*, 78. See also Okoye, "Sarah and Hagar," 167.

88. Wenham summarizes v. 12 as describing "Ishmael's future destiny, to enjoy a free-roaming ... existence. The freedom his mother sought will be his one day" (*Genesis 16–50*, 10–11). Wenham's translation shares with many other commentators' the sense of Ishmael's adversarial, defiant relationship with others (that is, it envisions Ishmael's hand "against" everyone's and his dwelling "opposite" all his brothers). For an in-depth explanation of the ambiguity of this verse and a case for an equally viable translation that envisions Ishmael's peaceful coexistence with others, see Heard, who concludes, "[T]he precise wording of the messenger's speech is such that readers may find it easy, even compelling, to perceive in this message things Hagar might well desire for her child: freedom, a relationship of mutual assistance with everyone, and proximity to kin" (*Dynamics of Diselection*, 69, 73).

promise of many descendants. Thus the comparison between Hagar's first interlude and the divine prediction results in a largely unified picture of sojourn. In both cases, the servitude and subjugation of the sojourn event yields to divine judgment in favor of the sojourner, who enjoys freedom and the prospect of a growing family.

The echo of sojourn in the first Hagar interlude derives not only from the divine prediction in Gen 15:13–14 but also from the preceding (and first) sojourn experience in Gen 12:10–20. If Gen 15:13–14 is taken as a definition and model of sojourn, then the story of Gen 12:10–20 might be understood as an instantiation of the sojourn experience. In its narrative representation of sojourn, Abram's fear of death precipitates a plan that places Sarai in the more vulnerable position (12:12–14); she is to say that she is Abram's sister, which effectively makes her available to the inhabitants. It is consequently Sarai who most markedly assumes the sojourner's role of subjection to the inhabitants, and so it is she whom Hagar most resembles. Sarai and Hagar, furthermore, conspicuously invite comparison in their inverted ethnic encounters: Sarai is an ancestor (a Hebrew; 14:13) in Egypt, and Hagar is an Egyptian in the ancestral family.

In Egypt, Sarai is an object of possession and speech, but is speechless herself. Pharaoh's leaders see her and praise her to Pharaoh, after which she is taken (לקח) into Pharaoh's house (12:15). Her situation finds resolution when God intervenes, causing Pharaoh to relinquish her to Abram and to send them away (שׁלח; 12:17–20). The reason for divine intervention is not entirely clear: על דבר שׂרי (12:17). Most translations render the phrase more figuratively along the lines of "because of the matter of Sarai."[89] The literal sense, "because of the word of Sarai," however, is not entirely out of the question[90] and in fact, as this study will show, assumes strength as a result of the comparison with Hagar's experience.

Like Sarai, Hagar begins as a voiceless object of speech and possession. Praise precipitated Sarai's move into Pharaoh's house; Sarai's command to Abram precedes Hagar's move into his bosom. Sarai takes (לקח) Hagar and gives her to Abram as wife (16:3), but Hagar soon changes hands as Abram returns her to Sarai's possession: "Look, your maidservant is in your hands" (16:6). Resolution to Hagar's plight results, as it does for Sarai in Egypt, from divine intervention—an intervention that

---

89. Schneider explains: "*D'var* can mean 'speech/word' or, as more suitable here, 'matter/affair'" (*Sarah*, 35).

90. Cf. Trible, "Ominous Beginnings," 37.

would appear to have come about because God has, as the divine messenger says, "paid heed (שמע)" to her subjugation (16:11). Translated most literally, this expression suggests that the LORD has "heard" Hagar, that in her subjugation she has verbally called out and he has responded. If this interpretive possibility is followed, then it corroborates the sense that God responded to Sarai's actual word in the similar sojourn experience in Gen 12:17. As vulnerable, speechless objects of foreign men's attention, of their words and hands, Sarai and Hagar find themselves passed from one party to the next. As objects of divine attention, however, they become—or so the text would imply—subjects of speech whose words solicit divine intervention.

The second Hagar interlude, like the first, echoes several elements of the ancestral sojourn experience that precede it. It most immediately echoes the preceding episode, in which Abraham "sojourned (ויגר) in Gerar (גרר)," a place whose name accents the significance of the sojourn.[91] This experience parallels the first ancestral sojourn in Egypt in several respects: Abraham fears death and so identifies his wife as his sister, the local leader takes her into his house, God intervenes, and the story finds resolution in Sarah's return to Abraham and the ancestral family's preservation. And as Hagar's first experience corresponds to Sarai's in Egypt, so her second corresponds to Sarah's in Gerar. First, both women are again voiceless objects. Sarah is an object of possession—first taken and then restored (20:2, 14)—while Hagar and her son are objects of sight and discourse respectively (21:9–10). Second, as God attends to "the word of Sarah (דבר שרה)" and intervenes on her behalf (20:18),[92] so he attends to Hagar and her son's voices and intervenes in their plight. Although the divine messenger only mentions that God hears Ishmael's voice (21:17), two corresponding narrative details suggest that he listens also to Hagar's voice. First, it is Hagar's distress that the narrative spotlights—she, not Ishmael, lifts her voice and cries out (21:16). Second, the divine messenger implicitly acknowledges her cry of distress by inquiring into her

---

91. Brodie suggests, "[I]n a narrative that plays with words, it [Gerar] tends, whatever its historical status, to strengthen the idea of sojourning, of living like a foreigner in transit, with a healthy nonattachment to things" (*Genesis as Dialogue*, 258).

92. This translation follows the interpretive possibility preferred in the above interpretation of 12:17. Although translations generally render the formulation in both verses as "the matter of Sarai/Sarah," this reading considers how the literal sense is equally as viable, particularly when one bears in mind the synonymous sojourn experience of Hagar, whose voice (and whose son's voice) commands divine attention.

state and commanding her not to fear (21:17).[93] Coupled with Hagar's preceding wilderness experience, where God had been listening to her since her subjugation under Sarai, these details bear out the likelihood that God is equally aware of Hagar's voice.

The basic parallels between Hagar's and Sarah's sojourn experiences—which consist in their vulnerability as objects before foreign subjects of power and their liberation by a God in front of whom they are transformed into speaking subjects—find dramatic expression in the preceding instance of sojourn, in which Lot finds himself at the mercy of the people of Sodom. When Lot attempts to safeguard the two divine messengers whom he has received into his home—ironically at the expense of his own two daughters (19:8)—the Sodomite men respond jeeringly: "This man came to sojourn, and he would actually judge! Now we will do worse to you than to them" (19:9). They then proceed to press (פצר) against him and attempt to break down his door (19:9). The Sodomites' words and actions confirm and give vivid illustration to the implications of sojourn, of living in a land that is not one's own. Sojourn means voicelessness, not being able to judge—or rather to speak a word that means something, that has consequence in the societal context. Sojourn means being an object of the inhabitants' judgments and desires. Sojourn means the potential of being forced into a corner, of having no choice but the one made by the inhabitants. The dramatic picture of sojourn in Lot's case finds particular resonance with Hagar's *second* experience in that here Hagar finds herself completely at the mercy of Abraham and Sarah. Whereas before, she flees Sarai's act of subjugation—suggesting that she assumes a modicum of autonomy—now she is sent away (שלח) by Abraham (21:14). But just as Lot receives divine aid at the moment when the inhabitants' threat reaches its apex and violence seems imminent (19:10-11), so too Hagar meets with divine rescue when the water supply runs out and death looms immediately ahead (21:17-19). Sojourn, at least in the context of these stories, means divine liberation after conflict with the inhabitants has "sent" (שלח; 21:14) or "pressed" (פצר; 19:9) the sojourner to the point of helplessness.[94]

93. Cf. Treacy-Cole, "Women in the Wilderness," 48.

94. Although there is no lexical connection between שלח and פצר, this study cites them together because they both connote the inhabitant's use of force, which puts the sojourner in a helpless situation. A faint resonance may be heard in the English equivalents of these words. One may speak of a helpless situation as one in which a person is "hard-*pressed*" by something or in which something "*sends*" one "to the brink of despair."

Before the story of Lot's sojourn lies one further mention of sojourn. At the start of Gen 17, when the LORD reiterates and confirms the covenant that he initiated with Abram, he declares, "I will give to you and to your offspring after you the land of your sojournings (מגריך), all the land of Canaan, as a holding forever. And I will be God for them (והייתי להם לאלהים)" (17:8). Preceding this declaration, furthermore, is the promise that Abraham will be a father of a multitude of nations (17:4–5).[95] Thus sojourn is conceptualized as an event that comes before nationhood, landedness, and divine partnership.

Of the three instances of sojourn that precede the second Hagar interlude, this one resonates the most faintly with Hagar's experience, and yet there is enough evidence to suggest that here again Hagar's sojourn experience mirrors that of the ancestral family. Once Abraham sends Hagar away from the family, she enters the wilderness. There the divine messenger comes to her aid and delivers the promise that God will make a great nation of Ishmael (21:18). Hagar and Ishmael's preservation, furthermore, is not limited to immediate rescue and the promise of a better future but also includes the continuing presence of God alongside Ishmael as he grows. The narration of God's presence—"and God was with the boy (ויהי אלהים את נער)" (21:20)—recalls the promise of God's partnership with Abraham's offspring: both posit God's being (היה) alongside (את and -ל) the offspring. The repeated notice that Ishmael "dwelt in the wilderness (וישב במדבר)" hints at a further parallel (21:20–21), as it is suggestive of the landedness that God promises Abraham's offspring. Of the five occurrences of "wilderness" (מדבר) through Gen 21:21, four refer to the location of Hagar or Ishmael's travels or residence. The wilderness setting's "limited distribution" in Genesis, and its almost ubiquitous association with Hagar and Ishmael, underlines its significance to their story.[96] It is a place of refuge for Hagar and Ishmael. It houses its own threats, such as lack of water—just as the promised land of Canaan houses threats to the ancestral family (e.g., the kings' war in Gen 14, and the conflict

---

95. This study limits the sojourn mention of 17:8 to the promissory declarations of the covenant, 17:1–8, which anticipate what will follow the ancestral sojourn. For a provoking look at the entire chapter, and particularly the complicated relation between the covenant and Ishmael, see Brett, who poses the question of the covenant's exclusivity: "[I]f circumcision is the 'sign' of the covenant (v. 11), and the covenantal line is to go through Isaac—not through Ishmael—why have the editors so blithely placed the 'obedience' of vv. 23–7 at the end of the chapter? The first person circumcised is Ishmael, the son excluded from the covenant" (*Genesis*, 63–64).

96. Dozeman, "The Wilderness and Salvation History," 24.

over wells in 21:25; 26:20–21)—but with God's provision, it becomes a place of residence.

To be sure, there is no explicit indication that God has promised or given them the land, as there is with regard to the ancestral offspring and the land of Canaan. But, in addition to the firm narrative correspondence between character and setting—Hagar and Ishmael and the wilderness—several details further the interpretive possibility. First, the divine messenger's earlier characterization of Ishmael as a "wild ass of a human (פרא אדם)" invites the idea that the wilderness is home for Hagar and Ishmael's family inasmuch as the פרא is understood as a native inhabitant of the wilderness (16:12).[97] Second, the wilderness functions as Hagar and Ishmael's own territory inasmuch as it is there that they exhibit their own subjectivity. In encounters between the inhabitant and the sojourner, the inhabitant is predominantly the subject, the character who sees, speaks, and acts. Hagar and Ishmael's transformation from objects within the ancestral household to subjects in the wilderness territory, to characters who live independently, suggests that they are residents in the wilderness.[98] Third, the details of Ishmael's marriage invite the interpretive prospect of the wilderness as Hagar and Ishmael's own land insofar as it signifies that Hagar and Ishmael eschew the obvious option of returning to Hagar's homeland, Egypt. In other words, the fact that Ishmael resides in the wilderness of Paran with his Egyptian wife rather than in Egypt insinuates that the wilderness has become Hagar and Ishmael's homeland. Lastly, the fact that Hagar's (and Ishmael's) wilderness experiences are associated with sites of water (16:7; 21:19)—the second of which is

---

97. Wenham, *Genesis 16–50*, 11. Wenham states that the פרא lives in the desert. See also Hamilton, *The Book of Genesis: Chapters 1–17*, 449, 454. Hamilton cites the work of lexicologists as a reason for interpreting אדם as "steppe." This translation, it is implied, confirms the wild ass' residence in the desert.

98. One might also remark on how the ancestral characters are generally objects in their sojourn encounters with the inhabitants and subjects in their own personal affairs (where they are not explicitly marked by the concept of sojourn). Take the ancestral family's experience in Gen 12 as an example of the distinction between its sojourn and non-sojourn experiences. Members of the ancestral family (Abram and Lot) are grammatical subjects of independent clauses fourteen times when they are outside Egypt. When the family is sojourning in Egypt, none of its members is the grammatical subject of an independent clause; Egyptians, on the other hand, are subjects of independent clauses eight times. When the family is outside Egypt, Abram speaks. When it is sojourning in Egypt, none of the ancestral family speaks. As explicit sojourners, then, the ancestral characters are objects. Otherwise, they assume a subjectivity that anticipates a more independent residence in the land.

explicitly identified as a well—implies a certain rootedness. Elsewhere in the ancestral narrative, water and wells commonly mark a place of residence—e.g., Beersheba, one of the primary ancestral sites of residence in the land, and the home of Nahor's family in Haran (24:10–11; 29:2–6). As wells and water sustain life for the ancestral family in their future land and for another branch of their family at their home in Haran, so it sustains Hagar and Ishmael in the wilderness.

To recapitulate, the echoes of the various ancestral sojourn experiences in Hagar's sojourn experience are deep and resonant. Embodying the definition of sojourn found in Gen 15:13–14, Hagar is a stranger amid the ancestral family, a servant who is subjugated until God judges in her favor, delivers her, and promises a future. Like Sarah, she is a voiceless object who finds a voice and audience before God. Like Lot, she is vulnerable to the wishes of those among whom she dwells; she is pressed to the point of helplessness, at which point God intervenes. As Abraham receives the promise of nationhood, divine partnership, and landedness, so she and Ishmael live lives suggestive of a similar promise: Hagar receives a promise of nationhood, God is present alongside Ishmael as he grows up, and Hagar and Ishmael dwell resolutely in the wilderness in a manner that implies their landedness there.

The Gendering of Sojourn

A significant correspondence worth flagging here is that the characters who best embody the experience of sojourn are females. Sarah (at the hands of the Pharaoh in Egypt and King Abimelech in Gerar) and Hagar (at the hands of the ancestral family) typify what it means to be a sojourner, an object at the mercy of the inhabitant's subjugating acts. The common realization of the sojourner role by female characters invites speculation into how the narrative genders sojourn. Is sojourn, as illustrated by Genesis, a feminine experience?

There are certainly male sojourners in Genesis. Abraham, Lot, Isaac, and Jacob are all explicitly associated with the concept. Upon inspection, however, their sojourns reveal experiences that elsewhere carry feminine connotations. In the three sister-wife tales (12:10; 20:1; 26:3), for instance, Abraham and Isaac are sojourners who resort to trickery—identifying their wives as their sisters.[99] Elsewhere in Genesis (and biblical narrative),

---

99. If Abraham's belated disclosure to Abimelech—that Sarah is indeed his sister (by shared father)—is true, his initial identification of Sarah as his sister may still be

trickery is arguably the female character's choice;[100] wit is her means of contesting male authority. Lot's daughters, Rebekah, Leah, Rachel, and Tamar all resort to one form or another of trickery,[101] as does Potiphar's wife. Abraham and Isaac's recourse to trickery in their sojourns thus figures them as similarly feminine characters: thinking that they are unable to achieve their ends through straightforward discourse and action, they resort to deceit. Lot's resemblance to the female character has less to do with what he does and more to do with what others intend to do to him and his visitors. As a sojourner in Sodom, he faces the threat of sexual subjugation: the Sodomites intend to "know" (ידע) his visitors, and likely him as well (as they promise to do worse to him than to his visitors). Inasmuch as the Sodomites' intention suggests the sexual act of penetration, Lot and his visitors are gendered as feminine.[102] Finally, Jacob, who identifies his entire life as sojourn (47:8–9), is characterized in various ways as both effeminate—he has smooth skin, lives in tents, cooks, and is his mother's favorite—and trickster—he deceives his brother, father, and father-in-law. Susan Niditch aptly identifies him an "effeminate trickster" who takes after his mother, Rebekah, in his various deceptions.[103] Jacob's life—or in his own words, sojourn (47:9)—thus bears many feminine associations.

This reflection does not indicate an essential connection between sojourn and the feminine but rather suggests the salience of their correspondence—a correspondence, furthermore, that might find more holistic expression in terms of power dynamics. Male characters in Genesis traditionally assume positions of authority, positions that facilitate the

---

construed as deceitful inasmuch as it purposefully hides the full nature of their relationship. In other words, by saying she is his sister, he is implying that she is not his wife.

100. This is not to say that male characters are not also tricksters. Cf. Jackson, *Comedy and Feminist Interpretation*, 41. Jackson notes that Abram and Joseph book-end the tales of tricksters in Genesis. But the correspondence between female characters and tricksters is notably higher than its counterpart statistic. As Niditch asks: "Why are so many tales of women in Genesis about tricksters who employ deception ...?" ("Genesis," 29). She implies the feminine gendering of trickery in her exploration of Jacob as both trickster and effeminate; from his story, she concludes, "women and their surrogates succeed in behind-the-scenes ways through deception and trickery" ("Genesis," 39).

101. Jackson explores this group of women as "trickster matriarchs" (*Comedy and Feminist Interpretation*, 41–66).

102. Cf. Carden, "Genesis/Bereshit," 37–38.

103. Niditch, "Genesis", 40.

realization of their intentions through word and action. The notable correlation between the sojourner role and female or feminized characters, then, is cause for little surprise. To be a sojourner means to be like a woman, which is to say, on the underside of the social balance of power. The characters of Sarah and Hagar exemplify so well the sojourn experience in part because their status as women already situates them on the underside of the power dynamic: they are thus doubly "woman" or "sojourner," in that their place as a sojourner woman entails an even greater power disadvantage.[104]

The gendering of sojourn—a noteworthy point on its own—caps the growing evidence linking Hagar to sojourn. Her name suggests sojourn. Her experience embodies sojourn. Her gender matches sojourn. These parallels suggest a significant relation between Hagar and sojourn, a relation that now comes to the fore.

Mise en Abyme

Hagar's experience provides an extensive reflection of ancestral sojourn in its various aspects and implications. The trajectory of her life follows the fundamental definition of sojourn outlined in Gen 15:13–14: living in a land not hers, she is a slave; her mistress subjugates her; and God ostensibly judges in her favor, attending first and foremost to her cause. Like Sarai in the sojourns in Egypt and Gerar, she is a voiceless and vulnerable object who, before the Lord, becomes a speaking subject whose voice occasions divine intervention. Like Lot, she is completely at the mercy of the judgments and actions of those with whom she lives, and only when pressed to the point of helplessness does she receive divine aid. Like the ancestral recipients of the promise of nationhood, land, and a special divine alliance, she and her son Ishmael live into a post-sojourn experience suggestive of the same promise. Hagar embodies a mirror image of ancestral sojourn to such an extent that, heeding the suggestion of her name, one might reasonably consider her "*the* sojourner" par excellence.[105] She is at the center of what it means to be a sojourner.

---

104. Consider, for the sake of contrast, Lot, a male sojourner. His attempt to resist the Sodomites' aggression may index the fact that he does not lie, or does not think he lies, at quite the disadvantage that female sojourners do. Similarly, Abraham assumes a more dynamic role than the average sojourner in his negotiations for a burial spot with the Hittites in Gen 23.

105. "The sojourner" is one possible translation for the consonantal makeup of her name, הגר.

Hagar's position, however, as a sojourner *within* the ancestral family presents a curious image: she is a sojourner amid sojourners; hers is a sojourning story amid sojourning stories. Her character and her stories are embedded respectively between other characters and stories of a parallel type. In literary discourse, such a situation has received analysis in the terms of *mise en abyme*, "setting in the abyss." A brief survey of the concept will assist in exploring the specific case of Hagar and her interludes and will illumine their relation to the ancestral narrative.

Scholarship generally attributes the origin of this concept to André Gide, who sketches the idea as the reflection of a narrative's "subject" in a particular narrative segment: "In a work of art I rather like to find transposed, on the scale of the characters, the very subject of that work."[106] Subject has been interpreted to mean either the narrative's theme or its narrating subject (i.e., narrator),[107] while "the scale of the characters" is generally taken to signify the diegetic realm (i.e., the story-world). Gide and other theorists following him would develop this seed of an idea into the concept of a work embedded within a work. (Gide, for instance, originally illustrated the concept through analogy to the heraldic phenomenon of a shield pictured within a shield.) Some degree of resemblance between the two works suggests a meaningful connection.

Theorists attuned to postmodern interests in metalepsis often specify the subject as the narrating subject.[108] For them, *mise en abyme* refers to a story told within a story. In these scenarios, *mise en abyme* reflexively suggests something about the nature of storytelling. What or how the embedded story signifies in the context of the main story suggests what or how the main story potentially signifies to its reader. Gide's definition of *mise en abyme*, however, allows for a broader application. It can also indicate a relation that occurs on one diegetic level alone (that is, a relation that does not entail a narration within a narration). If a segment of a story (for example, a character, an event, a place) resembles the theme of the story, then it too is placed *en abyme*. With reference to Gide's early sketch of the idea, Moshe Ron explains:

106. Gide, *Journals 1889–1949*, 30–31, quoted in Ron, "The Restricted Abyss," 418.
107. Ron, "The Restricted Abyss," 420.
108. Genette defines metalepsis as "any intrusion by the extradiegetic narrator or narratee into the diegetic universe (or by diegetic characters into a metadiegetic universe, etc.), or the inverse" (*Narrative Discourse*, 234–35). Many who study *mise en abyme* refer to the concept of metalepsis because they read the mirroring of narration to be suggestive of how what is inside a story (diegetic) might impinge on what is outside it (extradiegetic).

> It seems to me that it is at least as important to emphasize the other, apparently easier, sense of Gide's ambiguous *sujet*. For Gide talks about transposing the *sujet* (in the sense of the structured thematic whole) "on the *scale of the characters*." In this reading, nothing excludes the possibility of the entire *mise en abyme* relation occurring within the story (intra-diegetically, in Genette's terminology).[109]

Thus Ron offers his own formulation of *mise en abyme*: "Any diegetic segment which resembles the work where it occurs, is said to be placed *en abyme*"—where "'the work' (as that which is resembled) denotes any continuous aspect of the text, the narration or the story judged to be pertinent."[110]

Ron's formulation illumines how *mise en abyme* might play out in the Hagar interludes. The diegetic segment of the interludes, and particularly Hagar as a sojourner, resembles the narrative's continuous theme of sojourn, a theme that is otherwise consistently identified with the ancestral family. Put simply, then, Hagar is placed *en abyme* as a sojourner amid sojourners; her interludes are sojourn stories embedded in a sojourn story.

It might help to think of *mise en abyme* as the narrative quoting itself, citing one of its own key themes. The interpretation of a narrative segment as *mise en abyme*, in other words, confers quotation marks around the segment—quotation marks that suggest that the segment is purposefully, self-consciously narrated. *Mise en abyme* foregrounds the segment and suggests that it is not merely representational, but also functional as a guide for interpretation. It invites the reader to compare the quoted segment and the quoting context and to judge the relation.[111] Is the segment that is placed *en abyme* metaphorical? Does it affirm some element in the quoting context? Or is it ironic? Does it contest an element

---

109. Ron, "The Restricted Abyss," 420.

110. Ron, "The Restricted Abyss," 436.

111. White observes that "Gide's original heraldic analogy and Dällenbach's preferred metaphor of mirroring both suffer from the marked disadvantage of appearing to concentrate too exclusively on similarities and shared features." He observes that a case of *mise en abyme* can contrast with as well as parallel its quoting context; he contends that the differences are just as instructive as the similarities and posits that in *mise en abyme* there is "a creative interplay between elements of similarity and dissimilarity" ("The Semiotics of the Mise-en-Abyme," 49). Nonetheless, he still privileges the function of resemblance in *mise en abyme*. Similarity establishes a case of *mise en abyme*, and differences define it.

of the quoting context?[112] In the case of the Hagar interludes, one might ask: does the concept of sojourn confirm the ancestral family's identity, or does it challenge it?

Thematic Development: Ancestral Relationship with God

The theme of sojourn in the ancestral narrative contributes to the development of ancestral identity. Prevalent among the refrains of the ancestral story, its strains are also present within the Hagar interludes. But its sound in the interludes is defamiliarized. Transposed in part to the subjectivity of an outsider character, Hagar, the theme of sojourn no longer means what it did before for the ancestral family. The case of *mise en abyme* accentuates the thematic development of sojourn: amid an ancestral cast of characters, Hagar assumes the sojourner's role and structurally situates the ancestral family whom she otherwise resembles in an unfamiliar role—the role of inhabitant. Hagar and her interludes therefore invite the question of not only what it means for Hagar, a non-ancestral character, to be a sojourner, but also what it means for the ancestral family *not* to be sojourners, at least for the duration of the interludes.

The relation between Hagar and the ancestral family plots a few basic interpretive possibilities for the thematic development of sojourn and, correspondingly, ancestral identity. First, on the most immediate level, Hagar as sojourner would appear to function metaphorically as confirmation of the ancestral experience. As exemplar of the sojourn experience, she embodies what it means for the ancestral family to live in a land that is not theirs. Second, Hagar as sojourner may function ironically to contest the image of the ancestral family as sojourners. Hagar, in other words, positions the family in the role of inhabitant. While this interpretation dislodges the ancestral family from its thematic association with sojourn, it ultimately confirms another traditional theme: the ancestral family as future inhabitants of the land. Third, Hagar as sojourner may function ironically to contest not only the image of the ancestral family as sojourners but also the ideas that the members of the ancestral family are special recipients of divine promise and that the divine program centers on the ancestral family.

---

112. Cf. Ron: "[T]he occurrence of *mise en abyme* can either *contest* or *reveal* the proper functioning of a particular narrative" ("The Restricted Abyss," 434).

The first interpretive possibility does little to advance or develop the theme of sojourn. It serves rather to consolidate the conceptual contours of sojourn. If Hagar exemplifies the sojourn experience, then the parallels with the ancestral family's experience bear out the reality of the ancestral family's situation.[113] As Hagar is among them, so they are among the inhabitants of the land. Her life offers a sort of microcosm of what they are encountering on a grander scale: until the divine promise is realized, they will be living as sojourners, as vulnerable objects subject to the ruling inhabitants and reliant upon divine assistance. In this sense, Hagar and her interludes are little more than the foils that conventional interpretation posits. That is, Hagar's sojourn experience is significant only inasmuch as it illustrates the ancestral experience.

The second possibility expands on the theme of sojourn by delving into the structural implications of Hagar's sojourn. Hagar's position as sojourner entails that the ancestral family assume the role of inhabitant. For the duration of the interludes, it becomes like the anonymous nation to whom the ancestral offspring will be servants (15:13–14). It enjoys an advantage of power that entails the sojourner's experience of servanthood and subjugation, vulnerability and helplessness. Therefore Hagar as sojourner performs an ironic twist. The ancestral family's sojourning identity resounds dissonantly through Hagar's subjectivity. Hagar as sojourner contests the image of the ancestral family inasmuch as her experience entails a role reversal—the ancestral family's move from sojourner to inhabitant. But this contestation simultaneously works as a metaphor. It confirms a larger theme, namely the divine promise. Hagar's experience is a negative expression of the positive reality that the ancestral family seems to be on the verge of inheriting. Her interludes envision the ancestral family as inhabitants, showing what it will be like when the divine promise of land is realized. Thus Hagar and her interludes once again serve as foils: their significance lies not in Hagar as a sojourner but in the ancestral family as moving one step closer toward the realization of the divine promise of land.

---

113. Cf. McAfee, who notes this parallel in the inversion of sojourner roles in 12:10–20 and Hagar's experience: "Hagar's intervening sojourn among the Hebrew people is the inverse of the Hebrew Abraham's sojourn among her own (Gen. 12.10–20); in this Hagar again appears as a mirror image of Abraham, an image in which Israelite society could see its own reflection and define itself accordingly" ("Chosen People in a Chosen Land," 169).

The third possibility modifies the theme of sojourn most dramatically. Like the second possibility, it emphasizes the role reversal that Hagar's experience enforces on the ancestral family. But its imagination extends beyond that of the second interpretive trajectory. Rather than limiting the implications of the role reversal to the ancestral family's imminent inheritance of the land, it considers the full consequence of Hagar's assumption of the sojourner role. Scott K. Nikaido gives expression to the consideration that undergirds this interpretive possibility: "Conceptualizing their [Hagar and Ishmael's] plight merely as 'background' to Isaac's birth does not do justice to the literary dimensions of their characters nor explain the need for a detailed account of their circumstances."[114] The Hagar interludes, in other words, contain excessive detail about an outsider character. The interludes do not rest content with the ancestral side of the story, but instead focalize much of the story through the interest point of view of Hagar and Ishmael; "the story goes with [them] into the wilderness,"[115] outside the frame of the ancestral household, and details their individual dramas. So Niditch concludes:

> [W]hile reading this story, one has the distinct feeling it is being told from Hagar and Ishmael's point of view. One is moved by the portrait of the mother who places the child apart because she cannot bear to watch him die; the weeping mother (21:16) and the divinely protected boy ultimately rescued by God and promised a great future; the blessed child and mother, for whom God opens a well of water in the wilderness so that they might drink and live.[116]

The surprising level of attention given to Hagar and Ishmael invites consideration of their literary significance; their stories, it appears, are more than a backdrop to the ancestral narrative. The peculiar resonance of the concept of sojourn in their interludes, in particular, invites reflection on its significance for Hagar and Ishmael. Sojourn, in other words, does not echo here merely to illustrate some aspect of the ancestral experience— either to confirm the family's initial sojourning identity or to anticipate its later landedness—but also to suggest something distinctive about Hagar and Ishmael's experience.

---

114. Nikaido, "Hagar and Ishmael as Literary Figures," 241. See also Niditch, "Genesis," 34–36, in which Niditch reads the motifs of unusual conception and endangered upbringing as representative of a hero type story.

115. Frymer-Kensky, *Reading the Women of the Bible*, 229.

116. Niditch, "Genesis," 35.

Thus the recognition that, as Robert L. Cohn puts it, Genesis "valorizes outsiderhood over autochthony"[117]—that God is on the outsider's side[118]—assumes a deeper semantic layer. Genesis indeed valorizes outsiderhood, or sojourn, but not only as experienced by the ancestral family. The detail with which the narrative describes Hagar's sojourn experience confers upon it its own significance. Hagar's sojourn not only mirrors the ancestral family's. It not only anticipates their future status as inhabitants of the land. It also means that Hagar is just as much a sojourner as the ancestral family, that she herself assumes the sojourner's identity along with all its conceptual implications. Sojourn and its connotations of divine promise may be contained primarily *in* the ancestral family—but not *by* it.

That the sojourner role may be realized by opposed parties suggests the provisionality of the sojourn experience: in one iteration, a character may be the sojourner, and in another, she may be the inhabitant. The provisionality and reversibility of the sojourn experience is best understood in light of the effect of *mise en abyme*. The fact that the embedded representation of Hagar as sojourner and ancestral family as inhabitant reflects the larger picture of ancestral family as sojourner and others as inhabitants, evokes an infinite structure of sojourner-inhabitant transpositions.[119] This infinite structure, in turn, implicitly raises the questions: who can claim the role of sojourner and its attendant feature of divine partnership? And who can claim an inherent right to the land? The sojourner can become as the inhabitant—indeed, it may be more than mere coincidence that the narrative interrupts the first Hagar interlude with the notice that Abram has inhabited (יָשַׁב) the land of Canaan for ten years (16:3).[120] Tracing the reflection in the opposite direction, one might posit that the inhabitant can likewise become as the sojourner. In this

---

117. Cohn, "Negotiating (with) the Natives," 164.

118. Kennedy articulates this phenomenon as a "hidden loftiness concealed in the lowliness of sojourn" (*Seeking a Homeland*, 236).

119. Cohn discusses the distinction between "*pure* mise en abyme," in which a story would effectively cancel itself out (Cohn cites Jean Ricardou's *La Prise de Constantinople* as the best example), and lesser cases which do "nothing more than evoke this infinite structure" ("Metalepsis and Mise en Abyme," 109). While Cohn is explicitly concerned with *mise en abyme* of narration (that is, the instance of a narrative within a narrative), his remarks help to give expression to the general effect of *mise en abyme*, namely its suggestion of infinite reflection.

120. Cf. Wenham, *Genesis 16–50*, 8.

light, any claim to sojourn and special divine partnership based in one's inherited or long-assigned position becomes suspect.[121]

The provisionality of the sojourner and inhabitant roles has significant implications for ancestral identity. The divine program no longer centers on the sojourning ancestral family as essential participants, but rather on the sojourner, whoever that is. In contrast to the traditional claim that "[o]ne cannot be reconciled with God and be at odds with Abraham,"[122] the Hagar interludes show a sojourner who twice endures confrontation with and separation from the ancestral family, and yet is on equally intimate terms with God. Hagar effectively defamiliarizes the ancestral family's identity as privileged divine partner. She shows this aspect of ancestral identity to be permeable. Inasmuch as the ancestral narrative is a family story, a story about how the divine program is embodied by a family, Hagar's story "de-families" or deposes the ancestral family and replaces it with the sojourner. It decenters the ancestral family, reinscribing the ancestral–divine relationship along the lines of the sojourner's relationship with God. Concomitant with the defamiliarization of the ancestral family as privileged divine partners, then, is the familiarization of the sojourner. Whether it is the ancestral family or Hagar, the sojourner is the character in special relationship with God. It is not the ancestral family but the sojourner who enjoys a "secret high status."[123] The common identity of sojourners, ancestral or non-ancestral, consists in divine partnership and promise and suggests that in this narrative it is the sojourner through whom God funnels his purposes. The sojourners

---

121. Similarly, an inhabitant's claim to autochthony becomes suspect. A brief retracing of Genesis' account of the peoples' original relation to the land would appear to confirm this doubt. If it is indeed all the peoples (cf. "all the land"; 11:1) that journey and settle in the land of Shinar (שִׁנְעָר; 11:2), from which they are subsequently scattered over all the face of the earth (11:9), then no people is indigenous to a place—at least inasmuch as they all trace back to the same starting place. (The Table of Nations in Gen 10 does indicate territorial boundaries for some peoples, but it also indicates individual languages for different peoples, thus suggesting it is a proleptic genealogical account, outlining where the various peoples come to settle after the scattering from Babel.) Hagar's interludes thus dramatize the pliability of Genesis' concept of belonging to the land.

122. Hamilton, *The Book of Genesis: Chapters 1–17*, 52.

123. Kennedy explains that divine election, inextricably associated with sojourn, is the "secret high status" that the ancestral family enjoys (*Seeking a Homeland*, 236). For Kennedy, the ancestral family's privileged relationship with God as recipients of the divine promises is "secret" because the lowliness of sojourn conceals it.

become the familiar characters—familiar to God as his partners and to readers as protagonists.

It is, furthermore, interesting to observe that the common identity of sojourners suggests a unified divine purpose not only across the ancestral narrative but across all of Genesis. The frequently noted link between the primeval (Gen 1–11) and ancestral (12–50) narratives, the divine program for fruitfulness (פרה) and multiplication (רבה) of offspring (1:28; 9:1, 7),[124] joins the divine intention at creation with its particular outworking in—not the ancestral family—but the sojourner. In other words, it is the sojourner, whether ancestral or not, who receives the divine assurance of fruitfulness (פרה; 17:6, 20) and multiplication (רבה; 16:10; 17:2). Insofar as the divine program at creation unifies the narrative of Genesis, the sojourner comes into focus as its primary participant.

To analogize along the lines of sonata-rondo form, the Hagar interludes represent episodes among the recurring refrains of ancestral narrative. Within the refrains, sojourn is a consistent and constitutive theme of ancestral identity. Quoting this central thematic component, the Hagar episodes recontextualize it. They reverse the traditional subjectivities of sojourn, showing an Egyptian maidservant to be the sojourner who enjoys divine alliance and promise. Although the Hagar interludes are fleeting, a comprehensive consideration of their *mise en abyme* suggests a durable irony, the implications of which reverberate in each iteration of sojourn in the remaining ancestral narrative. In itself, the concept of sojourn has changed little; it "sounds" the same. But the role reversal that it accompanies in the Hagar interludes initiates a dialogue about what it can mean, because this reversal dislodges sojourn and divine association from the exclusive grasp of the ancestral family. In the context of this relativization, sojourn "sounds" different. Each time it sounds after the Hagar interludes, it reminds the listener that the ancestors are not the only sojourners and, more importantly, not the only recipients of divine promises. In other words, its irony pervades the remainder of the ancestral narrative; for while sojourn's each iteration would appear to suggest that the ancestral family is the privileged partner of the divine, the echo of Hagar's story reverberates within it and contests the ancestral family's

---

124. Kaminski indexes the iterations of the roots for "be fruitful" (פרה) and "multiply" (רבה) in the ancestral narrative (17:1–2, 6, 20; 22:15–17; 26:2, 4, 22, 24; 28:1, 3; 47:27; 48:3–4) and notes their association with the divine promises to the ancestral family. She concludes that the divine promises to the ancestral family are a "*particular outworking of the primaeval blessing*" (*From Noah to Israel*, 94–95).

exclusive relationship with God, pointing instead to the surplus meaning of this ancestral aspect of identity: it is not the ancestral family that enjoys a special divine relationship, but the sojourner, and the sojourner may be anyone.

Therefore, although Hagar and Ishmael fade from the ancestral narrative after the second interlude, they linger as ironizing specters in the unsaid spaces of the text, remembered in the following mentions of sojourn. The Hagar interludes ironize any assumptions that the ancestral family holds an exclusive claim to divine election—or to the land, on which the Dinah interlude has more to say. The recollection of Hagar and Ishmael's sojourn experiences pervades two enduring, interrelated elements of ancestral identity, divine promise and sojourn, and reminds the reader that, while the ancestral narrative may be promise-centered, it is not necessarily ancestor-centered. Readers commonly finalize their interpretation of Genesis according to the narrative that succeeds it in the Primary History, retrofitting the later interest in the people of Israel back onto their ancestors, making the ancestors into a specially chosen people that resemble their specially chosen descendants. But the Hagar interludes make the case that at this point in the story, although the ancestral family enjoys the lion's share of narrative attention, God makes promises to and allies with other people. What is later read as "the" promise is only "a" promise in Genesis.

At its root, the observation of the plurality of the divine program is a simple one. The reader need not appreciate the concept of sojourn or the precise mechanics of *mise en abyme* to see that Hagar is an outsider with whom God allies. Judith E. McKinlay articulates well the incongruity that many readers have puzzled over: divine election and divine care for the non-elect, the "message" and "counter-message" of the narrative, vie alongside one another.[125] God has chosen the ancestral family, but then God's care for the outsider Hagar, who is expelled from the ancestral family, would suggest another choice. The concept of sojourn and the workings of *mise en abyme* ultimately serve only to accentuate what is there in the first place, namely the plurality of the divine program. They strengthen the parallels between the ancestral family and Hagar and demonstrate the provisionality of sojourn and divine promise as markers of a special relationship with God. Amanda Mbuvi, explaining the universality of covenant in the flood story and the succeeding genealogical

---

125. McKinlay, "Sarah and Hagar," 173.

outlines, claims, "From this perspective, there are no outsiders beyond the range of covenant with God, only insiders of various stripes."[126] One might make a similar claim from the nuanced perspective afforded by the Hagar interludes. The ancestral relationship with God is, to appropriate Jon Levenson's words, "both unique and universal: no other people has it, yet all humanity has something of the same order."[127] In the ancestral narrative, the privileged divine partnership belongs to the ancestral family, but not only to it. It belongs more broadly to the sojourner—and, by suggestion of Hagar's *mise en abyme*, the sojourner may be anyone, even an Egyptian maidservant.

Summary

The conventional reading of the ancestral narrative takes the ancestral family to be the center of the narrative and thus also the center of the divine program. This interpretive preference for the ancestral family generally entails a reading that formulates the ancestral–divine relationship in exclusive terms. One consequence of the ancestor-centered readings is that the Hagar interludes, which shift the focus momentarily to non-ancestral characters and interests, are read as a narrative foil that accentuates the ancestral family's special status in God's plan. Hagar's name, however, suggests a meaningful connection between her identity and the family's, and her experience corroborates this parallel. She is a sojourner amid sojourners; hers is a sojourning story amid a sojourning story. This *mise en abyme* harbors different possibilities for thematic development, the most extensive of which sketches out an ironic progression of ancestral identity, particularly as it relates to God. Hagar as sojourner, that is, may function ironically to contest not only the image of the ancestral family as sojourners but also the ideas that the members of the ancestral family are exclusive recipients of divine promise and that the divine program centers on the ancestral family.

---

126. Mbuvi, "Belonging in Genesis," 226.

127. Levenson, "The Universal Horizon of Biblical Particularism," 147–48. Levenson makes this statement about Israel's covenant with God.

4

The Dinah Interlude

Traditional Interpretation

THE CLOSE READING OF the Dinah interlude commences with an exploration of the way that traditional interpretation has revolved around a series of evaluative comments within the story (vv. 2, 5, 7, 13, 27). These evaluative comments constitute the linchpin around which interpretation naturalizes the strangeness of the interlude. For most interpreters, these comments not only express the narrator's judgment of the events within the story. They also speak to a significant ancestral concern, namely ancestral relations to the land and its inhabitants. Therefore they offer a way to naturalize the strangeness of the story. The Dinah interlude may deviate from the local plot of Jacob's struggles with God and family, but its subtext offers an authorized commentary on how the ancestral family should relate to others. To account for this common interpretive naturalization, this study draws attention to the mechanics that underlie it. First identifying conventional interpretations' preoccupation with the evaluative comments, this study then explains the literary underpinnings of the authoritative narrator and explores how biblical scholarship conforms to this concept of the narrator. Finally, it outlines the particular consequences of reading the interlude according to an authoritative narrator. The Dinah interlude, as a story of judgment narrated by an authoritative narrator, becomes a verdict on how the ancestral family is to relate to the land and its inhabitants.

A Story of Judgment

The Dinah interlude is conspicuously distinct from the events that precede and follow it. Whereas the surrounding narrative centers on Jacob in his familial plights and his developing relationship with God, the interlude depicts a sequence of events in which Jacob is peripheral and God is absent. The story instead focuses on Dinah and the encounter between Jacob's sons and Shechem and the Hivites. Although Dinah as an active character commands little attention in the story, her identification at its introduction assumes paradigmatic significance. Her name announces what has become the crux of most interpretations of Gen 34. From the root דין, Dinah (דינה) means "judgment."[1] And as the story opens with an invocation of "judgment," so it closes in similar fashion.[2] Ending with Levi and Simeon's pointed question (v. 31), which remains unanswered, the story invites judgment.

Most readers concur that the story not only invites judgment, it also "passes 'judgment.'"[3] Sternberg, whose reading of the story serves as a point of reference for many modern interpretations, asserts that the story's "thematic structure" is one of "crime and punishment."[4] Two of Sternberg's most engaged interlocutors, Paul R. Noble and the duo Danna Nolan Fewell and David M. Gunn, echo his tone of discourse: the titles of their respective essays, "A 'Balanced' Reading of the Rape of Dinah" and "Tipping the Balance," call to mind the "balance," or scales, of justice, and their arguments accordingly revolve around the justifiability of the perceived offenses—namely Shechem's "rape" of Dinah and the brothers' retaliation.

These and other readings of judgment generally reach one of three verdicts. Ellen van Wolde summarizes: if the encounter between Shechem and Dinah is considered rape, "then the murder of the Shechemites can be defended, or is often defended, because of this unacceptable deed"; otherwise, "the murder of the Shechemites is to be judged as unacceptable, and

---

1. Bechtel, "Dinah," 69.

2. Hyman observes an *inclusio* of judgment: the story "concerns Dinah, whose name comes from the Hebrew word meaning judgment or law, thus underscoring the centrality of judgment within the story. In this way the story opens with 'judgment' and closes with a judgment" ("Final Judgment," 99).

3. Bechtel, "Dinah," 69.

4. Sternberg, *The Poetics of Biblical Narrative*, 469, 472.

the history of Jacob and his sons contains an ink-blank page."⁵ The three alternatives, then, are: Shechem's act is a crime, and the brothers' is not; the brothers' act is equally as grievous as Shechem's (the modality of van Wolde's "can be defended" implies the converse as well, that the brothers' act can be censured); or Shechem's act is not a crime, but the brothers' is. Furthermore, most readers sense in the story, alongside Niditch, a "strong impression . . . of insider versus outsider, us versus them."⁶ For this reason, they interpret the judgment of Shechem and Dinah's brothers synecdochically as a verdict on the question of interethnic relations.

Although these three lines of interpretation clash with one another, they share notably in one key hermeneutical aspect. Their readings of judgment all pivot on a common object of interpretation: the series of evaluative remarks that appear on the narrative level in vv. 2, 5, 7, 13, and 27. These remarks consist of the statement that Shechem "raped" or "humbled" Dinah (ענה; v. 2),⁷ the repeated charge that Shechem "defiled" Dinah (טמא; vv. 5, 13, 27),⁸ and the assertion that Shechem "had committed a foolish disgrace against Israel by lying with Jacob's daughter, and this should not be done" (v. 7).⁹ Because these evaluations transpire on the narrative level, readers normally attribute them to the narrator—either directly, as the narrator's own judgment, or indirectly, as the characters' judgment purposefully mediated by the narrator. Alternatively, a

---

5. Van Wolde, "Does *Inna* Denote Rape?" 530.

6. Niditch, "Genesis," 40.

7. Debate continues over the appropriate translation of ענה in this verse. This study gives voice to the various translations according to the interpreter under review. As will be explained later in the chapter, this study prefers the translation "humble."

8. While טמא (the root that, in its piel stem, is commonly translated "defile") applies to a broad range of purity matters, its usage in Gen 34 seems to pertain most closely to the issue of transgressing the boundaries of acceptable sexual relations. In the law codes, the root טמא applies to sexual relations between a man and women only in the context of marriage: in Lev 18:20, Num 5:11–31, and Deut 24:1–4, a married woman who has sexual relations with a man other than her husband "defiles" (imputes impurity to) either the man (Lev 18:20) or herself (Num 5:11–31 and Deut 24:1–4). In each case, the act described either is prohibited or entails punishment. It would thus appear that in the context of Gen 34 the report of Shechem's action implicitly portrays him in a negative light: he has transgressed a sexual boundary.

9. Some translations render בישראל as "in Israel" rather than "against Israel". In accordance with the endeavor to read Genesis on its own terms, and thus to avoid retrojecting concepts from subsequent biblical narrative (such as the land or people of Israel), this study chooses to limit the translation to "against Israel," which would indicate that Shechem's offence is against Jacob.

small minority dissociate the narrator from the evaluations in vv. 5, 7, 13, and 27—attributing these fully to the brothers' perspective—and read his voice and perspective only in v. 2. In either case, the comments attributed to the narrator possess a determinative power as they are seen to reflect the evaluative voice and perspective of the authoritative biblical narrator.[10]

The Authoritative Narrator in Literary Discourse

The literary assumptions underlying the concept of the authoritative biblical narrator clarify how the evaluative comments in the Dinah interlude acquire such interpretive weight. Therefore, before examining specific interpretations of the Dinah interlude, this study explores the literary conceptualization of the traditional narrator. In particular, it will trace the common interpretive tendency to accord omniscience to the traditional narrator.[11] The omniscient narrator is of special interest not only because it explains the authority that readers grant the traditional narrator but also because it points to the narratological roots from which this authority stems. That is, it reflects a couple of distinct narrative conventions—the performative convention and impersonal narration—that elucidate why the effect of traditional narrative is an authoritative narrator whose words are irrefutable, even as they communicate a subjective viewpoint.

Narratologist Mieke Bal summarizes the literary conceptualization of the narrator. She defines the narrator as "the ... subject, a function and not a person, which expresses itself in the language that constitutes the text."[12] In other words, the narrator is an *effect* of the text, an interpretive result, the agent of communication to whom—or to which—the reader attributes the narrative. Like a character, the narrator derives his/her existence from the words on the page. Furthermore, both narrator and character share the similar effect of conjuring in most readers' minds

---

10. By "authoritative biblical narrator," this study refers to the continuous identity of an authoritative narrator to whom is attributed not just Genesis but the entire narrative of the Primary History.

11. The mere mention of the "omniscient narrator" can detonate fierce debate among readers and narratologists. In order to qualify the purposes of this study, it should be made clear that the point of reviewing the concept of the omniscient narrator is not to determine whether or not the concept applies legitimately in Genesis, but rather to understand how interpretation confers on the narrator of Genesis an incontestable authority. The point, in other words, is not the validity of the concept but its effect.

12. Bal, *Narratology*, 15. Cf. Margolin, "Narrator," 351.

a person (unless they are explicitly indicated to be something else). This study's instinct to define the narrator in terms of "whom" rather than "which" betrays the common interpretive tendency to anthropomorphize the narrator. Monika Fludernik explains:

> When readers read narrative texts, they project real-life parameters into the reading process and, if at all possible, treat the text as a real-life instance of narrating. It then turns out to be a useful strategy to hypostasize the existence of a narrator figure who is telling us the story and whose presence and existence seem to be vouchsafed for by the stylistic features of authorial diction.[13]

In traditional narrative, the interpretive tendency generally does not stop at anthropomorphization, but proceeds to pseudo-deification of the narrator. Culler elucidates: "[W]e invent a person to be the source of textual details"—that is, we anthropomorphize the narrator—"but since this knowledge is not that which an ordinary person could have, we must imagine this invented person to be godlike."[14] This move is typified in the label commonly given to the traditional narrator, "omniscient."[15] Culler fleshes out the rationale for this identification: "The basis of 'omniscience' appears to be the frequently articulated analogy between God and the author: the author creates the world of the novel as God created our world, and just as the world holds no secrets for God, so the novelist knows everything that is to be known about the world of the novel."[16] (Although here Culler refers to the "author," he predominantly attributes the effect of omniscience to the narrator.[17] This study chooses similarly to attribute the illusion of omniscience to the narrator.[18]) According to such a for-

---

13. Fludernik, "New Wine in Old Bottles?" 623.

14. Culler, "Omniscience," 28.

15. Ska: "The classical narrator of ancient and traditional narratives is 'omniscient'. He is almost like God" (*"Our Fathers Have Told Us,"* 44).

16. Culler, "Omniscience," 23.

17. Culler refers to both the "author" and "narrator" throughout his essay, generally choosing the term of discourse employed by the interlocutor with whom he engages. He would in fact appear to prefer limiting discussion to the narrator, as he refers eight times to the "omniscient narrator" (three of which are quotes) and only twice to the "omniscient author" (one of which is a quote).

18. This study associates the effect of omniscience with the narrator rather than the author because the reader grappling with the question of omniscience must grapple first and foremost with the narrative. While the author remains outside the narrative—a matter of historical or psychological speculation—omniscience and the narrator are both effects of the narrative. To speak of omniscience is not to conjecture what the

mulation, the omniscient narrator is also authoritative. Receiving credit for the creation of the narrative world and thus assumed to command an exhaustive knowledge of the world, the omniscient narrator speaks an incontrovertible word.

While the terminology of the "omniscient narrator" continues to feature frequently in literary discourse, it has attracted critique for the manner in which it obscures or conflates a variety of distinct narratorial characteristics. Culler identifies four discrete "effects" of narrative that prompt readers to perceive an omniscient narrator:

> (1) the performative authoritativeness of many narrative declarations, which seem to bring into being what they describe; (2) the reporting of innermost thoughts and feelings, such as are usually inaccessible to human observers; (3) authorial narration, where the narrator flaunts her godlike ability to determine how things turn out; and (4) the synoptic impersonal narration of the realist tradition.[19]

To call a narrator "omniscient," in other words, is to extrapolate from more specific narrative features—features, moreover, that are not indicative of omniscience but rather of certain narrative conventions. The first three effects derive from the performative convention of narrative—what one might call the narrator's "omnipotence," his power to create a story-world through narrating.[20] (Indeed, one might say that the narrator *is* like God, at least as God is depicted in Genesis: he creates the world and appears to demonstrate supreme power but does *not* exercise omniscience.)[21] The fourth effect, impersonal narration, is a common narrative convention that evokes a semblance of the narrator's objectivity.[22] It is an effect akin to the "dramatic illusion" of theater, as "[t]he narrator deliberately leaves

---

historical author knew or did not know, but rather what the agent of narration appears to know.

19. Culler, "Omniscience," 26.

20. In other words, the performative convention confers upon the narrator the privilege of narrative creation: he creates the story-world, inhabits it with characters, fills those characters with thoughts and feelings, and so on.

21. E.g., he asks the whereabouts of the first man and woman (3:9), and explains that he must go down to see whether the outcry in Sodom and Gomorrah is legitimate (18:20–21).

22. Although Culler specifies the context of the realist tradition in his mention of impersonal narration, this study would argue that it applies equally as well to other literary contexts. More discussion on impersonal narration's illusion of objectivity (in contexts that are not of the realist tradition) will follow in this chapter.

no obvious trace of his presence in his text, so that the story can be read as though it were 'telling itself.'"[23]

The conventions of performative narration and impersonal narration both give rise to the impression of an omniscient, authoritative narrator, but the two conjure the illusion in different ways. It would appear that impersonal narration was the first to inspire talk of the narrator's omniscience. Jean Louis Ska traces the use of the term "omniscient" back to Percy Lubbock's *The Craft of Fiction* (first published in 1921).[24] There Lubbock suggests that the "omniscient author" should remain impersonal and unobtrusive, as this mode of narration retains the effect of objectivity and reliability.[25] "If the spell [of an unobtrusive narrator] is weakened at any moment, the listener is recalled from the scene to the mere author before him, and the story rests only upon the author's direct assertion."[26] Lubbock notes that, besides affecting a sense of objectivity, impersonal narration also can encourage identification with the characters through whom the story is focalized. "Think of the young man, for instance, in Dostoevsky's *Crime and Punishment*—there is a young man whose experience surrounds and presses upon the reader, is felt and tasted and endured by the reader; and any one who has been through the book has truly become Raskolnikov, and knows exactly what it was to be that young man."[27] Impersonal narration, therefore, conjures an objective agent whose knowledge and authority transcends that of a "mere" person at the same time as it subtly conveys a subjective perspective, sometimes associated with one or more characters.

As Lubbock notes, personal narration—or the breaking of the "spell" of impersonal narration—calls attention to the person of the narrator and invites the question of his reliability. Nevertheless, one form of personal narration can also function by convention as the authoritative commentary of an "omniscient" narrator. Wayne Booth identifies the "telling" mode of narration, as opposed to "showing," as a "form of artificial authority [that] has been present in most narrative until recent times."[28] The narrator tells the reader information, sometimes of an eval-

23. Gribble, "Narrative Interventions," 41.
24. Ska, "*Our Fathers Have Told Us*," 44.
25. Lubbock, *The Craft of Fiction*, 110–23. Lubbock's "author" is roughly synonymous with this study's "narrator."
26. Lubbock, *The Craft of Fiction*, 251.
27. Lubbock, *The Craft of Fiction*, 144. Italics added.
28. Booth, *The Rhetoric of Fiction*, 4.

uative nature, that would normally be qualified by what we know of the speaker (and therefore how much we trust them), but which "we must accept without question if we are to grasp the story that is to follow."[29] Such instances of telling actualize the performative convention by which the narrator structures the story-world. Booth cites as an example Homer's *Odyssey*, in which "Homer 'intrudes' deliberately and obviously to insure that our judgment of the 'heroic,' 'resourceful,' 'admirable,' 'wise' Odysseus will be sufficiently favorable."[30] While Lubbock's treatment of the authoritative narrator reveals one of its bases to be impersonal narration (the fourth facet of Culler's "omniscient narrator"), Booth fleshes out how the performative convention (which encompasses the first three facets of Culler's "omniscient narrator") serves as another basis. In order to make sense of the story, readers treat the narrator's word—including certain personal remarks that seem essential to the comprehension of the story—as authoritative.

In summary, the "omniscient narrator," which is also to say the authoritative narrator, derives from the more discrete narrative conventions of impersonal narration and the performative convention by which the narrator effectively creates the story-world. While these two conventions give rise to the sense of an omniscient narrator, they also serve as channels through which the narrator's ideological worldview might be smuggled into the story. Through impersonal narration the narrator subtly chooses vantage points, often character focalizors, through which readers make sense of the story. What the character focalizors see, feel, and think, takes on a factual quality that informs the readers' own understanding of the story-world. Through the performative convention, alternatively, the narrator proclaims not only the facts of the story but also the principles and norms through which the story might (or as Booth would say, should) be understood. By explaining who is bad and good, truthful and deceitful, and so on, the narrator predisposes readers to align their sympathies and expectations accordingly.

The Biblical Narrator

Modern interpretation of the biblical narrator has by and large followed the conceptual evolution of the "omniscient narrator." Traditional

---

29. Booth, *The Rhetoric of Fiction*, 3.
30. Booth, *The Rhetoric of Fiction*, 5.

formulations accord the biblical narrator authority on the grounds of a godlike omniscience—indeed, the narrator is not uncommonly depicted as an accomplice or counterpart to God. Sternberg, for instance, renders the biblical narrator "absolutely and straightforwardly reliable," and as analogous to God: "The narrator stands to the world of his tale as God to the world represented in that tale, each reigning supreme in his own sphere of activity."[31] For Sternberg, the narrator's omniscience serves the ideological function of glorifying God's omniscience.[32] For others, this ideological function is not so clear, and a subtle reversal is in order. The narrator is not subordinate to God, but rather vice versa: "[I]n a biblical story, God is to be trusted for reasons of faith, and the narrator is to be trusted . . . as above God and as the source of the report about God."[33]

The omniscience attributed to the biblical narrator reflects interpreters' awareness of approximately the same narrative effects that Culler identifies. On the one hand, the biblical narrator's general adherence to an impersonal mode of narration is seen to preserve a sense of objectivity and reliability. As Sternberg explains, "The narrator avoids all commentary that would invest him with the lineaments of an individual person or persona," for to make such commentary would "threaten the objectivity and authority of the disembodied voice mediating between God and his people."[34] Similarly Shimon Bar-Efrat explains the necessity of impersonal—or covert—narration for preserving a sense of immediacy, a sense of the events in themselves: "The narrative will be more vivid, dramatic, gripping, and realistic the less the narrator's existence is felt, the less aware we are of the fact that someone is mediating between us and

---

31. Sternberg, *The Poetics of Biblical Narrative*, 83.

32. According to Sternberg, the reading experience of gaps and ambiguities mirrors the narrative dramatization of human ignorance vis-à-vis divine omniscience. Thus he contends: "The combination of initial blurring and retrospective lucidity demonstrates to the reader, in terms of his own sense-making experience, the force of the generalization that 'man sees what meets the eye and God sees into the heart'" (*The Poetics of Biblical Narrative*, 99).

33. Amit, *Reading Biblical Narratives*, 95. See also Eslinger, who contests the practicality of labeling the narrator "omniscient" but nevertheless contends: "God, however supreme and omnipotent compared to the human denizens of the story world, is definitely implicated and subordinated by his involvement to the all-seeing wisdom and insight of the external unconditioned narrator" (*Into the Hands of the Living God*, 17).

34. Sternberg, *The Poetics of Biblical Narrative*, 123.

the events."[35] This sense of the narrator's impersonal sovereignty further manifests itself, according to Alter, in the way that the narrator's word assumes the status of objective reality while the character's word remains a questionable representation. The "narrator's authoritative report" is the touchstone against which a character's words are to be measured, and thus has the power to reveal the character to be mistaken, deceitful, or truthful.[36] Like Lubbock, biblical scholarship observes that while impersonal narration evokes a sense of objectivity, it nevertheless mediates particular subjectivities. Feminist scholarship, for instance, points out that much of the biblical narrative reflects an androcentric narrator, whose own perspective often aligns with the perspectives of his male characters.[37]

On the other hand, the biblical narrator's occasional commentary is read according to the performative convention of narrative and thus maintains a sense of the narrator's authority. Christopher T. Paris explains this phenomenon in terms of narratorial "obtrusion," which he distinguishes from the more impersonal omniscient comments: "Omniscient comments convey necessary information designed to assist reader understanding, whereas obtrusive statements attempt to form the response of the reader."[38] Obtrusive comments, in this sense, reflect the narrator's personal but performative and authoritative predisposition: they "represent instances where the narrator desires to exercise greater control over the text, perhaps because the narrator worries about losing power or giving too much freedom to the reader."[39] Corroborating this idea that obtrusions do not diminish but rather sustain the narrator's

---

35. Bar-Efrat, *Narrative Art in the Bible*, 31.

36. Alter, *The Art of Biblical Narrative*, 63–87.

37. E.g., Davies, who observes that "the biblical narrative tradition . . . was able to present male supremacy and female subordination as a normal, natural and inevitable part of human experience" (*The Dissenting Reader*, 49). Elsewhere Davies contends that the narrator of the Dinah interlude betrays his androcentric values through his choice to focalize much of the story through the brothers and other male characters (*The Dissenting Reader*, 56). See also Fewell and Gunn, who say that the narrator of the Dinah interlude exhibits the "limited viewpoint" of "an androcentric point of view" (*Gender, Power, and Promise*, 153).

38. Paris, "Narrative Obtrusion," xv. Paris' formulation of "obtrusion" suggests a personal narrator inasmuch as it envisions the narrator's overtness, or the reader's heightened awareness of the narrator, as an effect of a change in narrative style. Paris describes obtrusions as "those instances where a normally laconic narrator interrupts the flow of the text in an attempt to change the way a reader interprets" ("Narrative Obtrusion," 14).

39. Paris, "Narrative Obtrusion," 49.

authority is Bar-Efrat's remark on the biblical narrator's moments of overtness, which often overlap with a personal mode of narration. "[T]he effect of the explanations, judgments and interpretations ... is to create distance and reduce the reader's emotional involvement. A reader who is totally absorbed in the plot will be able neither to see the events dispassionately, nor to judge them and assess their significance."[40] In other words, an overt narrator—one whose narration may veer into a personal mode—can actually serve the purpose of detachment, as he pulls readers away from their personal inclinations into alignment with his own authoritative viewpoint. Booth's account of the biblical narrator's personal judgment in the book of Job captures this sense of the biblical narrator's performative authority well. "How do we know that Job sinned not? Who is to pronounce on such a question? . . . [T]he author pronounces judgment, and we accept his judgment without question."[41]

The Evaluative Comments in the Dinah Interlude

Readings of the Dinah interlude traditionally ground their judgment of its events and the events' implications for the question of ancestral relations in an authoritative narrator whose voice and perspective are perceived in one or more of a series of evaluative comments on the narrative level (vv. 2, 5, 7, 13, 27). This narrator resembles the omniscient narrator outlined in the preceding review, one whose personal commentary, carrying the authoritative weight granted to it by the performative convention of narrative, structures the story-world according to his principles, and whose impersonal narration lends a sense of objectivity and immediacy that allows him to guide readers indirectly—primarily through the means of focalization and word choice—to his own personal judgment. Thus interpretation generally classifies the relation between each evaluative remark and the narrator in one of three ways: (1) the evaluation represents the direct, unmediated judgment of the narrator; (2) it derives from the characters' perspective and serves the narrator's purpose of legitimating their feelings and engendering the reader's sympathy for their cause; or (3) it reflects solely the characters' perspective, which is distanced from the narrator and, therefore, of questionable validity.[42]

---

40. Bar-Efrat, *Narrative Art in the Bible*, 31.
41. Booth, *The Rhetoric of Fiction*, 4.
42. This third way, as will be seen, does not entail any loss of authority on the

Direct Evaluation

Readers hear the narrator's direct evaluation in several places. Offering one of the stronger readings of direct narratorial evaluation, Ronald T. Hyman claims that "[w]e have only the Narrator's words that Dinah was raped and defiled, that the rape was an abominable act in Israel, and that it ought not to have been done (vv. 2, 5, 7)."[43] While Hyman does not include vv. 13 and 27 as the narrator's words, one might assume that he implies their inclusion inasmuch as they repeat the general proposition of v. 5, namely that Shechem "defiled" Dinah. Thus Hyman would appear to take all the evaluative comments as directly indicative of the narrator's evaluation. Hyman's decision to capitalize the narratorial persona ("Narrator"), furthermore, is noteworthy, as it typifies the authority that he and most readers grant to the narrator. Hyman concedes, "The reader may not agree with the point of view of the Narrator,"[44] but the fact remains that it is the narrator's point of view that serves as the yardstick against which diverging perspectives (characters' or readers') are measured.

Most readers limit the narrator's direct evaluation to v. 2, in which Shechem sees, takes, "lies with" or "lays" (שכב את), and "rapes" or "humbles" (ענה) Dinah. The notice that Shechem "rapes" (ענה) Dinah in particular is read as the narrator's evaluative obtrusion into the story, while the formulation of the sexual act (שכב את) is considered to imbue the event with a negative tone. Sternberg voices the standard reading: this narration amounts to the narrator's own "unequivocal condemnation of the assault."[45] The unconventional formulation שכב את (in which את is read as a direct object marker), rather than just שכב, confers a negative charge upon the act, as it connotes forcefulness, and the use of ענה "speaks for itself."[46] He summarizes, "The verbs selected to describe the crime project a sharp judgment on the highest authority."[47] The narrator—or perhaps more appropriately, the Narrator—offers explicit

---

narrator's part. On the contrary, the narrator retains full authority. The evaluative remark's questionable validity results from its dissociation from the narrator's authoritative perspective.

43. Hyman, "Final Judgment," 98.
44. Hyman, "Final Judgment," 100–101.
45. Sternberg, *The Poetics of Biblical Narrative*, 446.
46. Sternberg, *The Poetics of Biblical Narrative*, 446.
47. Sternberg, *The Poetics of Biblical Narrative*, 446.

commentary on the moral nature of Shechem's act, pronouncing it a crime, and a rather reprehensible one at that.

Noble concurs with Sternberg, reading the narrator's candid evaluation of Shechem in שכב את and ענה,[48] and fleshes out the implications of this. "In my view, the key is provided by the narrator giving a forthright evaluation of Shechem's rape at the very beginning of the story, and this then becomes a yardstick by which the various characters are measured: Which of them share this perception?"[49] This early revelation, in other words, becomes the fulcrum of judgment. As Frank M. Yamada puts it, "The narrative start[s] out as a story about the rape of Dinah, an act that requires an ethical response from the reader and the characters in the story."[50] The "rape of Dinah," then, is a narrative fact received "on the highest authority," as Sternberg says. It grounds the rest of the story and its swirl of perspectives (Levi and Simeon's, the brothers', the Hivites', Jacob's) in an early verdict offered personally by the narrator, and it provides a solid criterion for weighing judgments, either characters' or readers'.

A smaller contingent of readers perceives that the narrator's initial condemnation is confirmed in v. 7, in which it is said that Shechem had done "a disgraceful folly," a thing "not to be done." According to van Wolde, here "the narrator presents his judgment openly," and Shechem's act is "condemned in the severest terms: it is a disgrace."[51] Ronald R. Clark, Jr. agrees, as he envisions the narrator volunteering his personal ruling: "The narrator is crying out for justice even if Dinah cannot."[52]

Indirect Evaluation: Character Perspective

While the narrator's direct word affords most readers the surest foundation for judgment, it does not act alone in guiding evaluation. As numerous interpretations make clear, the narrator's word is not necessarily undivided in its judgment, as it offers the possibility of positive evaluation of Shechem and negative evaluation of the brothers. The arguably

---

48. Noble, "A 'Balanced' Reading," 178–79. See also Rashkow, "The Rape(s) of Dinah," 61.
49. Noble, "A 'Balanced' Reading," 191–92.
50. Yamada, "Dealing with Rape," 156.
51. Van Wolde, "Love and Hatred," 443.
52. Clark, Jr., "The Silence in Dinah's Cry," 154.

sympathetic portrayals of Shechem in his love for Dinah (v. 3), his delighted eagerness to submit to the brothers' plan (v. 19), and his honored standing among family (v. 19), as well as the general representation of a trusting Hivite people (v. 24), complicate what might otherwise seem an easy verdict. (Indeed, for Sternberg, this complexity is purposeful: it captures the sense of dilemma in the story and, moreover, showcases the narrator's artful rhetoric in negotiating the complications to a final judgment in favor of Levi and Simeon.)[53] This complication calls for additional evaluative input, and although the narrator's direct word eludes most readers beyond v. 2, the narrator's authoritative stance is still sought and found in less direct communication. The impersonal narration that lends the story a sense of objectivity also affords it the opportunity to sneak in character perspectives that naturally assume the same sense of objectivity and thus authority.

For many readers, the narrator offers the necessary guidance covertly in three main ways. First, and most commonly, they claim that the narrator exercises his jurisdiction over the perspectives through which he mediates the story: he purposefully appropriates certain characters as focalizors in order to espouse their views and engender sympathy for them. Second, they make the distinction between vocalization and focalization, and aver that the focalized statements on the narrative level, while mediating the perspective of a character instead of the narrator, nonetheless remain under the linguistic jurisdiction of the narrator. The specific words that the narrator chooses to represent the character perspectives therefore reflect the narrator's own authoritative stance. Third, they call attention to the narrator's arrangement of perspectives, particularly his finalization of perspective in the brothers' last words. In summary, the narrator selects the perspectives through which he represents the story, chooses the words through which he mediates the perspectives, and arranges the perspectives—all in a purposeful manner.[54]

The reading of the narrator's practice of persuasion through focalization derives from a poetics that Wayne C. Booth popularizes in *The Rhetoric of Fiction* (a poetics, furthermore, that shares much of its

---

53. Sternberg accordingly titles the chapter in *The Poetics of Biblical Narrative* that addresses the Dinah interlude, "The Art of Persuasion."

54. Reflective of this understanding of the covert narrator is the assertion that van Wolde makes at the beginning of her study of the narrator in Gen 34: "A narrator tells a story, selects the material, arranges it and chooses the perspectives" ("Love and Hatred," 440).

understanding of focalization with Lubbock's *The Craft of Fiction*). In his chapter on "distance," Booth explores how Jane Austen simultaneously invites sympathy and judgment of Emma's character in *Emma*. "The solution to the problem of maintaining sympathy despite almost crippling faults," he explains, "was primarily to use the heroine herself as a kind of narrator, though in third person, reporting on her own experience."[55] Although Booth mentions neither perspective nor focalization here (indeed, "focalization" had not yet been coined),[56] he clearly means that Emma, "as a kind of narrator, though in the third person," serves as the focalizor for much of the narrative. "By showing most of the story *through Emma's eyes*, the author insures that we shall travel with Emma rather than stand against her."[57] Booth's general proposition, that focalization typically invites sympathy, echoes in biblical scholarship as well. In "Who Guides Whom?" van Wolde contends that "indirect narrator's texts," in which a narrator presents a character's point of view, entail the narrator's involvement (possibly identification) with a character and invite the reader to identify with the character as well.[58]

It appears that many readers of the Dinah interlude reach a similar conclusion to Booth's and van Wolde's, namely that by showing most of the story through the brothers' eyes, the narrator insures that the reader will travel with the brothers rather than stand against them. Van Wolde, who reads the evaluations in verses 5, 13, and 27 as "indirect narrator's texts" representative of Jacob and the brothers' perspectives, explains, "The narrator's influence on the representation of the story is . . . substantial."[59] By selecting the brothers' perspective as the lens through which he consistently portrays Shechem and the Hivites, the narrator encourages the reader to identify with the brothers.[60]

Sternberg makes the most comprehensive case for the interpretation that the narrator leads the reader into "complete identification with

---

55. Booth, *The Rhetoric of Fiction*, 245.

56. Genette introduces the term in *Narrative Discourse*, which was published after Booth's *Rhetoric of Fiction*.

57. Booth, *The Rhetoric of Fiction*, 245. Emphasis mine.

58. See her case study of 1 Kgs 3:23–28 in van Wolde, "Who Guides Whom?" 638.

59. Van Wolde, "Love and Hatred," 443.

60. Van Wolde infers, in large part from the evidence of the indirect narrator's texts, that the narrator "defends" the sons' position, that he "supports" their views ("Love and Hatred," 443).

the brothers at the expense of all the other characters."[61] He endeavors to show that the evaluative remarks of vv. 5, 7, and 13, while reflective of characters' perspectives, ultimately reveal the narrator's agenda.[62] The anonymous report in v. 5 that Shechem "defiled" Dinah, he avers, is "informationally redundant and syntactically omissible."[63] But the narrator purposefully includes it in order to remind the reader of the gruesome nature of Shechem's act with Dinah and to lessen sympathy for the unresponsive, and thus seemingly unmoved, Jacob.[64] Whereas the evaluative comment in v. 5 issues anonymously, Sternberg contends that those in vv. 7 and 13 stem from the brothers' perspective, which the narrator shares and into which he invites the reader. Key to Sternberg's reading of these verses is his concept of "controlled ambiguity," in which an ambiguity in representation meets with axiological certainty. Sternberg's explanation of v. 7 serves to outline the effect of controlled ambiguity in both verses:

> To whom does the judgment ... belong? It can be attributed both to the brothers and to the narrator himself. Needless to say, it is the narrator who communicates this sentence. The question facing the reader, however, is one of origination (and hence validity) rather than (possibly uncommitted) transmission. Does the discourse reflect the painful feelings of the brothers ("They were grieved and very angry because *they felt that* he had committed an outrage" etc.)? Or does it interpolate an evaluative comment on the narrator's own part, designed to justify their feelings ("They were grieved and very angry, *and no wonder*, since he had committed an outrage" etc.)? ... Where does the inside view end, or where does the narrator's voice begin? What

---

61. Sternberg, *The Poetics of Biblical Narrative*, 446.

62. As a side note, it is worth remarking on Sternberg's markedly different reading of the similar evaluative claim made in v. 27, which rationalizes the brothers' plunder of the city. See Sternberg, *The Poetics of Biblical Narrative*, 472. The notice that "they plundered the city because they [the Hivites] had defiled their sister" pluralizes the offender—it is no longer Shechem, but all the inhabitants of the city. Sternberg excludes Levi and Simeon from the character focalizors (i.e., the brothers) because the duo have already enacted their vengeance and, according to Sternberg, left the scene (v. 26). So, whereas the charge of defilement had stood previously as a righteous justification for the brothers' plan of revenge (v. 13), and specifically Levi and Simeon's enactment of it, it rings ironically here as the other brothers' cheap excuse for plundering the remains of the town.

63. Sternberg, *The Poetics of Biblical Narrative*, 449.

64. Sternberg, *The Poetics of Biblical Narrative*, 449.

is the narrator's standing in and attitude to the explanatory statement? Its weight crucially depends on the answer.[65]

This ambiguity, irresolvable as it is, need not trouble the reader, according to Sternberg, since ultimately either possibility yields the same effect. Read as a continuation of the brothers' perspective, the clause evokes sympathy for the brothers. Conversely, read as the narrator's evaluation, the clause relays the narrator's normative perspective.[66] Either way, the reader comes to the correct understanding of events: the brothers are justified in their emotional reaction to Shechem's offense, and Jacob is condemned by his non-reaction. (Shechem, of course, is even further reviled.) Sternberg proposes the narratorial motivation for this ambiguity: "[F]or rhetorical reasons the narrator chooses to ambiguate where he could elucidate, since the undecidable perspective enables him to elicit maximum sympathy for his heroes.... Subjectivity joins forces with objectivity to establish the most favorable climate of opinion for one of the tale's three parties," that is, the brothers.[67]

Sternberg's reading of the narrator's persuasive appropriation of the brothers' perspective proves instructive because it outlines a common effect of the evaluative remarks in vv. 5, 7, 13, and 27. This effect is the same one that Booth, van Wolde, and Lubbock note: focalization through certain characters invites sympathy for them and subtly suggests the alignment of the narrator's authoritative standpoint with them. In the case of the Dinah interlude, this effect often finds expression in the readers' conflation or confusion of the character-focalized evaluations with the narrator's perspective. Readings less narratologically inclined than Sternberg's forego the distinction between character and narrator and instead identify the character focalizors' and the narrator's perspectives as

---

65. Sternberg, *The Poetics of Biblical Narrative*, 454. Sternberg explains the phenomenon of controlled ambiguity in v. 13: "On the one hand, the *asher*-clause is so patterned as to suggest an inside view of the brothers (who indeed refer to Dinah as 'our sister' in the following verse). At the same time, its location after the *verbum dicendi* 'spoke' charges it with objective as well as emotive force. It is as if the brothers are about to reply but the narrator would not let them do so at once. Instead, he arrests for a moment the flow of events to remind us, on his own authority and in the strongest language, of the human ('their sister') and religious ('defiled') norms that should govern our judgment of the deceit.... By constructively ambiguating the viewpoint between subjectivity and objectivity, the narrator has again maximized the persuasive impact of a minimal piece of discourse" (*The Poetics of Biblical Narrative*, 463).

66. Sternberg, *The Poetics of Biblical Narrative*, 454–55.

67. Sternberg, *The Poetics of Biblical Narrative*, 455.

one and the same. Blyth, for instance, states: "[W]e read on three separate occasions (vv. 5, 13, 27) that, in the eyes of the narrator and the male characters, Dinah's sexual encounter with Shechem had rendered her 'defiled.'"[68] Robin Parry, who does not identify the narratorial perspective with that of the brothers, even while seeing some significant overlap between them, nonetheless overdetermines the judgment with reference to both. He first implies that the negative evaluation of Shechem issues from the narrator. Asking the question, "Does the narrator blame Shechem?" he implies an affirmative response: "Blame is always placed squarely on Shechem's shoulders. Shechem saw her, took her, lay her and shamed her (v. 2). Shechem 'defiled' her (vv. 5, 13, 27) and 'did folly in Israel (v. 7)."[69] He later traces the blame of Shechem to the brothers also: "[T]he sons (and Jacob?) saw the rape as an act which treats Dinah as a prostitute (v. 31) and thus 'defiles her' (vv. 5, 13, 27). It is 'folly in Israel' (v. 7)."[70] Specifically with regard to v. 7, there is a wealth of agreement that the narrator's perspective or voice is joined to the brothers': Shemesh contends that the "severe condemnation" of Shechem's act with Dinah is a case of "combined speech that reflects the feelings of Dinah's brothers as well as of the biblical narrator";[71] Turner classifies the evaluative comment as the "reaction" of "her [Dinah's] brothers and the narrator";[72] Mignon R. Jacobs declares that "the narrator's view . . . is seen in the brothers' evaluation of Shechem's act as 'vile'";[73] and Claudia V. Camp says, "The violation of Dinah is described from her brothers' point of view (with narratorial agreement) with the word *nebalah*."[74]

For readings that identify the narrator's judgment with the brothers', the disproportionate focalization of Shechem's act through the brothers solves an unsavory dilemma: "The trouble is that mass slaughter will not balance against rape according to conventional normative scales."[75] By drawing the reader alongside, and ultimately into "complete identification,"[76] with the brothers, the narrator obviates the otherwise

68. Blyth, "Terrible Silence," 501.
69. Parry, "Feminist Hermeneutics," 16.
70. Parry, "Feminist Hermeneutics," 19.
71. Shemesh, "Rape Is Rape Is Rape," 20.
72. Turner, *Genesis*, 150.
73. Jacobs, "Love, Honor, and Violence," 23.
74. Camp, *Wise, Strange, and Holy*, 302.
75. Sternberg, *The Poetics of Biblical Narrative*, 445.
76. Sternberg, *The Poetics of Biblical Narrative*, 446.

possible result, that the reader will disavow the brothers' violence.[77] In case anyone would doubt the effect of appropriating inside views to invite identification with a disreputable character, it is worth observing parallels in literature. Lisa Zunshine catalogues two similar cases in literary history in Samuel Richardson's *Clarissa* and Vladimir Nabokov's *Lolita*, in which contemporary audiences of the novels commonly identified with and approved of a character whom, by the author's account, was not be trusted.[78] In both books, the character in question enjoys the prerogative of first person narration; Lovelace in *Clarissa* shares portions of the epistolary narrative, and Humbert Humbert in *Lolita* is the homodiegetic narrator. Their privileged perspectives naturally invite the sympathy of the reader, despite the fact that Lovelace is "the man whom Richardson saw as a consummate stalker and rapist" and Humbert Humbert is, as Nabokov put it, "a vain and cruel wretch."[79] The cases of Lovelace and Humbert Humbert are not unlike that of Dinah's brothers: although the brothers in the Dinah interlude do not enjoy first person narration, the narrator's repeated focalization through them invites sympathy in their direction.

Readers who perceive the narrator's indirect evaluative guidance in character-focalized statements sometimes claim that the guidance extends beyond the perspectives mediated to the words selected for mediation. This line of reading entails a nuanced division between the narrator's voice and the character's perspective, which van Wolde's definition of an "indirect narrator's text" outlines: "[T]he character is represented as a thinking, observing, or speaking subject, but the representing is done by the narrator."[80] For readers who speculate on the lexical representation of the focalized perspective, it is as though, within the constraints of the focalizor's perspective, the narrator nonetheless discloses his own stance through the specific words he employs to represent the character's interiority. Thus Sternberg reads the lexical choice of "defile" (טמא) in vv. 5 and 13 as reflective of the narrator's own judgment. The narrator "prefers

---

77. I should note that Robin Parry, by seeing overlap rather than identification between the narrator's perspective and the brothers' perspective, argues that the text leads readers to condemn *both* Shechem's act *and* the violent response of the brothers. Parry, *Old Testament Story and Christian Ethics*, chapters 4–5.

78. Zunshine, *Why We Read Fiction*, 82–118.

79. The first quote is Zunshine's, from *Why We Read Fiction*, 101. The second is Nabokov's, quoted in *Why We Read Fiction*, 102.

80. Van Wolde, "Who Guides Whom?" 626.

to charge the report with the evaluative 'defiled,' which goes even beyond the emotive 'abused'. . . in implying moral and religious outrage as well,"[81] and his repetition of the same word in v. 13 "clearly indicates how lexical choice heightens both the intensity and validity of the brothers' motive for deception."[82] Van Wolde similarly reads the narrator's negative judgment in the lexical formulation of Jacob's and the brothers' interiority (in vv. 5, 13, and 27): "By the triple use of the term 'defile' the narrator places the Jacobites' mental awareness in a strong socio-religious condemnation of Shechem's behaviour," and because of this lexical choice—in addition to the fact that the narrator has selected the brothers' perspective as the lens through which to view Shechem's act—"one might conclude that the narrator supports Jacob's sons' views."[83]

In addition to the narrator's selection and lexical representation of character perspectives, readers also perceive the narrator's judgment in the arrangement of perspectives, most notably in the narrator's choice to give Levi and Simeon the last word. Hyman asserts: "The Narrator gives his over-all support to the brothers by giving them the last word for their judgment via their dramatic rhetorical question."[84] Van Wolde reads the last word as ratification of a perspective that has already dominated the narrative. It caps the evaluations that have preceded it and confirms that "the reader is encouraged to share the sons' point of view."[85] Sternberg concurs. Levi and Simeon's last word is the coup de grace to the narrator's rhetorical maneuvering: "[A]bove all, his giving the last word—and what a last word!—to Simeon and Levi, leaves no doubt where his sympathy lies."[86]

Indirect Evaluation: Impersonality That Yields a Clean Evaluative Slate

A small minority of readers dissociate the narrator from the evaluations in vv. 5, 7, 13, and 27—attributing these fully to the brothers' perspective—and read his voice and perspective only in v. 2. For them,

81. Sternberg, *The Poetics of Biblical Narrative*, 449.
82. Sternberg, *The Poetics of Biblical Narrative*, 461.
83. Van Wolde, "Love and Hatred," 443.
84. Hyman, "Final Judgment," 100.
85. Van Wolde, "Love and Hatred," 443. See also Parry, "Feminist Hermeneutics," 19, quoted on p. 170, which implicitly associates Levi and Simeon's last word with the focalized judgments (vv. 5, 7, 13, and 27) earlier in the story.
86. Sternberg, *The Poetics of Biblical Narrative*, 475.

the narrator is an exemplar of impersonality. In contrast to most other readers, who detect the narrator's judgment in commentary and/or the selection, lexicalization, and arrangement of character perspectives, they read a narrator whose own perspective is almost completely concealed. Danna Nolan Fewell and David M. Gunn's reading typifies this tendency. They rarely speak of the narrator's involvement in the text, and when they do, they discuss it more in terms of his "silence" and "reticence" than his presence.[87] Thus it is not the narrator who uses the term "defiled" in the repeated accusation against Shechem (vv. 5, 13, and 27), but the brothers.[88] And the narrator "seemingly couches" the evaluation of verse 7 "in their point of view."[89]

Yet even here the divorce between evaluation and narrator is not complete. Most indicative of their lingering association is the significance attributed to the interpretation of ענה in v. 2. Whereas readers like Sternberg identify this verse as the foundation to the negative evaluation of Shechem—as the narrator's own "unequivocal condemnation" of Shechem[90]—this third line of reading argues that the key word ענה is morally neutral in connotation. This case is made most famously by Bechtel, who contends that ענה (in the piel) indicates the social humiliation and relegation in status that results from a sexual act that either violates pre-established marital agreements or transpires with no prospect of marriage.[91] The term, in this view, acts as a descriptor of social consequence rather than as the narrator's moral judgment.[92] The contention that ענה neither means rape nor suggests the narrator's moral judgment testifies to the attempt to ground judgment in an authoritative narrator. Here, however, the argument rests not so much on what the narrator

---

87. E.g., Fewell and Gunn, "Tipping the Balance," 194.

88. See Fewell and Gunn, who remark on "[t]heir [the brothers'] use of the term 'defiled' to describe their sister" ("Tipping the Balance," 207). This stands in contrast to the common view that, regardless of its focalizor, "defile" bears the narrator's evaluation. Cf. Sternberg, *The Poetics of Biblical Narrative*, 449; Van Wolde, "Love and Hatred," 443.

89. Fewell and Gunn, "Tipping the Balance," 199.

90. Sternberg, *The Poetics of Biblical Narrative*, 446.

91. Bechtel, "What If Dinah Is Not Raped?" 19–36. See also Gruber, "A Re-Examination of the Charges." Paralleling Bechtel's argument, Gruber offers an original analysis of the word's use elsewhere in the Bible and in rabbinic sources, and he concludes that "there is no evidence that Shechem raped Dinah."

92. Brett echoes Bechtel's argument, noting, "Other verbs are normally used when violence is indicated" (*Genesis*, 101).

says, but rather on what he does not say. His morally neutral narration of Shechem's act places the events that follow on a clean slate. The events are then judged—generally in terms of the brothers' excessive violence and the ancestral family's diminished prospects for continued life in the land[93]—to reflect implied disapproval of the brothers' actions.

Thus Bechtel summarizes the story's events as harboring two implicit perspectives, one of which aligns with the "story's" own viewpoint:

> One element (Dinah and Jacob) is interested in interacting with outsiders . . . that show allegiance to their group values and customs. The other element is made up of militant folks (Simeon, Levi and the sons of Jacob) who are threatened by the impure outsiders and want to maintain strict group purity and absolute separation. The story seems to be challenging this attitude by showing the potential danger in which it places the group.[94]

For this study's purposes, how "the story" speaks is synonymous with how the narrator speaks. Although the narrator remains covert, his position is ultimately betrayed by the suggestive juxtaposition of ideological positions, which is illustrated against the colorless background of his neutral word choice. Brett, who follows Bechtel in reading ענה as morally neutral, concludes similarly that the narrator (in his terms, the Persian-era editor[s]) constructs the narrative in such a way as to cast the brothers in a tacitly negative light. He cites as evidence the brothers' deceptive use of circumcision, the excessiveness of their violence, Jacob's repeated censure of Levi and Simeon (34:30; 49:5–7), and the hypocrisy of Simeon's Canaanite marriage (46:10), which "point to the alternative interpretation, i.e., that they [the editors] favour the openness of Dinah, Jacob and Hamor, not Simeon and Levi's violent quest for purity. The dominant perspective, which legitimates ethnocentrism, has been quietly undermined."[95] While Fewell and Gunn do not work to amend the meaning of ענה, their reading too may be included as one that envisions an evaluatively silent narrator whose narrative representation nonetheless

---

93. The concern for these prospects is given voice by Jacob's character in v. 30. Interpretation often grounds its judgment on a foundation that encompasses more than Jacob's viewpoint, however. Several other justifications for a negative evaluation of the brothers are mentioned in the following paragraph.

94. Bechtel, "What If Dinah Is Not Raped?" 36.

95. Brett interprets a disproportion between the brothers' act of vengeance and Shechem's offense in light of Deut 22:28–29. He interprets their use of circumcision negatively because it "take[s] the sign of the divine covenant in vain" (*Genesis*, 101–3).

communicates an evaluation: "[I]t is not quite accurate to say that the rape is unequivocally condemned. The narrator calls it a rape, without passing further judgment."[96] Fewell and Gunn proceed to fashion a reading in which the brothers act irresponsibly and in a manner that does more harm than good.[97]

The common element in all of the above readings is the recourse taken to the narrator. Whether the narrator offers his judgment directly in personal commentary, indirectly through his selection, lexicalization, and arrangement of character perspective, or, alternatively, through an impersonal evaluative neutrality that allows for the story events to speak for themselves, it is ultimately his word that grounds the final verdict.

The Dinah Interlude as Judgment on Ancestral Relations

Even a cursory reading of the Dinah interlude flags the question of ancestral interethnic relations. As Niditch notes, the beginning of the story, in which Dinah goes out to see the women of the land and is then raped by Shechem, sets the tone: "A strong impression is conveyed of insider versus outsider, us versus them."[98] The question then finds explicit articulation in the negotiations between Hamor and Shechem and Jacob's sons, in which Jacob's sons envision becoming "one people" (v. 16). The terms of agreement, namely circumcision, further indicate the question of interethnic relations. Circumcision represents a physical boundary of ancestral identity; the prospect of circumcised Hivites would seem to herald a monumental shift in ancestral identity.

Thus many readings of the Dinah interlude interpret the story's judgment as one that impinges on ancestral relations. A general interpretive correlation holds: approval or disapproval for the brothers corresponds to approval or disapproval for their exclusivist mode of relations. While conventional readings privilege the evaluative comments as the basis for the judgment of the brothers, and by association as the basis for the judgment on ancestral relations, they also look elsewhere for evidence to substantiate the judgment on ancestral relations. A brief review

---

96. Fewell and Gunn, "Tipping the Balance," 195.

97. Fewell and Gunn summarize the main conclusion of this reading: "His [Jacob's] sons have usurped his authority, deceived him in the process, and acted without responsibility. They leave him to face the consequences, him and the rest of the family—the women and the children" ("Tipping the Balance," 208–9).

98. Niditch, "Genesis," 40.

of interpretation will clarify how these readings align their judgment of the brothers with their judgment on the ancestral mode of relations.

Although Sternberg depicts the Dinah interlude as a moral tale, the primary concern of which consists in redressing the injustice of Shechem's rape, he insists that the matter of exogamous marriage is inextricably bound to the quest for justice. It is, in large part, what justifies the brothers and incriminates Jacob. Jacob's "inaction amounts to an acquiescence in what a patriarch, whatever his paternal instincts, must fight tooth and nail: exogamous marriage. Dinah must be extricated even at risk."[99] Levi and Simeon, on the other hand, operate on the motive not only of redressing Shechem's initial violation but also of preventing "exogamous marriage, by hook or crook."[100] Where exactly does Sternberg detect the endogamous ideal, which is never explicitly indicated in Gen 34? Sternberg looks both backwards—to Abraham's and Isaac's marital preferences—and forward—to Deuteronomy's injunction against intermarriage with the Hivites, among others (Deut 7:1–4).[101] That such a strong tradition subsists from before the Dinah interlude to later in the life of Israel confirms, he argues, what remains unspoken in the text.

Joseph Vicek Kozar, who reads the narrative as supporting the brothers' actions,[102] suggests that the significance of interethnic relations is substantiated by symbolic imagery within the story. He points out that the homonym of Hamor's name (חמור) is donkey, an animal that "lives among the herd but is not one of them, lacking cloven hooves and not chewing the cud."[103] This, coupled with the fact that "[a]t the time of Dinah's rape, her brothers are out with the cattle (34:5),"[104] illumines the resultant confrontation: "The . . . clash of cultures (and slaughter) shows that the sons of herds and flocks cannot conduct social intercourse with the sons of the ass. This symbolism underlies the group or tribal nature

---

99. Sternberg, *The Poetics of Biblical Narrative*, 474.

100. Sternberg, *The Poetics of Biblical Narrative*, 472. See also Camp, *Wise, Strange, and Holy*, 279–322. Similar to Sternberg, Camp identifies the primary issue of the Dinah interlude as the brothers' sense of family honor, which, she contends, includes an impulse toward endogamy.

101. Sternberg, "Biblical Poetics and Sexual Politics," 482–85.

102. Kozar, "When 'Circumfession' Is Not Enough," 60–61. Kozar also, however, explores several ways of reading "against the text."

103. Kozar, "When 'Circumfession' Is Not Enough," 57.

104. Kozar, "When 'Circumfession' Is Not Enough," 57.

of the events behind the story."¹⁰⁵ Like Sternberg, Kozar also retrojects later narrative concerns of Israelite interethnic relations onto the clash between the ancestral family and the Hivites. He concludes that Dinah symbolizes Israel and Shechem represents the larger Canaanite culture, and that the story illustrates the danger of Israel's "being absorbed by the larger Canaanite culture."¹⁰⁶ Douglas Earl echoes this symbolic thinking in his own analysis, according to which "Dinah symbolizes Israel and Shechem the nations."¹⁰⁷ The narrative, Earl suggests, "serves to evoke affectually the disastrous consequences of exogamy and mingling, and the zeal with which exogamy is to be avoided."¹⁰⁸

Van Wolde also upholds the general move to see the encounter between the ancestral family and the Hivites as symbolic of the relationship between Israel and other nations. Indeed, she sees the story as the crucial narrative turning point between the ancestral family's relatively peaceful coexistence with the land's inhabitants and a proto-Israelite policy of exclusivity. First singling out the mention of "Israel" in v. 7, and treating it as a proleptic reference to the nation rather than to Jacob's recently received name, she explains: "In this way, Shechem's act is transferred to the world as the Israelite reader knows it, and, in this setting, Shechem's act is evaluated as disgraceful and unacceptable. This transfer is presented as a pretext for the text to come."¹⁰⁹ The narrator's repeated use of טמא, furthermore, invokes a "cultic and ritual cognitive domain"¹¹⁰ (again an Israelite domain) that suggests that Shechem and the Hivites threaten the ancestral family with their outsiders' impurity. Finally, the continuation of the narrative in Gen 35, in which Jacob commands his household to rid itself of its foreign gods, strengthens the negative socioreligious associations of Shechem. Where Jacob goes next, Bethel, stands in stark contrast: "Bethel, the place where Jacob met his God, represents the ideal of one place, one people and one God. It is opposed to the other place, Shechem, with alien people and alien gods, who have to be buried."¹¹¹ Thus the Dinah interlude is the "hinge" of the ideological reversal from

---

105. Kozar, "When 'Circumfession' Is Not Enough," 57.

106. Kozar, "When 'Circumfession' Is Not Enough," 57.

107. Earl, "Toward a Christian Hermeneutic," 40.

108. Earl, "Toward a Christian Hermeneutic," 42–43. See also Kunin, *The Logic of Incest*, 136.

109. Van Wolde, "Love and Hatred," 442.

110. Van Wolde, "Love and Hatred," 441.

111. Van Wolde, "Love and Hatred," 445.

the preceding narrative's "context of peace and mutual understanding with the Canaanites" to "a mono-ethnic position embedded in a mono-religious position."[112] Indeed, as van Wolde notes, in Gen 35 the ancestral blessing undergoes a notable revision, as "the blessing of other people is not mentioned any more," implying that the ancestral family is now the exclusive inheritor of the land.[113]

Readings that detect narrative censure for the brothers, conversely, perceive narrative support for interethnic ancestral relations. Bechtel, who devotes much of her argument to the immediate question of whether Shechem rapes Dinah, identifies ancestral relations as the ultimate question of the Dinah interlude. Like van Wolde, she highlights the recurrence of טמא as evocative of purity discourse. From the brothers' perspective, "Shechem is an uncircumcised, impure outsider. This outside pollution or outside impurity defiles the whole Jacobite community."[114] Bechtel perceives textual judgment against the brothers because, first, their act is the more violent one (compared to Shechem's indeterminate act with Dinah),[115] and, second, their rigid exclusivity undermines the group-oriented mode of living that is necessary to continuity in a land with other peoples. "Their behavior has made social intercourse and peaceful coexistence impossible. In the long run this kind of behavior violates group-oriented ideals and is condemned by Jacob, and the text, in Gen. 49.5–7."[116] Thus, for Bechtel, judgment against the brothers is associated with a broader judgment that challenges their ideology of "strict group purity and absolute separation."[117]

Like Bechtel, Brett—who detects implicit negative evaluation of the brothers in the excessiveness of their violence, their deceptive use of circumcision, Jacob's reprimands (34:30; 49:5–7), and Simeon's hypocritical

---

112. Van Wolde, "Love and Hatred," 447.

113. Van Wolde, "Love and Hatred," 447.

114. Bechtel, "What If Dinah Is Not Raped?" 32. Bechtel discusses the evaluative terms in v. 7 as relating more broadly to the ancestral family's customs for marriage.

115. Bechtel contends, "Ironically, if there is a rape in this story, it is Simeon and Levi who 'rape' the Shechemites. It is their behavior that is violent and hostile, carried out for the purpose of exploitation" ("What If Dinah Is Not Raped?" 34). It is important to remember that central to Bechtel's argument is her contention that ענה does *not* mean rape. Therefore it does not necessarily indicate a violent act.

116. Bechtel, "What If Dinah Is Not Raped?" 34.

117. Bechtel, "What If Dinah Is Not Raped?" 36.

Canaanite marriage (46:10)[118]—associates the judgment of the Dinah interlude with an ethnically inclusive perspective. Brett traces throughout the ancestral narrative an inclusivist stance toward outsiders, beginning in the initial divine call to Abram: "[T]he foundation of nationhood is apparently constituted by exogamy, not endogamy, since Abram was called to leave his kinship group, not to remain within it."[119] This strand resonates with the implicit criticism of the brothers, situating it firmly in the context of an ethnically inclusive perspective that prefers the "openness" of Dinah, Jacob, Hamor, and Shechem over against the brothers' apparent ethnocentrism.[120]

Whereas Bechtel and Brett read ethnic purity to be central to the brothers' concerns, Fewell and Gunn maintain that the brothers act primarily in the interest of preserving their family's honor. In their reading, טמא connotes a sexual, rather than ethnic, infringement. It refers to a sexual relationship "outside the proper boundaries of marriage."[121] Furthermore, the remark in v. 7 that Shechem had done a "disgraceful folly against Israel," something "not to be done," indicates the root of the brothers' anger: it is not Dinah, but rather a sense of familial honor.[122] The reading that Fewell and Gunn submit inclines toward a negative judgment of the brothers, whose sense of familial honor clouds practical considerations of security and the larger question of responsibility (i.e., their reckless and excessive act of violence entails a significant threat to the entire family). Fewell and Gunn's reading does not overtly identify the judgment against the brothers with a broader judgment against their exclusivist stance toward interethnic relations, but their interpretation nonetheless complements a reading of the interethnic question, as it indicates a preference for the union between Shechem and Dinah, and therein between the Hivites and the ancestral family.[123]

To summarize, the readings that approve of the brothers' actions approve also of an exclusivist mode of ancestral relations. Privileging the prior ancestral preference for endogamy, the future exclusivist Israelite policy, and symbolic imagery suggestive of this future policy, they see the

---

118. Brett, *Genesis*, 101–3.
119. Brett, *Genesis*, 51.
120. Brett, *Genesis*, 103.
121. Fewell and Gunn, "Tipping the Balance," 207, fn. 22.
122. Fewell and Gunn, "Tipping the Balance," 199.
123. Fewell and Gunn, "Tipping the Balance," 210–11.

brothers' mode of relations as validated by a larger pattern of exclusivist ancestral/Israelite relations. Readings that detect narrative disapproval of the brothers' actions, conversely, construe a judgment against their exclusivist mode of relations. Reading against a different background, one that privileges the exigencies of multiethnic living, the inclusivist implications of the divine promise, and practical considerations of family security, they see the proposed relations between Jacob's family and the Hivites as a positive model for the ancestral family.

The Dinah Interlude as Ventriloquy

The conventional reading—that the authoritative narrator's evaluative comments determine judgment in the Dinah interlude, not only moral judgment of the characters but also judgment on the matter of ancestral relations—turns the Dinah interlude into a definitive commentary on the ancestral relationship to the land and its inhabitants. It naturalizes the strangeness of the interlude's deviation from Jacob's story by unifying the interlude with the larger concern of ancestral relations. Foundational to this reading is the concept of the authoritative biblical narrator, often described as "omniscient." Also central is the presumption that this authoritative biblical narrator communicates in a straightforward fashion.[124] On these bases, the series of judgments on the narrative level assume the effect of a judge's gavel. They call order to the story, directly pronouncing the guilt of certain characters and implicitly delivering a decision on the matter of ancestral relations.

But what if the narrator in Genesis does not communicate in a straightforward fashion? Already in the Hagar interludes there have been indications of ironic equivocation. The motif of sojourn (גור) assumes strange associations with an outsider that contest its assumed significance as a mark of the ancestral family's exclusive relationship with God. This precedent destabilizes the narrative, leaving nothing completely safe, that is, straightforward. If the narrator has employed irony before, then why not again?

---

124. Sternberg gives voice to this presumption in his contention that the narrator does not "indiscriminately traffic in irony at the reader's expense: his ironies, many and diverse, are situational rather than verbal" (*The Poetics of Biblical Narrative*, 51). In other words, irony is restricted to the incongruity of events; it never touches what the narrator says. The narrator always says what he means.

This seed of doubt bears remarkable fruit in the alternative reading that this study advances. Instead of reading the interlude as an official narrative embodiment of the ancestral mode of relations, this study hears the evaluative comments to ring ironically. Attending to the narratological peculiarities of voice in the narrative, it detects a noteworthy resonance between the brothers' voice and the voice of the evaluative comments. Perhaps instead of delivering a straightforward judgment, the narrator is ironically ventriloquizing the brothers. This possibility readjusts the focus of interpretation. While the narrator maintains the mantle of authority that derives from creating the story world,[125] the question of omniscience no longer applies.[126] In other words, what the narrator knows (or does not know) no longer takes precedence in determining the meaning of the judgments. Instead, the focus turns to the effect of the act of ventriloquy, that is, to the dialogue evoked by the narrator's ironic appropriation of the brothers' voice.

Thus this study paves a way for reading the interlude not as an official verdict on ancestral relations but as a story that defamiliarizes the judgment on ancestral relations—as a story that, to appropriate Shklovsky's words, "increase[s] the difficulty and length" of the reader's "perception,"[127] both the aural perception of the evaluative comments and the mental perception of the question of ancestral relations. Unlike the conventional reading, this way of reading finds no simple resolution to the question of ancestral relations, because it hears in the evaluative comments not the narrator's straightforward judgment but rather the brothers' invective. It hears not an authoritative verdict but an equivocal act of ventriloquy.

Narratological Reflections on Voice

Interpretations of the Dinah interlude, as diverse as they are, all stand upon the foundation of the authoritative narrator's straightforward evaluation. Recent narratological discussions, however, stress an important

---

125. In the case of irony, the narrator's authority only matters insofar as it undergirds the doubt expressed toward the ironic proposition. That is to say, the narrator's authority no longer secures a definite, straightforward meaning.

126. Irony renders the question of omniscience irrelevant. It implies the impossibility of omniscience, because it relativizes propositions and thereby suggests that any piece of knowledge—anything that can be said—might be shown to be false or inappropriate in a different context.

127. Shklovsky, "Art as Technique," 12.

distinction in the concept of voice—a distinction that would question whether the narrator in the Dinah interlude pronounces his authoritative judgment in a straightforward way.

To preface the forthcoming narratological reflections, the distinction in the concept of voice consists simply in two different questions: Who speaks? And, whom does it sound like? The former understanding of voice, which has predominated in narratology until recently, informs conventional interpretation of the evaluative comments, which assumes that they issue from the narrator's voice. This study proposes moving the interpretive focus to the latter understanding of voice, which finds illumination in the metaphor of ventriloquy. A single speaker can affect two different voices, his and his dummy's, through different intonation, register, vocabulary, and other qualitative aspects. The metaphor of ventriloquy thus flags the prospect of double-voicedness. Any speaker, or narrator, may communicate in ways that recall another's voice. In the case that he does, the question arises: is his act of ventriloquy sincere or ironic? Does he endorse the perspective voiced, or does he challenge it?

Voice as Means and Voice as Effect

Narratology has traditionally identified voice by asking the question: "Who speaks?" Voice is fixed in presence—in a subject who speaks at a particular time and in a particular "place" (that is, a particular level of narration). Gérard Genette's classic typology of voice classifies voice accordingly.[128] Who is the source of the narration, and is she involved in the story (homodiegetic) or not (heterodiegetic)? Does she speak during or after the story? And does she relate the principal story (a diegetic narrator), a story within the principal story (a metadiegetic narrator), or something outside the principal story (an extradiegetic speaker)?[129] Seymour Chatman reinforces this typology with his concept of a voice's "audibility," by which he effectively identifies the voice of a statement with the subject who pronounces the statement. A voice that is audible is a subject whose presence is distinguishable. Therefore personal commentary and

---

128. Aczel, "Hearing Voices," 468, summarizes Genette's typology of voice as a classification of person (homodiegetic/heterodiegetic), time (the relationship between the time of narration and the time of the story), and level (extradiegetic, diegetic, metadiegetic, etc.).

129. For a discussion on the terminology of diegetic classification, see Genette, *Narrative Discourse*, 228–29, 245.

explicit self-mention make a voice particularly audible; the reader can distinguish a personal subject to whom the voice should be attributed.[130]

The traditional typology, then, restricts its analysis of voice to a particular speaker in a definable instance of speech. Who, when, and where is this voice? It emphasizes the presence of the voice's speaker. What this typology neglects, however, is the "question of *how* a narrator speaks."[131] Setting aside concerns with fixing voice in a single person and instance, this alternative question chooses instead to attend to such matters as "tone, idiom, diction, speech-style"[132] in order to explore what might be called the otherness of voice. Voice, in other words, is always invoking other voices, through qualitative features such as its register, vocabulary, subject matter, and syntax.[133] This understanding of voice implicitly acknowledges the traditional definition of voice, inasmuch as the qualitative aspects of voice are understood to recall previous speakers and instances; but it does not finalize the boundaries of voice according to particular speakers and instances, because there is a wider acknowledgment that the qualitative aspects of voice are indefinitely shared, that the voices of previous speakers and instances recall yet previous speakers and instances (whether or not they are known).

These two different perspectives on voice suggest a basic distinction between voice as "means" and voice as "effect."[134] The traditional typology of voice assists in defining voice as a means of communication, as the property and tool of a speaker who uses it to convey a message. Here voice refers to *what*. It is fixed in an instance of speech—in a person, a time, and a place. Voice as effect, however, unfixes voice. The "effect"

---

130. Aczel, "Hearing Voices," 470. A similar understanding of voice, specifically with regard to the narrator, prevails in biblical studies. See, e.g., Berlin, who states: "The most blatant intrusions of the narrator's voice are in etiologies, geographical notes . . . and similar information . . . . The narrator steps out of the story, as it were, to say something to his audience" (*Poetics and Interpretation of Biblical Narrative*, 57).

131. Aczel, "Hearing Voices," 468.

132. Aczel, "Hearing Voices," 469.

133. For a detailed discussion of the qualitative aspects that help to distinguish voice, see the chapter "Register and the Plural Text" in Fowler, *Linguistic Criticism*, 185–209.

134. Cf. Aczel, who advocates "distinguishing between narrator as function and narrative voice as effect" ("Hearing Voices," 492). See also Walsh, "Person, Level, Voice," 49–51. Walsh explores the idea of voice as means and effect in terms of the narrating instance (in which Walsh interprets voice as the means of narrative) and character discourse (in which Walsh interprets voice as an effect, a feature of characterization).

here alludes to the qualitative aspects of a voice that affect how an utterance is interpreted. So voice as effect looks beyond the fixed particulars of an utterance to *how* an utterance sounds, which incidentally liberates voice from a single subject and utterance. Whereas voice as means might be characterized as centripetal—it centers voice in a single person and instance—voice as effect might be characterized conversely as centrifugal. Its interest in the suggestive qualities of voice, in how a voice recalls other voices, steers it outside a single person and instance of speech and toward other persons and instances. Whereas voice as means assumes that a voice issues from a person, voice as effect assumes that other persons—or rather, their trace—issue from a voice.

Ventriloquy as a Metaphor for Voice as Effect

Attending to voice as effect rather than as means opens up possibilities of interpretation because the quest for meaning extends beyond identifying a subject and the circumstances of his speech to investigating the trace of others' voices and how the speaker might appropriate them. Ventriloquy offers an illustrative metaphor for this hermeneutical dimension of voice. Although speech is emitted only from a single set of vocal chords, it is alternately inhabited by two subjects with their own respective "voices." First one hears the ventriloquist's voice, then the dummy's, and so on, as the ventriloquist stages the two in dialogue. Attending to a ventriloquist, then, would entail listening for two different voices and considering how the ventriloquist employs them in a meaningful interchange. Similarly, attending to voice as effect in a narrative would mean listening for different voices and considering to what effect the narrator appropriates them. The clearest cases of multiple voices in a narrative are, of course, in character discourse, where the narrator might be said to ventriloquize the characters' voices; but close attention to the qualitative aspect of narrative discourse may reveal traces of other voices on the narrative level itself.

Richard Aczel provocatively pushes the boundaries of this metaphor to make the point that every utterance is, to an extent, an act of ventriloquism, that no utterance is without the trace of another's voice:

> Imagine [that a ventriloquist] has the dummy tell a story in several voices; not only the voices of the characters he portrays, but also other voices pertinent to aspects of their characterization. Describing one he waxes ironical, or lyrical, or mock-heroic;

> portraying another he adopts a voice that is bumptious, unctuous, outrageous, shy, or coy. These voices are intended to tell us something about the characters in question without either directly quoting them or making explicit statements about them. To whom, if anyone, are we to attribute these voices? To the dummy? Can the dummy really be said to have a voice or voices of his own?[135]

Aczel effectively identifies the speaker or narrator not as a ventriloquist—that is, not as a subject who could presumably cease ventriloquizing and speak in a natural voice unaligned with any other—but as an ever-changing dummy, as a constant medium for other voices. Aczel's extension of the ventriloquy metaphor dovetails nicely with Bakhtin's reflection on the inherent otherness of language: "[T]he word ... exists in other people's mouths, in other people's contexts, serving other people's intentions: it is from there that one must take the word, and make it one's own."[136] Therefore every utterance is a quotation, or as Aczel puts it, "[E]very act of speech is an act of ventriloquism, and the source of the voice can never finally be fixed in the presence of the speaker."[137]

It is worth pausing here to observe that the narrative in Genesis demonstrates a marked awareness of voice as effect, of speech as an instance of ventriloquy, and thus would appear to accommodate readings attentive to the qualitative dimensions of voice. First, in Gen 27:22–23, Jacob attempts to mislead his father into identifying himself as Esau so that he can receive the blessing. Isaac is deceived, but not without hesitation. He comments: "The voice is the voice of Jacob, but the hands are the hand of the Esau" (27:22). The narrative then relates Isaac's conclusion: "And he did not recognize him, because his hands were like the hands of Esau, his brother—hairy" (27:23). By identifying the voice as Jacob's but the person as Esau, Isaac acknowledges that a voice is not fixed in one source, that it can be appropriated by, or at least heard in, another voice.

Gen 42:7–8 offers another example of the narrative's awareness of voice as effect, albeit in converse fashion. Whereas in the first story Isaac recognizes that a voice is *only* an effect and need not be identified exclusively with one person, in this story Joseph exploits the common identification of voice and person in order to deceive his brothers. He appropriates another voice—another register, another tone—in order

135. Aczel, "Throwing Voices," 704.
136. Bakhtin, *The Dialogic Imagination*, 294.
137. Aczel, "Understanding as Over-hearing," 599.

to appear as another person. "He acted as a stranger and spoke harsh words with them" (42:7). Joseph's pretense proceeds primarily from his utilization of voice as effect. He speaks as if he were a stranger, as if he were not Joseph—with "harsh words." The act continues as, immediately afterward, he asks his brothers where they have come from—a question whose logical presupposition, given the context, would be that the speaker does not know the people whom he addresses. To the brothers, Joseph's voice is the voice of a stranger, and they treat him as such.

In addition to reflecting a narrative awareness of voice as effect, both stories underline the potential for an incongruous relation between voice and person. Isaac seemingly understands Jacob to be Esau ventriloquizing (or less actively, sounding like) Jacob. Joseph ventriloquizes a stranger. In neither case is the ventriloquy meant to be recognized as such; in the first case, it is not meant at all, and in the second case, it is meant to deceive. And yet speakers commonly ventriloquize with the intention that the listener hear both their voice (as means) and a distinctly different voice that they appropriate—that is, that the listener distinguish between their person and the voice of another person whom they ventriloquize. Indeed, ventriloquy as a metaphor accentuates the potential for a speaker's ironic appropriation of voice. One need only think of the amusement that the ventriloquist's act offers in its celebrated dramatization of conflict between ventriloquist and dummy—the ventriloquist's surprised expression as the dummy "says" something with which he disagrees. The audience's enjoyment of this drama derives precisely from its appreciation for the irony of voice, for hearing two conflicting voices in one utterance. On the one hand, it identifies the voice as the ventriloquist's. (Here the audience interprets voice according to voice as means.) On the other hand, it suspends disbelief and attributes the voice to the dummy. (Here the audience interprets voice according to voice as effect.) Thus the audience witnesses not merely a conflict of opinion, which would hardly constitute irony by itself, but rather a conflict of voice in which the ventriloquist's voice appropriates the dummy's and says things that the ventriloquist himself would challenge. The ventriloquial speech, like any ironic statement, stages a debate within itself.

Double-Voiced Discourse

The possibility that a speaker may overtly appropriate another voice complicates the listener's process of interpretation. Or in the case of narrative, the possibility that a narrator may do so complicates a reading of the text. Narratology identifies this possible difficulty as free indirect discourse,[138] in which a narrator appropriates a character's voice on the narrative level without explicitly attributing it to the character. Free indirect discourse thus entails what has been called "dual voice":[139] the narrator's voice (primarily voice as means) and character's voice (primarily voice as effect) inhabit the same words. Besides causing confusion in the identification of voices (where does the narrator's voice end and the character's begin?), free indirect discourse more importantly encourages a comparison or contrast between the perspectives attributed to the respective subjects of these voices. As a ventriloquist stands toward her dummy's "voice," so the narrator stands toward the character's: in a dynamic, undetermined relationship.

Bakhtin's concept of "passive double-voiced discourse" focuses the awareness of this relationship into a consideration of the different configurations of intention that inhere within such an utterance. On one end of the spectrum, there is "unidirectional double-voiced discourse," in which the speaker's voice and the voice he appropriates run along the same semantic lines. The speaker, in other words, confirms the original intention of the discourse he invokes.[140] On the other end of the spectrum, there is "vari-directional double-voiced discourse," in which the speaker exercises "a semantic intention that is directly opposed to the original one. The second voice [i.e., the speaker's], once having made its home in the other's discourse, clashes hostilely with its primordial host and forces him to serve directly opposing aims."[141] Bakhtin observes that the device of irony falls into this latter category of double-voiced discourse, and that

---

138. Pascal explains the linguistically derived foundations of the term "free indirect speech" (a designation basically interchangeable with free indirect *discourse*): "free" indicates the formal freedom of the phenomenon (it can take many different syntactic forms), "indirect" signals "that both a narrator and a character are involved," and "speech" denotes "a mode of discourse" (and is consistent with other terminology for discourse, namely direct and indirect speech) (*The Dual Voice*, 31–32).

139. Thus the title of one seminal work on free indirect discourse, Pascal's *The Dual Voice*.

140. Bakhtin, *Problems of Dostoevsky's Poetics*, 189–93, 199.

141. Bakhtin, *Problems of Dostoevsky's Poetics*, 193, 199.

is indeed quite frequent: "In the ordinary speech of our everyday life such a use of another's words is extremely widespread, especially in dialogue, where one speaker very often literally repeats the statement of the other speaker, investing it with new value and accenting it in his own way—with expressions of doubt, indignation, irony, mockery, ridicule, and the like."[142] As a concept, passive double-voiced discourse facilitates analysis of the pronounced cases of free indirect discourse, when a narrator appropriates a character's voice. The appropriation might function as the narrator's confirmation or contestation of the character's voice.

The distinction between voice as means and voice as effect leads this study to shift its interpretive focus from the narrator's ownership of the narrative (in terms of voice as means) to the traces of other voices that can be detected within the narrative (in terms of voice as effect). It invites awareness of the possibility that the narrator ventriloquizes another voice. Consequently it raises some unsettling questions for the reading of an authoritative narrator's straightforward evaluation in the Dinah interlude. Whose voice is heard in the evaluative comments? If it is not the narrator's, then why does the narrator appropriate it? Does the narrator ventriloquize in order to confirm or to contest the appropriated voice?

Hearing the Brothers in the Evaluative Comments

Conventional interpretation of the Dinah interlude treads a relatively continuous semantic pathway that is activated by anticipation. The perceived evaluation (or not) in v. 2 communicates with a reliable degree of narratorial authority the nature of Shechem's act. The evaluations that follow in vv. 5, 7, 13, and 27 then either confirm the reprehensibility of Shechem's deed or showcase the misguided anger that leads the brothers to their wrongdoing. Both lines of reading anticipate judgment, insofar as they weigh Shechem's act and the brothers' feelings in the balance—a balance weighted by the narrator's authoritative evaluation, wherever it is read—and reach an early verdict. In this sense, these readings already have an answer prepared for Levi and Simeon's closing question—"Should he treat our sister like a prostitute?" (34:31).

This study proposes, however, that Levi and Simeon's closing rejoinder can actually be read not to confirm but rather to complicate the anticipated determination. Listening carefully to their voice activates a

---

142. Bakhtin, *Problems of Dostoevsky's Poetics*, 194.

potentiality that remains otherwise hidden in the narrative.[143] That is, it invites a retrospective reading through the garden-path of the evaluative comments[144]—a reading that encourages a rehearing: comments that may have once sounded like evaluation tinged with the narrator's voice and perspective now resound with the judgment of not only the brothers' perspective, but more importantly their voice.[145] If the brothers' voice indeed inhabits the comments, then they are liberated from their more immediate association with the narrator. That is, although they issue from the narrating instance—from the narrator's voice as means—they bear no close ties to the narrator's voice (as effect) or perspective.

The evaluative comments echo Levi and Simeon's question in various aspects of its register: field of discourse, syntax, and tenor. The retrospective reading, or rehearing, that follows will explore these similarities in order to demonstrate the viability of reading the brothers' voice in the evaluative comments of vv. 2, 5, 7, 13, and 27.

It is worth remarking that this reading argues for the possibility of hearing the *brothers'* voice as opposed to exclusively Levi and Simeon's, whose voice is heard in v. 31. This is for three reasons. First, apart from v. 31, the brothers speak as a collective unit (vv. 13–17). Second, apart from Levi and Simeon's acts of killing Hamor and Shechem and taking Dinah away, the brothers act as a collective unit (vv. 5–7, 27–29).[146] Third, three of

---

143. Here this study draws from Iser's exploration of the reader's continual modification of meaning: "[T]he reader, in establishing these interrelations between past, present and future, actually causes the text to reveal its potential multiplicity of connections" (*The Implied Reader*, 278).

144. Sperber and Wilson, *Relevance*, 242. Sperber and Wilson introduce the phrase "garden-path irony" to refer to a particular case of retrospective interpretation in which what first appears as an ordinary assertion is later adjudged to be "irrelevant" (and ultimately ironic) in its context. The garden-path irony that this study reads in the Dinah interlude stems not only from the retrospective interpretation of the brothers' voice resounding on the narrative level, but also from the perception of the narrator's dissociative stance toward the brothers' judgment—which this study will explore shortly.

145. It should be acknowledged here that Fewell and Gunn's reading in "Tipping the Balance" also follows this path, as it appears to attribute the character-focalized evaluations solely to the brothers, divorcing them from association with either the narrator's voice or perspective. Hence they speak of the brothers' "use" (i.e., vocalization) "of the term 'defiled'" (see "Tipping the Balance," 207). What separates this reading from Fewell and Gunn's is its emphasis on the brothers' voice, particularly as it is appropriated on the narrative level.

146. While some readers contend that Levi and Simeon are excluded from the brothers' plundering of the city (vv. 27–29), the text gives no explicit indication of this:

the five instances of potential double-voiced discourse (vv. 7, 13, and 27) offer a rationale for the feelings or actions of the brothers as a collective unit. The primarily joint nature of the brothers' speech, actions, and feelings, therefore, suggests that Levi and Simeon's voice is a representative subset of the brothers' voice. Their one separate act—killing Hamor and Shechem and taking Dinah away—may reflect a heightened concern for retribution, but if so, this concern is based more broadly in the brothers' shared outrage and planned retaliation.

Vv. 13 and 27

Reading backward from Levi and Simeon's closing question—"Should he treat our sister like a prostitute?" (v. 31)—the evaluations in vv. 27 and 13 echo the brothers' voice in several aspects of register. First, "he/they had defiled their sister" (vv. 13, 27) mirrors Levi and Simeon's question in its basic syntactic pattern. Both utterances represent the same understood subject (Shechem) as acting upon the same direct object ("sister"). Second, the evaluative comments inhabit a similar field of discourse. Their representation of Shechem's action through the verb "defile" (טמא) corresponds to the adverbial clause "like a prostitute," as both suggest Dinah's social diminishment.[147] Third, the evaluative comments match Levi and Simeon's question in their justificatory tenor.[148] As Levi and Simeon's question offers a rationale for their attack on Shechem, so the evaluations in vv. 13 and 27 offer a rationale for the brothers' collective acts of deceit and plunder.[149] Furthermore, as their question sounds

---

"the sons of Jacob" are the subject of the pillaging acts, and it is only by inference that one can interpret Levi and Simeon to be excluded (perhaps on the basis that in the preceding verse, after killing Hamor and Shechem and taking Dinah, they "went away").

147. See fn. 8 in the present chapter (p. 128). While the particular connotations of טמא are ambiguous, it seems clear that Shechem's act is understood to have imputed a sort of impurity to Dinah. As the justificatory tone of these evaluations would suggest, being rendered impure in this manner entails some sort of dishonor or social diminishment.

148. Cf. Fowler, who describes tenor as consisting in the "relationship between the people concerned" and "the intentions of the speaker" (*Linguistic Criticism*, 191–93).

149. It is important to note that the evaluations in vv. 13 and 27 both follow the word אשר. Generally serving as a relative pronoun in biblical Hebrew, אשר can also indicate a causal clause. Joüon, *A Grammar of Biblical Hebrew*, 2:638, offers the cases in Gen 34:13 and 27 as examples of אשר indicating a causal clause. Most commentaries interpret vv. 13 and 27 likewise, although little explicit rationale is given. Speiser,

also in a proscriptive tenor—the implied answer to their question is an emphatic, "No!"—so the evaluative comments' use of טמא reverberates with a prohibitory timbre. In the word's application to transgressions of proper marital boundaries elsewhere (Lev 18:20; Num 5:11-31; Deut 24:1-4), טמא describes an act that should not be done. In each case, the act—which is variously described as sin, causing guilt, and an abomination to God—is either explicitly prohibited or implicitly so, as it entails punishment.

V. 7

This retrospective reading of the brothers' voice weaves back further to v. 7, where the brothers' anger is explained in this way: "For he had committed an outrage against Israel by lying with Jacob's daughter, and this should not be done." Again the general syntactic representation, field of discourse, and tenor corresponds to Levi and Simeon's question. Shechem is the understood subject, and the evaluation revolves around his act with Dinah—although this time the object of Shechem's transgression is widened to include Israel, that is, Jacob.[150] The tenor is both justificatory, as it accounts for the brothers' anger, and proscriptive, as it unambiguously proclaims that Shechem's act is the kind that should not be done. Besides these similarities, however, the evaluation in v. 7 also employs personal language,[151] which imparts the sense that here a personal subject, most likely a character, is speaking. The personal language is reflected first in the comment's modal nuance of obligation:[152] hence the common translations "should not be done," "must not be done," and

---

Genesis, 265-66, implies that the interpretation of אשר as initiating a causal clause in both verses derives from an assumption of stylistic consistency. This study surmises that the logic underlying the move to read these clauses as causal is as follows: the syntax of v. 13 strongly suggests such a usage, as the relative pronoun would make little sense. While v. 27 allows for either usage, the precedent set in v. 13, along with the use of evaluative comments as motive clauses in vv. 7 and 13, invites the reading of another causal (motive) clause.

150. See fn. 9 in the present chapter (p. 128).

151. Bal, *Narratology*, 51-52. Bal outlines a basic distinction between personal and impersonal language situations. Among the markers that Bal suggests for distinguishing between personal and impersonal language situations are *deixis*, emotive aspects, conative aspects, verb tense, and modal verbs and adverbs.

152. For more on the modal nuance of obligation, see Joüon, *A Grammar of Biblical Hebrew*, 2:371-72.

"ought not to be done." It is also evidenced in the colloquial dialect. The phrase לא־יעשׂה appears elsewhere in biblical narrative consistently in the mouths of characters rather than the narrator (e.g., Gen 20:9 and 29:6).[153] Finally, the lack of an immediate antecedent for the third masculine singular pronominal subject implies a shift to personal speech, to a personal interiority that is already absorbed in the details of a matter (i.e., Shechem is already "on the mind," so to speak). These indications of personal language would suggest mediation of either the narrator's or a character's personal viewpoint. The typical covertness of the biblical narrator, the brothers' emotional reaction immediately preceding the evaluation, and the modal equivalence between the evaluation in v. 7 and Levi and Simeon's closing retort suggest that this personal language aligns more closely with the brothers' voice than with the narrator's.

V. 5

This retrospective reading winds back next to the evaluative comment in v. 5, where Jacob hears that "he [Shechem] had defiled Dinah, his daughter." The evaluative comment's near-identity to the evaluations in vv. 13 and 27 confer upon it a voice that has come to be associated with the brothers. Of course, in the chronology of the story, the brothers have not yet heard the news—they do not hear until v. 7. So this voice in v. 5 cannot be theirs in the voice-as-means sense. But listening for voice as effect does not heed the boundaries of chronology in this retrospective reading. Because the judgment of v. 5 is qualitatively indistinguishable from the evaluations of vv. 13 and 27, its voice may be said to be the same.

And in fact, there is good reason to believe the voice in v. 5 actually cross-pollinates the brothers' voice—i.e., that it is a voice that they come to appropriate or ventriloquize. When the brothers first "hear" about what happened in v. 7, the narration withholds an explicit report, raising the question: what exactly did the brothers hear? The precedent of hearing in v. 5 encourages the reading that they hear what Jacob heard, namely that Shechem had defiled Dinah. The boundaries of voice therefore begin to blur, as what the brothers hear becomes what the brothers say in vv. 13 and 27. So although what Jacob hears in v. 5 is decidedly not the brothers' report, it nonetheless resounds in this retrospective reading with the echo of what becomes the brothers' voice.

---

153. See also 2 Sam 13:12.

V. 2

This retrospective reading ends its course at the first evaluative comment in v. 2: "And he humbled (ענה) her." First, as both Bechtel and van Wolde demonstrate,[154] the semantic range of ענה does not suggest that the term by itself indicates rape. Rather it denotes social debasement or humiliation, a lowering of a person's status. While this study translated it as "subjugate" in and around the Hagar interlude, where it seemed to refer to one party's act of bringing another party into subjection, it opts for "humble" in the Dinah interlude, where it seems to refer more broadly to a social consequence rather than to an intentional act of subjugation. In other words, Shechem has transgressed a marital convention and therefore humbled, or perhaps devalued, Dinah. The evaluative overtone, while not as strong as "rape," is nevertheless notable—and notably consistent with the brothers' voice. The syntactic representation, field of discourse, and tenor of the utterance resonate with the other evaluative comments and Levi and Simeon's question. Shechem is the implied subject and Dinah the implied direct object. Shechem's act is one that diminishes Dinah's worth. And the tenor is understatedly prohibitory, as the previous uses of ענה in the ancestral narrative refer to acts that invite negative judgment: the subjugation of ancestral descendants, which results in their divine deliverance (15:13–14); the subjugation of Hagar, which precipitates God's close involvement with Hagar (16:6, 11); and Laban's warning to Jacob not to humble or devalue Rachel and Leah by marrying other women (31:50).

At the end of this retrospective reading, then, the brothers' voice can be heard ringing almost as clearly in the evaluative comments of vv. 2, 5, 7, 13, and 27 as in Levi and Simeon's closing words.[155] Alter the pronouns and tense accordingly,[156] and the brothers can be heard vociferating, "He

---

154. Bechtel, "What If Dinah Is Not Raped?" 19–36 and van Wolde, "Does Inna Denote Rape?" 528–44.

155. Parry, "Feminist Hermeneutics," 19. Parry broaches this possibility in terms of perspective, as he links the viewpoint of Levi and Simeon's final comment with that of the previous evaluations. See his quote on p. 170. The distinction between the present study and Parry's is a subtle but significant one. It is not merely the brothers' perspective that is echoed in the evaluative comments; it is their voice.

156. Pascal, *The Dual Voice*, 136–37. Pascal observes that free indirect discourse commonly distinguishes itself by ventriloquizing another voice while *retaining* tenses and pronouns appropriate to reported speech. The tenses and pronominal forms, in other words, evidence the voice of the appropriator, while the voice as effect (idiom, tone, style, etc.) evidences the voice appropriated.

humbled her!" (v. 2), "He/They defiled our sister!" (vv. 5 and 13, and v. 27, respectively), and "He has committed an outrage against Israel by lying with Jacob's daughter, and this should not be done!" (v. 7).

The Evaluative Comments as Double-Voiced Discourse

Bakhtin's delineation of double-voiced discourse indicates two possible effects: either the speaker upholds the invoked voice, or he dissociates himself from it. The effect of the brothers' voice in the evaluative comments, therefore, would appear to suggest two basic possibilities for interpretation. Either the narrator appropriates their voice in order to confirm it, in which case judgment favors the brothers, or the narrator mimics their voice in order to contest it, in which case judgment goes against the brothers. The former possibility largely treads the path of conventional interpretation, as it reads a straightforward authoritative narrator. Although the narrator appropriates another voice, he does so only in order to authorize it. The brothers' voice is, ultimately, indistinguishable from his voice. The latter possibility, however, uncovers the unexamined interpretive prospect of a dissimulating narrator, one whose judgment is not so straightforward.

Several narrative aspects of the Dinah interlude suggest that the evaluative comments constitute this latter type of double-voiced discourse—that is, that they are ironic. In particular, incongruity, change in register, repetition, and exaggeration imbue the evaluative comments with ironic potential.[157] First, the narrator in Genesis traditionally focalizes cases of wickedness that merit lethal punishment through God's evaluation. Thus the narrator prefaces the flood and the destruction of Sodom (and later, the deaths of Er and Onan) with the notice that God perceives the offenders' wickedness (6:5, 11; 13:13; 19:13; 38:7, 10). The absence of divine judgment—or indeed God's character—in the Dinah interlude marks an incongruity in evaluative practice and calls into question the validity of the evaluative comments. Second, the typically covert biblical narrator's allowance for evaluative excess on the narrative level marks a change in register and invites the question of its function. A change in voice, in the way of speaking, often indicates irony, as it signals

---

157. Hutcheon, *Irony's Edge*, 156–59. Hutcheon includes incongruity, change in register, repetition, and exaggeration on a list of "generally agreed-upon categories of signals" of irony.

the potential for mimicry. Third, the repetition of the evaluative comments in vv. 5, 13, and 27 flags the possibility of exaggeration. Repetition and hyperbole regularly work hand in hand, pushing a point to an absurd extreme in order to suggest something in the opposite direction. Indeed, theorists of irony commonly invoke the example from Shakespeare's *Julius Caesar* of Mark Antony's speech, in which his repeated phrase, "Brutus is an honorable man," is first heard by the audience within the story as an innocuous remark but progressively assumes a more ironic tone as its overemphasis jars against the increasingly embittered sentiments expressed toward Brutus.[158] Similarly the repeated judgments of vv. 5, 13, and 27, as well as the comparable judgments in vv. 2 and 7, might be heard as progressively ironic, for they lead to increasingly incongruous events in the story-world: first the judgment stands alone as narration and hearsay (vv. 2 and 5); next it explains the brothers' anger (v. 7); then it justifies their deceit (v. 13); and lastly, it rationalizes the massacre and pillaging of the town (v. 27). From report and rumor to rationale for mass murder and pillaging, the judgment finds itself linked to an increasingly ill-matched consequence.[159] If the judgment is indeed the brothers' evaluation, ventriloquized repeatedly by the narrator, then its transformation—from a guileless account of events, to a calculated premise for deception, to a battle cry—invites consideration. Perhaps like Mark Antony, who repeats approbation within a larger speech that would question it, the narrator parrots judgment against progressively questionable deeds in order to question the sentiment itself.

In addition to these common markers of irony—of incongruity, change of register, excess, and repetition—this study also identifies the brothers' dominance as a significant mark of ironic potential. The brothers dominate the story in several different aspects. First, they dominate within the story, in both voice and deed. They effectively usurp their father's voice in negotiations with Shechem and Hamor, they might be said to drown out Dinah's voice as they exclude her from their talks, and they determine proceedings according to their terms. Then, after the negotiations, they violently enforce their will over Shechem, Hamor, and all the Hivites, massacring and plundering the town. Hearing the brothers'

---

158. See, e.g., Hutcheon, *Irony's Edge*, 147; Sperber and Wilson, "Irony and the Use-Mention Distinction," 315.

159. The last evaluative comment marks another line of incongruity. It pluralizes the offending party—"they defiled" Dinah (v. 27)—thereby suggesting that the entire town is responsible for what Shechem alone did.

voice in the evaluative comments, however, means that their domination extends from within the story-world to without, from their words and deeds to the narration itself. In their claim to authority, they have not only deceived and invaded Shechem, they have "deceived" (insofar as their words pass for the narrator's) and invaded the narration.

The brothers' comprehensive dominion might be described as monologic: their one word, their judgment against Shechem, determines the story. As Bakhtin says of monologue in general, so one might say of the brothers' judgment in the interlude: it "pretends to be the *ultimate word*."[160] This is certainly the case with the brothers, who enjoy literally the final word of the story. Further, monologue "closes down the represented world and represented persons."[161] Again, this is literally the case with the brothers, whose violence finalizes the world according to their judgment. Ironically, though, the brothers end up lacking the one thing they need to consolidate their claim to power: a listener. According to the logic that discourse is a claim to power, monologism—which strives for power through the elimination of other voices—paradoxically achieves no power precisely because it has removed the other voices. There is no difference by which it can be defined, no other voice to validate its claim.[162] Thus the monologic evaluation that rings throughout the Dinah interlude in the brothers' voice and actions fails to find the power it seeks and implodes on itself.

To illumine the ironic effect of this monologism, one might liken the relation between the narrator and the brothers to an adult who, suppressing response, allows a child to fabricate an intricate lie. The child, having eaten from the forbidden jar of cookies, manufactures an elaborate story, punctuated throughout by the refrain, "But I did not eat the cookies." The child's monologue meets with no acknowledgment from his addressee and so founders on the rocks of meaninglessness. Why does the child even speak in the first place, one might ask? There is a gentle irony, already, in the child's claim to speak a meaningful word. But the irony magnifies when one draws out the implications of his monologue. His insistent refrain exposes his concern and the adult's silence

---

160. Bakhtin, *Problems of Dostoevsky's Poetics*, 293.

161. Bakhtin, *Problems of Dostoevsky's Poetics*, 293.

162. Cf. Bal, who discusses negotiation as a "speech-act of and for power" (*Death & Dissymmetry*, 162). As a claim *for* power, an utterance finds its power realized in the response it seeks. Power, in this sense, is two-sided. It involves a claim and an acknowledgment.

only accentuates this. The refrain rings ironically as its insistence suggests the very opposite, namely, that the child *did* eat the cookies. In other words, the child's monologism actually conceals a dialogue, as it anticipates the accusation or objection of another voice.[163] The irony of the child's monologic insistence, then, becomes apparent from the perspective of the adult, who might be said to imagine a set of ironic quotation marks around the child's words. The more the child asserts his innocence, the more the authority he claims is undermined. So too the brothers' evaluative refrains reverberate ironically in the context of their monologic control. Without an alternative voice to define and give substance to the brothers' voice, their unrelenting judgment of Shechem collapses in on itself. Moreover, it exposes the point of their anxiety and suggests an alternative perspective, one that places ironic quotation marks around their judgments.

Thematic Development: Ancestral Relations

Reverberating throughout the Dinah interlude are motifs thematically resonant with the ancestral family's relationship to the land and its inhabitants: motifs of the promise of land, the promise of universal blessing, and intermarriage. In the refrains of the ancestral sonata-rondo, these motifs harmonize in an equivocal counterpoint on how the ancestral family might inherit the land and relate to its current inhabitants. God promises both land and the blessing of all families (presumably including those inhabiting the land), but does not specify how these promises are consistent with one another;[164] the ancestral family retains an ambiguous stance itself, as it exercises the isolationist practice of endogamous marriage but nonetheless integrates peacefully among, if not within, the neighboring communities.

Conventional interpretation reads the episode of the Dinah interlude as a means of thematically reconfiguring these motifs into a more concrete position on ancestral relations. The evaluative comments in particular suggest this thematic resolution. For most readers, the comments present a straightforward authoritative commentary not only on

---

163. This internal dialogism is what Bakhtin refers to as the "active" variety of double-voiced discourse, which he described as an "intense sideward glance at someone else's word" (*Problems of Dostoevsky's Poetics*, 199, 203).

164. On more than one occasion, these promises sit side by side (26:4; 28:13–14), begging the question of how they accord with one another.

the matter of Shechem's act but also on the ancestral family's relationship to the land and its inhabitants. The comments either validate the brothers' exclusivist mode of relations, or they reveal the brothers' misguided perspective and affirm a more inclusive stance. Attending to the voice of the evaluative comments, however, this study proposes a thematically richer reading, one that traces how these motifs might resound ironically in the narrator's act of ventriloquy, how they might develop not toward a finalized model of ancestral relations but rather toward a more open dialogue on the matter. A brief overview of the motifs will outline how the interlude might engage them—how it may either resolve them according to an authoritative narrator's straightforward evaluation or develop them through the ironic ventriloquizing of the brothers.

The motif of the promise of land frames and punctuates the Dinah interlude. Immediately prior to the story's beginning, Jacob sets up camp at Shechem (33:18), where Abram first received the promise of land (12:6–7). Then Jacob purchases a portion of land from the sons of Hamor (33:19). Together, the site's history and Jacob's purchase of land recall the promise and flag up the theme of land. The motif later repeats with even greater force when Hamor invites the ancestral family to dwell in the land and take possessions (אחז) in it (34:10).[165] Hamor's words invoke the same language with which God promises Abraham the land of Canaan as a perpetual "possession" (אחזה) (17:8), soliciting the interpretation that the prospect of dwelling in Shechem anticipates at least a partial realization of the divine promise of land.

The motif of the promise of universal blessing also frames and suffuses the interlude. Just before the interlude, the narrative relates, "Jacob came to Shalem (שלם), the city of Shechem" (33:18). Most commentators render שלם as an adverb meaning "safely," but, as Wenham notes, nowhere else in the biblical text does the word function as an adverb qualifying a verb.[166] The word can, however, serve as a place name. In fact, earlier in the ancestral narrative, after Abram rescues Lot from Chedorlaomer and his alliance of kings, the priest-king Melchizedek comes from Shalem (שלם) and pronounces Abram and God[167] blessed (14:18–19). In this scene, Abram demonstrates amicable relations with several different people groups: in addition to the Shalemite king, Abram

---

165. Wenham, *Genesis 16–50*, 312.
166. Wenham, *Genesis 16–50*, 300.
167. Or "El Elyon," whom Abram shortly thereafter identifies with Yahweh.

confers peaceably with the Sodomite king and mentions his alliance with the Amorite brothers Aner, Eshcol, and Mamre (14:21–24). Collocated with Melchizedek's pronouncement of blessing, Abram's peaceful interaction with others is charged with the echo of God's earlier blessing of Abram, and particularly the promise that all the families of the earth will find blessing through Abram. It seems indeed that the divine promise has found fruition in Abram's relations with these different peoples. Jacob's arrival at Shalem thus reverberates not only with the lexical connotation of peace but also with the memories of Abram's encounter with the king of Shalem and the promise of universal blessing that achieves a measure of fulfillment in that scene. In addition to the setting at Shalem, the interfamiliar backdrop of the Dinah interlude calls to mind the promise of universal blessing. For the first time in Genesis, the ancestral family engages specifically with another *family* (rather than with another people), inviting remembrance of the promise's formulation, namely that all the "families" of the earth will somehow find blessing through the ancestral family (12:3; 28:14).

Thus two promise motifs—of land and universal blessing—confront one another in the Dinah interlude. Particularly illustrative of this confrontation is the coupling of Shechem and Shalem. Their identification as one and the same place suggests a startling equivalence between the motifs. Shechem as a catchword for the promise of land and Shalem as a byword for peaceful relations join together. Their identification weds the ideas of land and peaceful relations—or, in the context of the divine promises, land and universal blessing. As the ancestral family comes to "Shalem, the city of Shechem," they broach the possibility of living into these two promises together.

A third motif, intermarriage, joins the thematic mix midway through the story and hints at one avenue through which the promises of land and universal blessing might find joint realization. After requesting Dinah's marriage to Shechem, Hamor offers, "Make marriages with us. Give your daughters to us, and take our daughters for yourselves" (34:9). In their response, Dinah's brothers affirm this outcome and comment on its implications of union: "We will live with you and become one people" (34:16). This proposed union appears to be egalitarian; that is, neither family explicitly envisions the union as a compromise of identity but rather as a welcoming of the other family into its own fold. Thus the brothers stipulate circumcision, the requisite physical mark of ancestral identity,[168] as the condition of intermarriage and becoming "one people" (34:15–16). It is as though the brothers are saying, "You will become one of us." Similarly Hamor and Shechem envision the ancestral family as part of their own, as they proclaim to the men of their city, "These people are שלמים" (34:21). Consistently translated as "peaceful," שלמים carries within it a significant semantic alternative. Recalling that שלם likely identifies the name of the city (33:18), one might also translate שלמים as the gentilic, meaning Shalemites. Therefore Hamor and Shechem's proclamation may be doubly meaningful. It is as though they are saying, "These people are already like us Shalemites—they are peaceful."

As a viable means for the joint realization of the promises of land and universal blessing, intermarriage is not without its difficulties. Previously in the ancestral narrative the motif of intermarriage is heard in the ancestral ideal of endogamy. Abraham forbids the idea of Isaac's marriage to a daughter of the Canaanites, preferring instead that the wife come from his kindred (24:3–4). Isaac follows his father's example, as he proscribes Jacob's marriage to a Canaanite and instead commands him to marry one of Laban's daughters (28:1–2). Although the brothers verbally assent to the idea of intermarriage in their negotiations with Hamor and Shechem, they too appear to hold to the endogamous preference of their forefathers. In particular, the discourse of purity that resounds in their voice on the narrative level—Shechem "defiled" their sister (34:5, 13, 27)—suggests their aversion to the idea of intermarriage. Although the aspect of "defile" is ambiguous—does it refer to the transgression of marital conventions or ethnic boundaries?—its use in a story rife with associations to the promise of land and to the ancestral relationship with other families would at the very least hint at interethnic unease. Furthermore, the disproportion between the alleged offense, committed by a single man, and the act of retaliation, committed against the entire city, implies that the brothers are concerned with more than a single act of sexual transgression. Indeed, the last evaluative comment pluralizes the offender: "they had defiled" Dinah (34:27). Heard in the brothers' voice, this comment points up an incongruity in their logic and suggests an underlying anxiety toward the entire city. The brothers act not out of their desire to avenge Dinah, but rather out of their ethnocentrism, out of their aversion to interethnic union.

168. Cf. Gen 17:14.

Thus the brothers reject intermarriage as a way forward for living into the promises of land and universal blessing. Their massacre and pillaging of the city suggests their eagerness to take possession of the land and its goods at the expense of its inhabitants, whom they will not admit into the ancestral family. So, whereas previously the motifs of the promise of land, the promise of universal blessing, and intermarriage hang together in a configuration open and undecided on the matter of ancestral relations with the inhabitants of the land, in the Dinah interlude the brothers' actions and voice join them in an unequivocal case for an ethnically exclusive mode of relations. The brothers evidently assume the right to the land, but they take their forefathers' endogamous preference to its violent extreme, thus precluding the possibility of another family's blessing. While earlier the ancestral family merely avoids intermarriage, here it kills the idea, so to speak, massacring all the males and destroying the very opportunity for intermarriage. The brothers' voice and actions univocally delineate a violently exclusivist mode of relations, one that rejects intermarriage and disregards the prospect of universal blessing.

For most readers, the motifs of the promise of land, promise of universal blessing, and intermarriage find thematic resolution in the brothers' course of action. Either the narrator offers straightforward evaluation that affirms the brothers in their judgment and actions, and thus endorses an exclusivist mode of relations, or the narrator remains relatively neutral and endorses an inclusivist mode of relations by allowing the events to speak for themselves. In either case, the motifs do not so much develop the theme of ancestral relations as they finalize it.

The narrator's ironic ventriloquization of the brothers, however, invites an indefinite dissociative stance toward the brothers' exclusivist ideology, a stance that challenges their mode of relations and invites further dialogue on the matter. The brothers take the ancestral rule of endogamy to its extreme limit, but the ironic echo of their zealous voice and the irony of their excessive actions—an irony which reaches its zenith in the stark incongruity between Shalem as a place name connoting peace and universal blessing, and the brothers' actions, which turn Shechem into a byword for violence—contest the certitude of their ethnocentric conviction and unravels their configuration of the motifs of promised land, promised blessing, and intermarriage. In "Shalem, the city of Shechem," they exercise an aggressive form of endogamy that yields neither peace nor land. The motifs of land, universal blessing, and intermarriage ring ironically in the brothers' voice and actions, kindling a pervading doubt about their exclusivist ideology. The irony points away from the brothers' domineering subjectivity to the glimpses of Shechemite subjectivity; it entertains their voice, their perspective, the idea that the families' union might indeed be desirable. Perhaps—it proposes—the interfamilial negotiations and terms of agreement actually represent a viable, even preferable, mode of ancestral interethnic relations. Perhaps endogamy, which prior to the Dinah interlude has kept the promise of land and the promise of universal blessing in a precarious, unresolved relation, is not the best way forward for the ancestral family. Perhaps the preference for Israelite ethnic purity in subsequent narrative is not as consistent with the ancestral narrative as it first appears.

Coalescing around the motifs of land, universal blessing, and intermarriage, the irony of the Dinah interlude suffuses the rest of the ancestral narrative. After the episode of the Dinah interlude, the three motifs no longer sound the same. They now resonate with associations and implications that disturb the thematic trend of an exclusivist mode of ancestral relations. So when they sound in ancestral refrains, they tremor with irony. They express doubts toward the brothers' way of living into the promises. A couple of examples suffice to show the invasive ironic effect of these developed motifs.

First, after the Dinah interlude, Jacob leads his family from Shechem to Bethel. Already one may hear a faint irony in the family's departure from a land that had previously assumed a close thematic connection with the promise of land. In other words, the brothers' violent conquest, which on the surface might seem a more immediate way of securing the land, has actually deprived them of it. A more biting irony, however, reverberates in the promise that God delivers to Jacob at Bethel. God repeats the common terms of the ancestral promise with one notable exception: the promise of universal blessing.[169] The echo of the brothers' voice, which now inhabits the motifs of land and universal blessing, edges about God's new promise and recalls the same judgment it evoked in the irony of the Dinah interlude. It is as if the motifs append to God's promise the muttered aside, "With that kind of exclusivist rhetoric, there cannot be universal blessing." In other words, the promise now resounds

---

169. Van Wolde traces the iterations of the promise and contends that this particular promise reflects a momentous shift in ancestral relations: "[T]he blessing of other people is not mentioned any more; the land is exclusively given to the Jacobites" ("Love and Hatred," 447).

with a degree of irony; it draws from its own motivic history a measure of judgment against the brothers' exclusivist mode of relations.

Second, shortly after Jacob's stop in Bethel, the narrative pauses to relate the genealogy of Esau, at the beginning of which it flags the motif of intermarriage: "Esau took his wives from the daughters of Canaan" (36:2). Again, the motif echoes with its recent history, with the brothers' exclusivist ideology. And again, the motif resounds ironically, for Esau's inclusivist mode of relating to the peoples of the land in fact bears the fruit of the divine promise more quickly than does the ancestral mode: as the narrative conspicuously relates, Esau's lineage includes kings—a recurring object of promise in the divine promise[170]—before Jacob's does (36:31).[171] The irony of the Dinah interlude thus rings within Esau's genealogy, reemerging from the motif of intermarriage to suggest judgment of the brothers' mode of relations and invite consideration of Esau's contrasting example.

In both examples, the semantically excessive character of irony is apparent, for the motifs' suggested judgment only points away from the brothers' exclusivism—it itself does not identify with any particular mode of ancestral living. Strictly speaking, irony only says what it does not mean. What it means remains a question. The irony of the brothers' voice therefore resists simple identification with an authoritative narrator's preference for an inclusivist mode of relations. It can only hint in this direction. In the wake of the brothers' failure to live into God's promises of land and the blessing of other families,[172] the irony's skepticism toward the brothers' exclusivist ideology raises the question, "What could have been?" It, in effect, replaces Levi and Simeon's rhetorical question, which leaves little room for discussion, with an open question inflected in the opposite direction. Whereas Levi and Simeon's question echoes with their self-righteousness, this irony lingers with a sense of the brothers' misguidedness and an inquisitiveness into other possibilities. It suggests that, despite the brothers' vociferations and violence, the silence—of God, of the victims' voices—speaks just as loudly and deserves to be heard. What remains unsaid—the possibility of a more inclusive relation

---

170. Cf. Gen 17:6; 35:11.

171. Brett, *Genesis*, 106.

172. Contrary to the terms of God's promise and covenant (Gen 12:3; 26:4; 28:14), another family of the earth is not blessed via the ancestral family but rather massacred and pillaged. Moreover, the ancestral family does not receive the land in Shechem (cf. Gen 12:6–7), but rather must leave it under the threat of attack (cf. Gen 34:30; 35:5).

with the inhabitants of the land—remains a question that the brothers' dominating voice cannot dispel.

Summary

Conventional readings of the Dinah interlude interpret it as a story of judgment—judgment, moreover, that extends from matters of morality to the question of ancestral relations. They ground their readings of judgment in an authoritative narrator whose perspective they detect in one or more of the evaluative comments on the narrative level. Thus they are able to naturalize the interlude, to transform it from a plot deviation into a definitive commentary on ancestral relations. The peculiarity of voice in the evaluative comments, however, invites reflection on whether these comments issue as the authoritative verdicts of the narrator. The voice resonates qualitatively with Simeon and Levi's last word in several ways, suggesting that it may in fact represent a case of double-voiced discourse in which the narrator ventriloquizes the brothers. This case of ventriloquy, which engages a motivic medley bearing on ancestral relations, harbors significant potential for thematic development. Before the Dinah interlude, the motifs of the promise of land, the promise of universal blessing, and intermarriage harmonize in an equivocal counterpoint of how the ancestral family might inherit the land and relate to its current inhabitants. In the Dinah interlude, the brothers' excessive claim to power, embodied not only in their actions but also in their ventriloquized voice, joins the motifs in an unequivocal case for an ethnically exclusive mode of relations. While the conventional reading construes an authoritative affirmation or rejection of the brothers' ideology—a finalization of the motifs and a conclusive resolution to the question of the land and interethnic relations—the ironic echo of the motifs in the brothers' voice and actions suggests otherwise. Eliciting doubt toward the brothers' exclusivist mode of relations, it invites further dialogue on the possibility of a more inclusive alternative.

5

The Tamar Interlude

Traditional Interpretation

THE CLOSE READING OF the Tamar interlude begins with an investigation of how conventional readings center on the dynamic of agency. The question of agency dominates interpretation of the latter portions of the ancestral narrative and the Joseph story in particular, as God's character recedes from the narrative and invites the question of who is in control of events and their outcomes—God or humans? Conventional interpretation typically subjects the Tamar interlude to this interpretive concern and reads it as an instructive example. The Tamar interlude, according to most readers, assumes significance primarily as an interpretive key that points up either the outworking of divine providence in the narrative or the priority of human agency, or conversely, the irrelevance of the question of agency in light of the more immediate significance of the story's results, which bear on the matter of ancestral inheritance.

The Dynamic of Agency in the Ancestral Narrative

The Joseph story revolves around the drama of fraternal conflict, which ultimately resolves in a reconciliation that ensures the ancestral family's survival. Many interpretations of the Joseph story, however, read a narrative interest that underlies the drama of fraternal conflict: namely, the balance of divine and human agency in the ancestral narrative. This line of reading derives from the observation that, as the ancestral narrative progresses, God gradually disappears as an active character and the human characters inversely assume a more distinct presence and agency. The Joseph story throws the dynamic of agency into marked relief: the narrative frames events as the result of human characters' motivations and actions, and yet Joseph insists that God receive credit for the end result (45:5, 7–9; 50:20). Thus interpretation of the Joseph story, which invariably addresses the surface drama of fraternal conflict, also conventionally wrestles with a deeper anxiety regarding the question, "Who is really in control of events?" Because readings traditionally perceive the Tamar interlude as subordinate to the Joseph story, this question comes to determine interpretation not only of the Joseph story, but also of the Tamar interlude's relation to it.

Readers generally make sense of the balance of agency in the ancestral narrative in one of three ways. First, they read the progressive absence of the divine character against narrative resolutions that accord with the divine program as an aporia. Whether God is accomplishing his purpose behind the scenes in the latter portions of the ancestral narrative is indeterminate. Alternatively, they detect the subsistence of divine agency in the plot logic. Divine providence explains why events, although apparently determined only by human characters, resolve in a way that is consistent with the divine program. (Or conversely, the events, resolving in a manner consistent with the divine program, explain divine providence.) Third, they conclude that God's disappearance means that, quite simply, human agency prevails. Whether or not God is amenable to this shift in agency, the human characters clearly control the course of events.

While the dynamic of agency in the ancestral narrative remains a tacit or unfocused concern for many readers, Richard Elliott Friedman, W. Lee Humphreys, Everett Fox, Jack Miles, and Hugh White openly address it and evidence among their work the three general ways of reading it. A survey of their readings of agency will therefore facilitate an exploration of the more specific ways that readers understand the Joseph story and the Tamar interlude's place within it.

The Hidden Face of God by Richard Elliott Friedman attentively traces the progression of divine and human agency in Genesis and implicitly points up the three ways of explaining God's diminishing presence. Friedman maps out a general reversal in determination: whereas God determines the place and role of human characters in the beginning, the human characters gradually assume positions that determine the place of God's character—or rather, his lack of place. Friedman highlights this progression in the characters of Adam, Noah, Abraham, Jacob, and Joseph.[1] Noah's responsibility and initiative exceed Adam's: whereas Adam receives divine instruction only with regard to what he can and cannot eat, Noah receives detailed instructions about building an ark; whereas Adam eats the fruit, Noah plants a vineyard, makes wine, and gets drunk, after which he confers curses and blessings upon his children. Similarly Abraham's agency outstrips Noah's, particularly in his relationship with God; engaging in dialogue with God on multiple occasions, Abraham occasionally voices doubts (15:2, 8) and questions the God's judgment (18:22–33). The development of human responsibility and agency advances further in Jacob's story. In contrast to before, when God directly selects Isaac as heir to the covenant, Jacob along with Rebekah appears to play a decisive role in directing the covenantal succession through his own line. Jacob, furthermore, sets conditions on God's developing relationship with him (28:20–22) and even fights with a character whom he identifies as God. The divine-human balance shifts a degree further in the story of Joseph. In Joseph's character, "Genesis arrives at a point at which God is working behind the scenes (39:2–3, 21, 23; 45:5–9) while a man controls a divine power enough that he must persist in informing people that the power is really God's and not the man's."[2]

Friedman's characterization of Joseph as one who possesses "a divine power" but insists "that the power is really God's" spotlights the hermeneutical crux for the interpretive resolutions of God's diminishing presence. Joseph's declaration of divine agency marks the point at which the three lines of reading diverge. The fact that Joseph, a human character, makes the assertion of divine agency leaves the question of divine agency indeterminate inasmuch as the assertion lacks the authoritative determination of the narrator. If, however, readers privilege the word of the protagonist Joseph, then they may retrospectively detect the determining influence of divine agency at work behind the scenes. On the other hand, if they treat Joseph's words as no more than an illocutionary act calibrated to his own ends, then they may read human agency as the determining factor of the course of events.

The Character of God in the Book of Genesis: A Narrative Appraisal by W. Lee Humphreys typifies readings that appreciate the indeterminacy

---

1. Friedman, *The Hidden Face of God*, 31–40.
2. Friedman, *The Hidden Face of God*, 39.

of divine agency in the latter parts of the ancestral narrative. Humphreys observes that, according to Alter's scale of reliability for the various means of characterization, the narrative characterizes God through increasingly unreliable means. "We move from a preponderance of narrator's notices of God's actions and speeches, occasionally tempered by notices of God's thoughts and feelings, to a significance [sic] reliance on what other characters say about God as a character in stories they construct."[3] In other words, as the narrative progresses, the representation of God's character shifts hand from narrator to characters, thereby losing a degree of its dependability. Humphreys summarizes the characters' various representations of God and stresses their constructedness:

> The depiction of a God who guides Abraham's servant to the right place and woman to secure a wife for his master's son, and who nicely observes the script set by the servant as a sign of God's designs [Gen 24] is appealing. Appealing in their own way are Jacob's and his wives' constructions of God as one who takes their side to secure their rights in the face of Laban's alleged exploitation and appropriation of their talents and goods [Gen 31]. Even more so is Joseph's construction of a God whose providential designs for life and good can catch up and transpose the desires and actions of a family, apparently bent on self-destruction, into relief and regeneration for the elect family [Gen 45]. But as appealing as these depictions are, we cannot forget that they are constructions by other characters in the story-world of Genesis.[4]

He concludes, perhaps tongue-in-cheek, "In the end, God sustains precisely those who, in fact, so construct God as Super Agent."[5] There is, in other words, a sort of circularity in the characters' constructions of God, which begs the question: is God actually as they represent him? Or does the fact that their representation confirms their own program suggest that God is merely a tool that they use toward their own ends?[6]

---

3. Humphreys, *The Character of God*, 241.
4. Humphreys, *The Character of God*, 240.
5. Humphreys, *The Character of God*, 242.
6. Humphreys acknowledges a fundamental tension between the narrator's characterization of God (as a complex, conflicted, full-fledged character) and the characters' representation (as a one-dimensional agent confirming their purposes). He offers one possible explanation: that God's diminishing presence in the latter parts of Genesis corresponds to his acquiescence to the ancestral characters' appropriation of him. In other words, he effectively compromises: in order to "engage humans who in

In his article "Can Genesis Be Read as a Book?" Everett Fox reads similarly to Friedman and Humphreys, observing a general progression of diminishing divine presence—"as the book progresses, there is notably less and less human contact with the deity"[7]—and increasing narrative attention to human characterization and agency: "[T]he further one reads in the text, the more complex and human the heroes become."[8] Unlike Friedman and Humphreys, however, Fox reads firmly in favor of a determinative divine agency that operates even in the narrative absence of God's character. Indeed, he implies an inverse correlation between divine presence and divine control: "By the second half of the book of Genesis, God appears more decisively in control of events, manipulating them with the skill of a master puppeteer (whose puppets are allowed at least a modicum of free will)."[9] Although Fox does not elucidate how God appears in control of events, one might reasonably assume that he reads God's character within a theological frame of reference that is keen to attribute realization of the divine program to God's agency. One may further conjecture that he reads Joseph's assertions of divine providence as the narrative's confirmation of the divine program's realization. An observation by Goldingay illuminates the theological perspective that Fox ostensibly takes. The stories of Genesis, says Goldingay, "illustrate the theme [of God's promise], often by showing how God overcomes the obstacles to the fulfilment of his commitment."[10] That is, even though God does not feature in some stories, the correspondence of their denouements with his promises points to his involvement.

Jack Miles' *God: A Biography* stands opposite to this reading of divine providence. Tracing the progression of God's diminishing presence and the ancestral family's increasing agency, Miles provocatively reads a process of divine domestication. Early in the ancestral narrative, he construes God as striving for Abraham's trust, and Abraham as resisting God's purposes. In Gen 22, the relationship achieves a delicate compromise in which neither Abraham nor God acts to the full extent of his

---

their own ways seem intent on becoming like God as they seek to set and shape the course of their lives on their terms," he allows them to assume his place—provided that they recognize his sovereignty (*The Character of God*, 243–56). Cf. Miles, *God*, which conceives of God's diminishing agency in Genesis as a sort of a divine domestication.

7. Fox, "Can Genesis Be Read as a Book?" 34.
8. Fox, "Can Genesis Be Read as a Book?" 33.
9. Fox, "Can Genesis Be Read as a Book?" 33–34.
10. Goldingay, "The Patriarchs in Scripture and History," 22–23.

intentions: Abraham goes through the motions of obeying God, but in ambiguous enough fashion that his ultimate obedience (i.e., sacrificing Isaac) remains a question, while God stops short of demanding Abraham's unequivocal trust—he does not allow Abraham to follow through with the sacrifice of Isaac (perhaps because he is afraid that Abraham will not, and thus he will have no claim to Abraham's trust). Abraham exhibits (or feigns?) trust, but not full trust, and God demands obedience, but not full obedience.[11] This seed of divine domestication—whereby God cuts his losses (i.e., in his quest for full trust) and makes provision for ancestral desires—grows in the narrative that follows: God assumes a more domesticated role within the lives of the ancestral family, responding just as much as (if not more than) he demands response. For example, Abraham presupposes divine assistance in his servant's search for a wife for Isaac;[12] Rebekah approaches God with an inquiry into the status of her pregnancy; and Jacob sets conditions to the promise God delivers at Bethel. In fact, Jacob uses God much more than God uses Jacob. Miles muses:

> It almost seems that it is Jacob, rather than God, who is showing a degree of steadfast love and faithfulness, attributing to divine assistance happy outcomes that, by the word of the narration, come from his energies alone. Whether in tricking his father, outwitting his uncle, or appeasing his hostile brother, Jacob acts, to all seeming, on his own.... It is as if, since the Lord God is on Jacob's side, Jacob is free to lie about the Lord God or insult him when it is in his interest to do so. The Lord God seems willing to tolerate much so long as, in the end, he accomplishes his purposes.[13]

Miles concludes that, in terms of agency, the relationship between God and the ancestral family ultimately reverses: "The Lord God is active and articulate in his relationship with Abraham; it is Abraham, not the Lord

---

11. Miles, *God*, 58-66.

12. Miles postulates divine agency at work in Gen 24: "At the beginning of the Abraham cycle, Abraham belonged to the Lord; by the end of it, the Lord belongs to Abraham, or at least *he mysteriously acts* as if he does at certain points" (*God*, 64; emphasis mine). This study would contend that here Miles interprets in a manner counter to his method elsewhere by treating character discourse to and about God as reflective of divine agency. Whereas he understands Jacob's and Joseph's words about God to constitute their own assumptions and to reflect their own objectives, he takes Abraham's (and implicitly his servant's) words to indicate God's actual activity.

13. Miles, *God*, 74.

God, who keeps silent. In the story of Joseph, by contrast, the Lord God is neither active nor articulate."[14]

One might supplement Miles' analysis of the Joseph story with Hugh White's argument that Joseph uses God, rather than vice versa. Reading the Joseph story within the narrative framework of fraternal conflict and the potential alternate resolutions of either Joseph's triumph (as suggested by his dreams) or his demise (suggested by the antagonism between him and his brothers), White perceives the determination of events not in any narrative accounts of divine agency (indeed, there are only a few isolated mentions of God's presence) but rather in character discourse. Appropriating Stanley Fish's image of a self-consuming narrative, White proposes that in the Joseph story, "the content of the closed perspective of the narrative framework [is] taken up into the direct discourse of the characters and subordinated to the ongoing dialogical process which prevents the narrative from achieving closure."[15] In other words, character discourse keeps the question of the narrative's determination alive and open; it continually frames and reframes events. In fact, it becomes the means of the narrative's (unfinalized) determination, not only framing events but actually constituting a key event itself. Thus White concludes that when Joseph attributes the outcome of events to divine agency (e.g., 45:8),

> this view is being presented to the brothers in direct discourse as a means of persuasion. It is not being offered in the narrative framework as a final 'explanation' for the curious turns in the plot, but rather is a part of the plot that is not yet concluded.... It is the utterance by Joseph of this statement which releases the power to bring about this end. Thus even the most encompassing explanation is subordinated to (and thus 'consumed' by) the open dialogical process.[16]

Double Plot Logic and Representation/Metarepresentation

The three approaches to the balance of agency in the ancestral narrative proceed from the same observation—God's diminishing presence—to different conclusions primarily by their configuration of two common interpretive concerns: the story's relation to the divine program and the

14. Miles, *God*, 78.
15. White, "The Joseph Story," 54–55.
16. White, "The Joseph Story," 67–68.

reliability of character discourse. One might account for these approaches, then, by exploring how these two concerns are variously configured. In particular, two principles of poetics clarify the ways these concerns are configured: the double logic of *fabula* and story, and the distinction between the readerly acts of representation and metarepresentation.

The "double logic," as presented by Culler and expounded by Peter Brooks,[17] holds that there are two opposite logics operative in reading a plot. The *fabula*, or the actual story-world events (and often one decisive event in particular), determines the story, or the meaningful representation of events. And conversely the story determines the *fabula*. Providential readings of the ancestral narrative, which hold the promises of the divine character in high regard, evidence both arcs of this double logic. On the one hand, they prioritize the event of the divine program (God's proclamation of his plan for the ancestral family). It becomes a sort of narrative map that outlines the *fabula* and undergirds the story with the fundamental meaning that God is continually operating toward the fulfillment of certain promises. Whatever the perspective given later in the story—e.g., the relative absence of God in the story of Jacob's family's survival—the reader "knows" that God sustains the ancestral family. The event of the divine program determines the story of the ancestral family's struggle toward its fulfillment: indeed, its continual triumphs over the obstacles in its way only confirm this determinative event. On the other hand, there are portions of the narrative that betray little awareness of this fundamental event, or even of divine presence and activity. In these segments especially, the story's *peripeteic* developments (whereby characters do the opposite of what they intend, but in so doing reach a happier end)[18]—in their "implicit claims to significance"[19]—comprise a story whose unforeseeable twists and turns, whose structures of meaning, demand priority. The divine program no longer explains the story; the story, rather, explains the divine program. In other words, these

---

17. Culler, *The Pursuit of Signs*, 188–208; Brooks, *Reading for the Plot*, 3–36.

18. Consider, for instance, what one might call a double *peripeteia* in Judah's case. Desiring progeny, he precludes its possibility by sending Tamar home. Then, desiring to keep Tamar at a safe distance from his family, he unwittingly becomes intimate with her himself. The end result realizes Judah's original intention, but only in a manner completely contrary to Judah's own plans.

19. Culler, *The Pursuit of Signs*, 198. Culler indicates by this phrase the sense that the story's thematic structure is priority and thus determines the events that ostensibly underlie the plot. The events, which constitute the *fabula*, are not a given but are rather "justified" by the meaning of the story.

portions of the ancestral narrative appear so decisively determined by its human characters' intentions and actions that the story—far from being a predetermined outworking of a divine program identical with the *fabula*—would seem to be the foundation from which the *fabula* and its fundamental divine program would have to be constructed, or "justified."[20] Indeed, the narrative itself betrays an acknowledgment that the story can be seen to determine the *fabula* inasmuch as one of its protagonists, Joseph, makes sense of the humanly determined events by the retrospective explanation of divine providence. Joseph, in this sense, serves as a surrogate reader—a character "within a fiction who represents the reception of the narrative"[21]—positing a *fabula* of divine providence only after the human drama has unfolded.

Thus both *fabula* and story can be read as determinative of the other; either way, the divine program is upheld. On the one hand, the *fabula*—particularly the divine proclamation of the divine program—appears to determine the story. On the other hand, parts of the story appear as the unique and unforeseeable results of human determination, and yet these unforeseeable results align with and thus point back to the divine program. The ancestral narrative ultimately reaches conclusions that suit and thus, depending on the logic, either derive from or justify the *fabula* and its centerpiece, the divine program.

The distinction between the readerly acts of representation and metarepresentation, however, complicates this understanding of the divine program. In providential readings, readers represent the divine promises. They read the divine program as the *narrative* program. Consequently the promises become "architectural truth" and adequately bear the *fabula*.[22] Whether the divine program is read as the event that determines the subsequent stories of the ancestral narrative, or the event that is ineluctably deduced from their endings—with which it accords[23]—it becomes the foundation on which divine agency is read in the latter stages of the ancestral narrative. As Goldingay says, the stories

---

20. Culler, *The Pursuit of Signs*, 198.
21. Currie, *Postmodern Narrative Theory*, 53.
22. Zunshine, *Why We Read Fiction*, 75.
23. Culler explains the second logic—story's determination of *fabula*—in terms of how well the ending fits the events supposed to have precipitated it: "We adopt the second perspective when we discuss the appropriateness or inappropriateness of an ending (when we debate whether these actions are appropriate expressions of the thematic structure which ought to determine them)" (*The Pursuit of Signs*, 198).

of Genesis "illustrate the theme [of God's program], often by showing how God overcomes the obstacles to the fulfilment of his commitment":[24] that is, these stories' resolutions, whether they proceed from or point to the divine program, necessarily correspond with it. If, however, readers metarepresent the divine promises—that is, if they qualify them with the source tag, "God says," and treat God as a character and not an authoritative accomplice of the narrator—then they can entertain the possibility that the divine program does not constitute the narrative program, that it does not bear the *fabula*. Similarly, by metarepresenting characters' propositions of divine providence, readers confront the indeterminacy of the characters' claims. The dual plot logic remains at work: the *fabula* still determines the story, and the story still determines the *fabula*. But now the reader can construct a *fabula* and story not of the divine program, but of indeterminate or, more positively, human agency. Jacob's tricksterism, the antipathy between Joseph and his brothers, Judah's selfishness and subsequent transformation—these and other human elements can become the *fabula* (or more specifically the decisive event[s]) from which the story derives, or which derives from the story.

The Tamar Interlude as an Interpretive Key

Because the Tamar interlude seems like a narrative outsider amidst the Joseph story, an intruder with little import to the embedding narrative, interpretation conventionally rationalizes its inclusion as an instructive incident that illumines the Joseph story. Somehow its story informs the Joseph story. It is little surprise, then, that interpretation of the Tamar interlude's relation to the Joseph story engages the concern that underlies much of the interpretive interest in the Joseph story: namely, the balance of agency. In rough correspondence to the three approaches to the balance of agency in the ancestral narrative, there are three overlapping ways that interpreters relate the Tamar interlude to the Joseph story. A recent article by Hans-Georg Wünch, "Genesis 38—Judah's Turning Point: Structural Analysis and Narrative Techniques and Their Meaning for Genesis 38 and Its Placement in the Story of Joseph," can serve as a primer to these three ways, for in its review and development of past scholarship on Gen 38 it models each way of linking interlude and embedding narrative.

24. Goldingay, "The Patriarchs in Scripture and History," 22–23.

First, Wünch focuses on divine agency, unseen and yet providentially at work, as the determining factor of the Tamar interlude's events. Although God only intervenes in the story to kill Er and Onan, and Tamar engineers the turnaround that resolves the procreative dilemma, Wünch considers the serendipitous turn of events, in which Judah's ignorance highlights his lack of control over the course of events, to reflect divine agency: "The structure reveals what determines the whole story"—here, one might interject, Wünch reads according to the second plot logic, interpreting thematic structure as determinant of the events—"Judah, who seems to be the actor, does not really know the reality. He acts, but in reality it is Yahweh who is the final actor and who pulls the strings."[25] Although Wünch does not draw an explicit parallel between divine agency in the Tamar interlude and the Joseph story, readings calibrated to the determinative influence of the divine program easily make that link (as will be shown below). To such readings, the correspondence between the *peripeteia* of the Tamar interlude (Judah intends to isolate Tamar, but his actions instigate their eventual union and the resolution to the procreative dilemma) and the *peripeteia* of the Joseph story (Joseph's brothers intend to wreck Joseph's dreams, but their actions ultimately lead to the dreams' realization as well as the family's survival) suggests that the outcome of events is more than coincidence: in their ignorance, Judah and Joseph's brothers act unwittingly to mediate the divine agency.

Conversely, Wünch also highlights the significance of human agency. The Tamar interlude, Wünch notes, provides an essential key to Judah's characterization. As "the starting point for a change in the character and mind set of Judah,"[26] it illumines the process by which he moves from selfishness to selflessness. Underlining the verbal link (the rare root ערב; 38:20; 43:9; 44:32) between Judah's conduct in both stories, Wünch sketches the reversal in Judah's character. In the Tamar interlude, "Judah had only himself and his desires in mind and was prepared to give his very personal marks of identity as deposit for it. Now [later in the Joseph story] he mortgages himself and is prepared to go to jail or slavery in the place of his brother (remember that he was the one who was prepared, without hesitation, to sell Joseph into slavery)."[27] This second approach to the interlude's relation to the embedding narrative thus centers the

---

25. Wünch, "Genesis 38," 794.
26. Wünch, "Genesis 38," 785.
27. Wünch, "Genesis 38," 797.

reader's attention not on the clandestine movements of divine agency but on the increasingly distinct human characters and their decisive intentions and actions.

Third, Wünch regards the Tamar interlude as an integral piece to the puzzle of who will succeed Jacob as primary heir. "Who will take the lead under the sons of Jacob?"[28] This question ultimately allows for the indeterminacy of divine/human agency—or disregards the question altogether—choosing to focus on the effect or result of the stories' events rather than on the potential causes. It appropriates the Tamar interlude as a character sketch of Judah that is purposefully juxtaposed to the more extensive profile of Joseph's character. The Tamar interlude thus becomes a voice in the dialogue of how privilege and power might be apportioned to Jacob's sons.

Having outlined these three main interpretive appropriations of the Tamar interlude, this study will now explore each in greater detail. Surveying representative readings from each approach, it will attend to how each places the Tamar interlude in a position of service to the embedding narrative.

Divine Agency

Like many commentators, von Rad contends that "the story of Judah and Tamar has no connection at all with the strictly organized Joseph story"[29]—that "the Joseph story knows nothing at all about Judah's separation from his brothers."[30] Nevertheless, he implicitly posits a significant relation between the Tamar interlude and the embedding ancestral narrative. God, he acknowledges, is a relatively absent character in the Tamar interlude. The interlude, rather, consists in "a complicated human event."[31] "[I]ts essence," he explains, waxing lyrically, is "its wonderful openness to what is human—passions, guilt, paternal anxiety, love, honor, chivalry, all churning up the narrow circle of one family in labyrinthine entanglement!"[32] This reading of the interlude's humanness, however, concludes with a note on its providential backdrop and its fundamental

---

28. Wünch, "Genesis 38," 783.
29. Von Rad, *Genesis*, 356.
30. Von Rad, *Genesis*, 357.
31. Von Rad, *Genesis*, 361.
32. Von Rad, *Genesis*, 361.

connection to the larger narrative: "One can recognize the theological substance of this story only if one knows about the material character of the saving gifts toward which Israel's ancestors directed their life. In contrast to the majority of Abraham and Jacob narratives this story is not concerned with the Promised Land but with the blessing of great progeny."[33] Here, von Rad not only mimics the theological coda that Joseph appends to the course of events that brings his brothers to Egypt (45:8), but also models a common interpretive move among providential readings. After commenting on the particulars of the interlude's human drama, he concludes that its significance ultimately consists in its reflection of divine agency. Thus, although he does not explicitly draw the parallel, von Rad effectively interprets the Tamar interlude as analogous to the Joseph story—a story also told in "secular style"[34]—the "incorporation [of which] into the larger complex of the patriarchal stories ... is of great theological significance, for the guidance of divine providence, which the Joseph story portrays in so many mysterious ways, is now part of the great historical plan which Yahweh drew up in order to call his people Israel into existence."[35] The message of the Tamar interlude is synonymous with that of the Joseph story: behind and through the agency of the human characters, God works in mysterious ways.

While von Rad's reading demonstrates little interest in the narrative integration of the Tamar interlude with the Joseph story, recent theological readings have inclined more toward a narrative-critical approach that seeks a purposeful relation between the stories. They generally subordinate the interlude as a sort of theological key to the Joseph story. Arnold demonstrates this tendency in his reading. He begins alongside von Rad, acknowledging the human interests that predominate in the interlude.[36] He furthermore construes these interests as a purposeful contrast to the human interests in the Joseph story: "[M]ore likely this text was originally incorporated ... as a means not only of creating suspense, but as a foil for Joseph. Judah's indiscretion and callousness, which he himself acknowledges make him less than righteous, are contrasted with Joseph's unsurpassed morality in the very next chapter (39:8–12)."[37] Like von Rad,

33. Von Rad, *Genesis*, 362.
34. Von Rad, *Genesis*, 398.
35. Von Rad, *Genesis*, 439.
36. Arnold, *Genesis*, 325.
37. Arnold, *Genesis*, 325.

Arnold ultimately sees the human interests subtended by divine providence. Unlike von Rad, Arnold explicitly links the divine providence that he reads in the interlude with that which he reads in the Joseph story. The former, he would suggest, points to the latter: "[T]he text [of Gen 38] demonstrates that God can and will use the misguided decisions and behavior of his people to accomplish his purposes, working good out of evil. In a vastly different way, the Judah and Tamar episode buttresses the central theme of the Joseph Novel: God turns good from evil in order to preserve life (45:5–8; 50:20)."[38] The evil that Judah does in the Tamar interlude parallels that which the brothers do against Joseph, and the perceived divine agency in the interlude thus proleptically hints at a parallel providential resolution to the Joseph story. The divine program succeeds in both cases, regardless of the foibles of its human mediators.

Esther Marie Menn parallels Arnold in supplying a providential link between the interlude and the Joseph story. Like Arnold, she attends particularly to the felicitous outcomes of morally questionable deeds: "Perhaps, as in the larger Joseph story, God may be present despite his narrative absences in Genesis 38, working through the morally ambiguous matrix of human lives for more comprehensive purposes."[39] Menn supplements this speculation with an exploration of the play of knowledge and ignorance. She suggests that the deaths of Er and Onan mark God's omniscience over against the characters' (particularly Judah's) ignorance, and that this juxtaposition invites a providential interpretation: "[A]n examination of this biblical narrative in terms of the theme of concealed and revealed knowledge gives rise to a compelling theological understanding of the human condition. Although people make decisions and follow courses of action in the half-light of partial human knowledge, there may be a greater purposefulness to their lives visible only to the divine gaze."[40] Judah, in other words, assumes a position of ignorance that accentuates the potential play of providence—a play, furthermore, that repeats in the Joseph story, as the brothers' ignorance yields to a purportedly providential resolution.

Like Menn and Arnold, Judy Fentress-Williams also advances a purposeful relation between the Tamar interlude and the Joseph story. Observing several thematic parallels between the human drama of both

---

38. Arnold, *Genesis*, 329.
39. Menn, *Judah and Tamar*, 43.
40. Menn, *Judah and Tamar*, 48.

stories—including the use of garments, deception, and revelation—she situates the main thematic nexus in the two heroes, Tamar and Joseph, both of whom "function as the links between the promise of God and the fulfilment of God's promise."[41] Fentress-Williams treats the Tamar interlude as a distinct voice in dialogue with Gen 37 and 39–50, and she distinguishes in it a particular "lesson," namely that "the path to God's promise is a circuitous one."[42] Thus the interlude serves as a sort of analogue for the Joseph story, indicating that "Joseph's path to the fulfilment of God's promise to Abram will be" circuitous as well—that is, comprised of "delays, imprisonment, exile, and reversals."[43]

While the above providential readings acknowledge the significance of human agency in the Tamar interlude—highlighting the selfishness of Judah's character or the deception that figures so integrally into the plot's twists—they nonetheless focus on the unseen divine agency as the significant link between the Tamar interlude and the Joseph story. Whether the divine program is read to buttress the interlude's felicitous conclusion, or the peripeteic twists are read to confirm a providential outworking of the divine program, divine agency is read as the ultimate focus of the story. The Tamar interlude serves the larger narrative purpose of showing that God is guiding events according to the divine program—in this case, the program's promise of offspring, or more generally the survival and preservation of the ancestral line.

Human Agency: Characterization and Human Drama

Other readings, however, concentrate on characterization and the development of human drama as the main link between the stories. Devoting more attention to the increasingly distinct human characters and their decisive intentions and actions than to the possibility of divine agency operating in the notable absence of the divine character, they shift their gaze from God to the human cast. In these readings, Judah generally takes center stage as a full-fledged, dynamic character who changes in the course of the Tamar interlude and the Joseph story, although sometimes Tamar also attracts attention as a potential analogue to Joseph.

---

41. Fentress-Williams, "Location, Location, Location," 20.8.
42. Fentress-Williams, "Location, Location, Location," 20.2.
43. Fentress-Williams, "Location, Location, Location," 20.7.

The focus on human agency and the focus on divine agency, however, are not mutually exclusive, as Richard Clifford demonstrates in his article "Genesis 38: Its Contribution to the Jacob Story." Clifford in effect weds the two points of interest together in his interpretation, interweaving divine providence with Judah's transformation and the subsequent transformation of Joseph's character. He perceives divine providence operating in the Tamar interlude primarily by way of the numerous ancestral echoes that he hears: "exogamy, difficulty in begetting children (appearing elsewhere in the form of the barren wife), naming of the son, sons contending for firstborn status, the divine requirement that the father 'give up' his only son, mourning that incites the bereaved man to procreation, and meeting one's future wife at a spring."[44] These resonances, he proposes, suggest that the misadventures of Judah and Tamar fall firmly within the frame of the divine plan for the ancestral family. Clifford also detects resonances between the characters of Joseph and Judah: both "go down," are caught up in deceptions involving a kid from the flock and clothing, marry foreign women, beget "rivals for firstborn status," and are involved in recognition scenes.[45] For Clifford, these correspondences suggest that just as Judah and Tamar's story is situated in the larger divine plan for the ancestral family, so too the Joseph story progresses within the structure of divine providence. The Tamar interlude, therefore, both reflects and anticipates divine providence. Clifford's reading, however, does not rest content with seeing God's critical influence in the story. It emphasizes the determinative power of human agency just as much as that of the divine. For Clifford, Judah's transformation at the conclusion of the interlude—a transformation that, Clifford contends, includes recognition not only of Tamar's righteousness and his wrongdoing but also of "God's strange and previously hidden activity in propagating the family"[46]—anticipates[47] and indeed precipitates Joseph's own transformation:

44. Clifford, "Genesis 38," 528.

45. Clifford, "Genesis 38," 521.

46. Clifford, "Genesis 38," 530. This assertion seems tenuous: nowhere does Judah insinuate that the turn of events has derived from some providential force. Perhaps Clifford reads Judah's later attribution of events to divine agency (Gen 44:16) back into the recognition scene between him and Tamar. In other words, what Judah articulates later in the story represents, for Clifford, what Judah comes to understand earlier (in Gen 38).

47. Clifford states, "Judah's conversion is a paradigm, told quickly and completely before the Joseph story unfolds at its more leisurely pace, so that readers might learn at the very outset that it is possible for the sons to change" ("Genesis 38," 532).

> Scholarly emphasis on Joseph as a wise man testing his brothers to see if they have changed has obscured *Joseph's* need to change. In family affairs, no one is a cool sage. Judah's speech in chap. 44, the longest in the Book of Genesis, demonstrates only one brother's change of heart. The reader knows only that Joseph loves his father and his only full brother; the reader is not told about Joseph's attitude toward the other ten. One must assume that he is truly undecided. The outcome of the story hangs in the balance.... Joseph wavers until he hears Judah offer to take Benjamin's place lest his father be destroyed. Joseph then recognizes that God has indeed brought good out of evil; his envious and murderous brothers have truly changed and become sons of Israel, willing to give up their own lives that the family might survive.[48]

Like Clifford, Ackerman points to Judah's transformation as determinative of parallel transformations in the Joseph story. Ackerman suggests that, without the Tamar interlude and Judah's transformative experience, "history [would likely] repeat itself" in the Joseph story.[49] To elucidate this likelihood, Ackerman first points out a deep "structural doubling" in the Joseph story,[50] whereby the initial events of the plot (the brothers' crime and Joseph's subsequent suffering) repeat in "chronological reverse": Joseph leads his brothers first to suffer what he suffered and then to re-enact their crime (i.e., to leave a brother behind and go home to their father).[51] Then, in a third stage of plot doubling, Joseph offers them the chance to commit the crime anew (i.e., to leave the next favored son, Benjamin, behind).[52] What, if anything, has changed between the initial events and their doubles? Ackerman insists: Judah. He posits that Judah's involvement in the brothers' initial crime stems from the desire to eliminate his "rival."[53] Because Levi, Simeon, and Reuben have already fallen outside the bounds of Jacob's good grace, Judah stands "next in line" for special status.[54] But as long as Jacob's favorite son remains,

---

48. Clifford, "Genesis 38," 532.
49. Ackerman, "Joseph, Judah, and Jacob," 94.
50. Ackerman, "Joseph, Judah, and Jacob," 86.
51. Ackerman, "Joseph, Judah, and Jacob," 93.
52. Ackerman explains, "The plot doubling has structured events so that history can repeat itself and they [the brothers] can again be rid of the favored son" ("Joseph, Judah, and Jacob," 94).
53. Ackerman, "Joseph, Judah, and Jacob," 100–101.
54. Ackerman, "Joseph, Judah, and Jacob," 100–101.

Judah's place is not secure; thus he acts to ensure his removal from the family. In the second portion of the story, however, Judah operates in a completely different manner. Acting selflessly, he works for the survival of the family. According to Ackerman, Judah's experience with Tamar has led to a fundamental transformation of his character. In the Tamar interlude, Judah learns that trying to safeguard the life of his youngest son has almost cost him the continuation of his family line: it was wrong for him to withhold Shelah from Tamar (38:26). He echoes the lesson of this experience when he persuades Jacob to relinquish Benjamin—"so that we might live and not die" (43:8)[55]—and subsequently when he leads Joseph, a son who was not withheld, to a similar realization.[56] (In other words, according to Ackerman, Judah helps Joseph to realize that his experience in Egypt has been necessary for the family's survival. Because of the lesson that Judah imparts, Joseph articulates his own experience as part of the divine plan to ensure the life of Jacob's family.)[57] Like White, Humphreys, and Miles, Ackerman is keen to read the plot logic in terms of character dialogue. For him, it is not so much God who is at work as it is Judah's persuasive capabilities.[58]

Readings that center on characterization and the development of human drama typically view the Tamar interlude as a condensed narrative that mirrors and helps to bring into focus narrative elements that play out across the longer Joseph story. Alter helped to pioneer this line of thinking with his observations of numerous verbal and thematic parallels between Gen 38 and its "frame-narrative," the Joseph story.[59] Strongest among these are the lexical parallels in the recognition scenes. Just as Joseph's brothers direct their father Jacob to recognize Joseph's coat—"recognize please (הכר נא)"—so Tamar calls Judah to recognize his items

---

55. Ackerman claims that Judah "shows Jacob that Jacob's efforts to save the life of the younger, favored son are threatening the continuation of the entire line" ("Joseph, Judah, and Jacob," 103).

56. Ackerman, "Joseph, Judah, and Jacob," 103–7.

57. Ackerman, "Joseph, Judah, and Jacob," 106–7.

58. It should be noted, however, that Ackerman reads the determinative agency of human characters within an encompassing frame of divine agency. Thus he concludes, "The characters brought the story to its fitting conclusion. But the narrator makes it clear that the characters were able to learn and grow only because they were placed in a cosmos that, given proper cooperation from its supporting cast, brings life out of death and transforms evil into good" ("Joseph, Judah, and Jacob," 112–13).

59. Alter, *The Art of Biblical Narrative*, 4.

of surety (37:32; 38:25).⁶⁰ Alter also calls attention to a correspondence of motifs associated with the acts of deception that precede these recognition scenes. Garments conceal the truth;⁶¹ and goats, in one way or another, play an important role in the deceitful schemes. These lexical and motivic parallels invite a comparison of the roles that Judah, the common character, assumes in each story: deceiving in the first scene, Judah is deceived in the next. He is thus "the deceiver deceived."⁶² Although Alter primarily addresses the links between Gen 37 and 38, he also remarks on the similarities between Gen 38 and the narrative that follows. For instance, he observes an inverse relation between Judah's mishaps in Gen 38 and Joseph's adventure in Egypt. The former is "a tale of exposure through sexual incontinence," while the latter is a tale about "ultimate triumph through sexual continence."⁶³ Alter also notes a broader thematic connection between the Joseph and Judah stories. Both are "about the reversal of the iron law of primogeniture."⁶⁴ If nothing else, Alter seems to say, the Tamar interlude through its various repetitions of theme and motif opens the reader's eyes to the finer nuances of the human characters and their actions in the Joseph story.

Alter's reading hints at the possibility of identifying the Joseph story and the Tamar interlude as two instances of the same or similar type. Recent narrative readings pursue this possibility, drawing attention specifically to the stories' broader structural parallels that highlight the synonymous role assumed by Tamar and Joseph. My study "The Type-Scene Connection between Genesis 38 and the Joseph Story," for instance, postulates a basic sequence of events that the two stories share—deception, counter-deception, an acknowledgment of wrongdoing, and an *anagnorisis* (recognition scene).⁶⁵ Tamar and Joseph resemble one another in their

---

60. Alter, *The Art of Biblical Narrative*, 10.

61. For more on the parallel significance of garments in these stories, see Huddlestun, "Divestiture, Deception, and Demotion," 47–62.

62. Alter, *The Art of Biblical Narrative*, 10.

63. Alter, *The Art of Biblical Narrative*, 10.

64. Alter, *The Art of Biblical Narrative*, 6.

65. Kruschwitz, "The Type-Scene Connection." For a similar structural comparison, see Noble, who postulates that the stories of Joseph and his brothers and Tamar and Judah—as well as the preceding story of Jacob and Esau—are "type-narratives" that "manipulate a set of shared motifs in such a way as to provide meaningful variations on essentially the same underlying plot." Noble outlines the type-narrative as follows: an "unsatisfactory relationship" leads to wrongdoing, which precipitates a "lengthy separation"; the separation ends when need reunites the two parties, the

synonymous role of the victim-turned-counter-deceiver. Their eventual triumphs, furthermore, follow from *peripeteias* in which their antagonists act toward the opposite of their intention. That is, whereas Joseph's brothers intend to rid themselves of Joseph and wreck his dreams (37:20), their action precipitates his dreams' realization and the family's eventual reconciliation. Similarly, whereas Judah intends to keep Tamar at a safe distance from his family, he unwittingly engages in sexual relations with her, which, in turn, leads ultimately to reconciliation. This reading once again interprets the Tamar interlude as a narrative device for clarifying the contours of the human drama in the Joseph story: "In its compact plot rich with irony, Genesis 38 may operate as a lens through which its audience might better understand the longer—but similarly shaped and irony-filled—plot of the Joseph novella."[66]

Like the providential readings, interpretations that treat the Tamar interlude as a clue to the workings of human agency make the story to serve the perceived interest of its embedding narrative. Here, however, attention shifts from God to the human cast. Whether human motivations like antipathy and selfishness and actions like trickery and counter-deception are read to determine the story's progression, or the story is read to confirm these motivations and actions as the reason for its outcome, human drama rather than providence takes center stage.

The Question of Inheritance

The two previous approaches take opposite positions toward the relative void of divine activity in the Joseph story and the Tamar interlude. The providential readings focus on potential indices of divine agency, and the readings of human drama concentrate on the increasingly defined human characters, on their motives and actions. In contrast to these two lines of reading, a third effectively allows for the indeterminacy of divine/human agency—or simply overlooks the question altogether—as it speculates less on the possible causes of events and more on their effect or result with regard to the matter of inheritance. Prioritizing the

---

wronged of which is transformed and thus not recognized; the wrongdoer attempts payment, which is rejected, and finally a disclosure of identity transpires, along with a confession by the wrongdoer(s) and a narrative summary of the two parties' subsequent relationship. In this type-narrative, Tamar and Joseph are synonymous characters ("Esau, Tamar, and Joseph," 219–52).

66. Kruschwitz, "The Type-Scene Connection," 410.

theme of covenant, this line of reading proceeds from the recognition that previous stories have tackled the question of inheritance as it relates to Abraham's and Isaac's offspring and the assumption that Gen 37–50 is the next step in the narrative, the story that addresses the question as it relates to Jacob's offspring.

Goldingay begins with a deduction common to these readings: the primary competition for inheritance must be between Judah, the oldest son who has not yet disqualified himself, and Joseph, Jacob's favored son.[67] For Goldingay, the brothers' act of selling Joseph into slavery accomplishes, among other things, the removal of Joseph from the line of inheritance, thus setting the stage for a story about Judah. "Now Joseph, supposedly destined to be leader, seems to be out of the way. So Judah becomes the focus for a while."[68] Goldingay ultimately interprets the Tamar interlude as a portrait of the disqualified. Reading the interlude and the Joseph story along the parallel of sexual in/continence (a correspondence highlighted commonly by readings of human agency), he infers a negative judgment of Judah, from which he interprets Judah's disqualification. "The chapter's function is once again to tie off the story of a supplanted older brother by telling us of the fulfilment of the promise in the birth of his sons. It seems that Judah is disqualified from leadership by his marrying out and his recourse to an apparent prostitute: in the realm of marriage and sex he behaves more like Reuben . . . than Joseph."[69]

In contrast to Goldingay, Goldin does not read Judah's disqualification: "With Joseph gone (seemingly for good), Reuben, Simeon, and Levi out of favor, who but Judah is left? Forthwith the editor inserts chap. 38, to inform us of events in Judah's life. Here the *vita* of the chosen one belongs."[70] Goldin nuances this portrait of the "chosen one," however. Not only does it affirm Judah as heir to Jacob, it also upholds the providential "theme of the youngest triumphant," as Judah begets twins and "the younger gets ahead of the older."[71] This overturning of primogeniture, according to Goldin, affirms the "inscrutable" divine will[72] and anticipates

---

67. Goldingay explains: "Since Reuben, and Simeon and Levi, have disgraced themselves (34, 35:22), Judah is in a sense Jacob's senior son" ("The Patriarchs in Scripture and History," 21).

68. Goldingay, "The Patriarchs in Scripture and History," 21.

69. Goldingay, "The Patriarchs in Scripture and History," 21.

70. Goldin, "Youngest Son," 43.

71. Goldin, "Youngest Son," 43.

72. Goldin, "Youngest Son," 44.

the eventual triumph of Joseph, a younger son, as well: "The pattern [of overturned primogeniture] survives. Having been informed of this, we can return to the Joseph story and learn that God's designs are never destroyed."[73] Goldin thus does not assert the priority of either Joseph or Judah, but rather reads both as triumphant heirs, as dual inheritors whose legacy ultimately results from divine agency.[74]

Friedemann W. Golka converges with Goldin in reading both Judah and Joseph as heirs, but he goes a step further to distinguish between the natures of their inheritance. He deduces from Jacob's blessings (Gen 48-49) that Joseph's inheritance is "worldly" and Judah's is "spiritual."[75] Wünch offers a similar interpretation. He contends that, while Gen 48:17-19 indicates that Joseph "received the primogeniture" (a double portion, evidenced by the blessing bestowed upon his two sons), Gen 49:8 indicates that "the time when the brothers bow down to Joseph is coming to an end. The leading position belongs to Judah and his descendants."[76]

The Tamar Interlude as an Ancestral Birth Story

The foregoing analysis reveals the ways in which interpretation typically explains away the Tamar interlude's difference. It appropriates the interlude as a key to the embedding narrative—the Joseph story and the ancestral narrative—and subjects it to the prevailing question of agency. Readers inclined to perceive divine providence as an underlying concern of the Joseph story identify in the interlude's serendipitous turn of events a proleptic analogy to what will befall Joseph in Egypt. They make the Tamar interlude conform to the interests of the divine program—namely its concern with ancestral survival and the continuation of offspring. Readers attuned to the particularities of the Joseph story's human drama and the determinative role of human agency draw attention to the transformation of Judah's character as well as the parallels between either him or Tamar and Joseph. They make the Tamar interlude

---

73. Goldin, "Youngest Son," 43.

74. Goldin, "Youngest Son," 43. Here it appears that the histories of Ephraim and Judah (in the narrative of the Primary History) inform Goldin's reading. The fact that Joseph (through Ephraim) and Judah both father leading tribes suggests their dual inheritance in Gen 37-50.

75. Golka, "Genesis 37-50," 160.

76. Wünch, "Genesis 38," 784. See also Alexander, "Genealogies, Seed," 260; Williamson, *Abraham, Israel and the Nations*, 266.

into a lens that illumines the human drama of the Joseph story. Readers who allow for the indeterminacy of agency or neglect the question altogether, focusing instead on the outcome of events, speculate on the question of inheritance. They make the Tamar interlude into a puzzle piece that completes the logical competition between Joseph and Judah as heirs (assuming that Reuben, Simeon, and Levi have been disqualified). In each case, readers risk minimizing the strangeness of the Tamar interlude: the unconventional relations and identities of its characters, the peculiarity of their actions, the oddity of its inclusion in the ancestral narrative. The quest for the interlude's integration with the surrounding narrative leads to interpretations that accentuate the story's connections and potentially analogous relation to the embedding narrative at the expense of its difference.

The interlude, however, does not relinquish itself so easily to these various interpretive appropriations. This study draws attention to one narratological peculiarity, in particular, that suggests that the interlude's difference bears a significant meaning of its own, that there is more to the story's odd twist of events than the dynamic of agency or the question of inheritance. The interlude harbors within it the curious echo of the ancestral birth narrative. It reverberates with motifs suggestive of past ancestral birth stories. Yet these motifs are defamiliarized in the particularity of their strange circumstances: (presumably) Canaanite mothers, a wayward patriarch, a God that acts contrary to expectations, and several other twists on the procreative drama. Thus, even as the motifs invite a comparison with previous ancestral birth stories, they distance themselves from them and throw into relief the stark difference of the interlude. Attending to the distinctiveness of these motifs allows for a reading that does not subordinate the interlude to the interests of the surrounding narrative but rather considers it on its own terms. As this study will demonstrate, these motifs pose the question of what qualifies as an ancestral birth narrative and thus, by implication, what qualify as matriarchal and patriarchal identities and a proper mode of preserving the ancestral lineage.

Ancestral Birth Narrative Motifs

Feminist readings lead the way in identifying the ancestral birth narrative motifs in the Tamar interlude. Yet they do little to situate the story within its narrative context. Either the interlude becomes an object for intertextual comparison with other stories that feature female characters in similar roles—e.g., Melissa Jackson compares Tamar and Lot's daughters as tricksters,[77] and Fokkelien van Dijk-Hemmes compares the two Tamars (Gen 38; 2 Sam 13)[78]—or it comes under focus as an isolated birth narrative, replete with the drama for which previous birth narratives have primed the reader, in which one obstacle or another (e.g., age and barrenness) threatens the continuation of the family line. Thus Esther Marie Menn, Anthony J. Lambe, and Diane M. Sharon offer unique structural interpretations of the story's plot as a basic movement from death to life, from procreative dilemma to resolution.[79]

This study will take its cue from these feminist readings and other related interpretations, paying particular attention to the aggregate of ancestral birth narrative motifs. At the same time, it will seek to position the Tamar interlude more comprehensively within its narrative context. Rather than resolve the interlude's difference by subordinating it to the central thematic strains of the main ancestral narrative, however, it will show that the aggregate of ancestral birth story motifs—as a central thematic element within the interlude—can subvert the ancestral narrative. In other words, rather than allowing the center—the main ancestral narrative—to determine the different, it will explore how what is different might determine the center.

Before exploring the ancestral birth narrative resonances in the Tamar interlude, a prefatory note on the subject of motifs is in order. Read as purposeful allusions, motifs lend meaning to the unsaid. They invoke assumptions and expectations that can either confirm or contest their quoting context. In the latter case, the motif usually is *ironized*—quoted in a dissociative manner that highlights the incongruity between its assumptions and expectations, and the diegetic reality.[80] For example, in 2 Sam 11:1, when the narrator explains that David remains

---

77. Jackson, "Lot's Daughters and Tamar as Tricksters."

78. Van Dijk-Hemmes, "Tamar and the Limits of Patriarchy."

79. Menn, *Judah and Tamar*, 15–28; Lambe, "Genesis 38"; Sharon, "Some Results." While Lambe's reading does not present itself as feminist, this study includes it here because its analysis closely parallels the structural analyses of feminist-inclined readings.

80. In her book *The Triumph of Irony*, Klein demonstrates this dynamic in Judges. The exposition, Klein explains, introduces a number of motifs that illustrate Israel's proper relationship with Yahweh. These motifs are later ironized to great effect, illustrating the ever-increasing waywardness of the Israelites.

at Jerusalem at the time when kings go to battle, the motif of David's kingship is ironized; the expectations attendant on David as a king are not realized in the present narrative. Less commonly, the motif *ironizes*. Particularly when multiple motifs work collectively, their cumulative effect can render the quoting context suspect. The ironic quotations marks turn inside out. The motifs that before stood inside them as the ironized material now stand outside them as that which ironize. The quoting context—the appearance of things—is thrown into question; it becomes the ironic proposition, and the motifs become the background that sets the irony in relief. Brett's reading of Gen 22 illustrates this phenomenon. He reads the recurrent divine mention of Abraham's "only son" as an apparent piece of exclusivist discourse stemming from the ideological interests of the ruling class in the Persian period. However, a host of motifs recalling the story of Hagar and Ishmael—divine sight, naming scenes that emphasize the divine deliverance of Abraham's sons, and inhabitance in Beersheba—"subvert" (or we might say ironize) this apparent exclusivism. "In short, the names of Hagar and Ishmael are mentioned nowhere in chapter 22, but their ghostly presence is everywhere. The reader is faced with a choice: either hear their voices, or else read with the exclusivist ideology of Genesis 22 and ignore them."[81]

This study proposes that the motifs of Gen 38 are ironizing. First, however, it will treat them individually and demonstrate how, taken independently of one another, they are ironized. Each motif finds itself in an uninhabitable context—that is, its assumptions and expectations meet with contradiction, and so it cannot take root. Each motif falls short of its own suggestion, and so the story is decidedly *not* an ancestral birth story. It is, rather, quite *un*ancestral.[82]

Patriarchal Migration (נטה)

Matriarchal birth stories in the ancestral narrative proceed from patriarchal stories. Their interest, the birth of offspring, proceeds from patriarchal interest—specifically, fulfillment of the divine promise of offspring

---

81. Brett, *Genesis*, 74–76.

82. The choice of terminology here—"unancestral" instead of "non-ancestral"—is deliberate. The ironized motifs do not merely show the interlude to be different from the previous ancestral birth narratives. They show it to be a failure of an ancestral birth narrative. Whereas the prefix "non" might convey a more neutral sense of difference, "un" connotes more clearly the negative judgment implied by the ironized motifs.

and the transfer of the divine covenant from father to chosen son. In this sense, the Tamar interlude is little different. The story begins with Judah, not Tamar. In little time, a couple of motifs hint that Judah is a sort of patriarchal "black sheep," straying from both his ancestors' example and instruction.

In the story's opening, Judah leaves his brothers and "turns aside" (נטה) to Hirah, the Adullamite (v. 1). The same root in the present stem (*qal*) features only four times before the Tamar interlude, and three of its occurrences collocate the migration of a patriarch—Abraham, Isaac, and Jacob—with the building of an altar to the divine character as well as some form of calling (upon) him (12:8; 26:25; 33:19–20).[83] As a *Leitwort*, or "leading word," נטה carries implications constructed by its patterned use in a common sequence modeled by the patriarchs.[84] Thus Judah's initial act of turning aside portrays him as a patriarch, following in the footsteps of his ancestors. What follows this initial act of emulation, however, diverges considerably from their example. Instead of turning aside to a place where he worships God, Judah turns aside to an Adullamite man, suggesting that from the start Judah falls short of the patriarchal archetype.[85]

Patriarchal Marriage (בת כנען)

The deviance from patriarchal standards that Judah's initial action mutedly suggests finds near-explicit confirmation in his ensuing behavior: taking for a wife "the daughter of a Canaanite man" (38:2), an act against which both Abraham and Isaac make unequivocal prohibitions.[86] His actions with the Canaanite daughter compound the suggested negative evaluation of his conduct. By "seeing" (ראה) and "taking" (לקח) her, Judah acts in a manner that has previously referred to "the Woman's eating

---

83. In the other case, Gen 35:20–21, נטה collocates with Jacob's establishment of a pillar, but to Rachel rather than God.

84. Buber, *Schriften zur Bibel*, 1131, translated by and quoted in Alter, *The Art of Biblical Narrative*, 93.

85. Menn supplements this reading with the observation that "since this verbal root [נטה] in the causative stem can express the idea of leading someone astray, its use may imply that Judah erred in his alliance with the foreign population" (*Judah and Tamar*, 37).

86. See Gen 24:3 and 28:1, where Abraham and Isaac make injunctions against taking a wife "from among the daughters of (a) Canaan(ite)."

of the forbidden fruit (3.6); the sons of God cohabiting with the daughters of humans (6.2); the Pharaoh taking Sarai into his harem (12.15) and Shechem's rape of Dinah (34.2; though see 22.13; 30:9)."[87] As Laurence A. Turner concludes, "[C]an Judah's marriage spell anything but trouble?"[88]

These two early thematic echoes, of patriarchal migration and marriage, appear *ironized*. Judah's imitation of the previous patriarchs' conduct pales in comparison. The reader may indeed laugh, for if anything Judah seems to be an anti-patriarch, inasmuch as his patriarchal behavior opposes the spirit of that of the previous patriarchs. He "turns aside," but does not worship God; he marries, but against the traditional model of endogamy.

Childbearing (הרה *and* ילד)

The sequence of Judah's actions proceeds logically: after settlement and marriage, he procreates. For a moment, the spotlight shifts from him to his Canaanite wife, the daughter of Shua, who conceives and bears three sons. The immediate succession of conceiving (הרה) and bearing (ילד) echoes a common matriarchal pattern and indicates the routine, unhindered nature of the births.[89]

It is of particular note that the routine sequence of conception and birth is frequently collocated with an implication of God's agency in the matter. The first birth in Genesis—when Eve conceives and bears Cain and declares, "I have acquired a man with [the help of] the LORD" (4:1)—establishes the pattern of God's involvement in the procreative process. The narrative accounts of the conceptions and births of Sarah, Leah, Bilhah, and Rachel confirm the model: the narrator explains Sarah's childbearing experience as a result of the divine word (21:1–2); the narrator prefaces Leah's childbearing with the notice that God opened Leah's womb, and Leah herself alludes to God's role in the process in five of the six names she gives; Rachel attributes the first surrogate birth of Bilhah to God's judgment in her favor; and the narrator introduces Rachel's first conception and birth with the notice that God opened her womb, before

---

87. Turner, *Genesis*, 164.
88. Turner, *Genesis*, 164.
89. The routine cases of conception and birth are in Gen 4:1, 17; 19:36–38; 21:2; 29:32–35; 30:5, 7, 17, 19, 23. The interrupted cases (in which both הרה and ילד appear, but are separated by a narrative impediment) are 16:4, 15; 25:21, 24.

Rachel herself ascribes her son's birth to God's involvement and gives him a name that expresses her desire that the LORD give her another son.[90] It is worth observing, furthermore, that in stories of a barren matriarch God often appears to usurp the husband's procreative role. As Menn notes, "The substitution in three out of four cases [i.e., Sarah, Rebekah, Leah, and Rachel] of masculine verbs with a divine subject for masculine verbs with a human subject emphasizes God's decisive role in the births."[91] This substitution, Menn contends, contributes to the sense that the births represent "the fulfillment of God's promise to Abraham" and thus signify "divine benevolence and loyalty."[92]

The births of Judah's second and third sons tighten the motivic association between childbearing in the Tamar interlude and the previous matriarchal cases, in which God's facilitation is so often implicated. The formulation of Onan's birth—ותהר עוד ותלד בן (v. 4)—repeats verbatim the familiar refrain used in Leah's spate of childbearing, which transpires as a result of God's opening her womb (29:31, 33–35). Then the use of the root יסף in the account of Shelah's birth—ותסף עוד ותלד בן (v. 5)—recalls the name of Joseph (יוסף), who was born as a result of divine intervention and whose name echoes Rachel's call for further divine mediation: יסף יהוה לי בן אחר (30:24).[93] (Indeed, with Joseph starring in the preceding story, the motivic connotations evoked by his name and its origin may be the freshest of any of the childbearing motifs.)

The connection between matriarchal childbearing and divine facilitation ultimately suggests that the childbearing of Judah's first three sons is *ironized*, just like Judah's patriarchal conduct. The varied allusions to past instances of childbearing—uninterrupted conception and birth, the refrain of Leah's childbearing, the root of Joseph's name—contribute to a background rife with suggestions of divine promise and involvement, a background that is discordant with the diegetic reality. What is seen in the narrative, or rather what is not seen—divine presence, ultimately

---

90. The exceptions to the collocation of conception (הרה) and birth (ילד) with the implication of divine agency are the births of Cain's first son (4:17), the sons of Lot's daughters (19:36–38), Leah's third son (29:34), and Bilhah's second son (30:7).

91. Menn, *Judah and Tamar*, 88, fn. 169. Menn cites Gen 21:1, 25:21, and 30:22 (in the stories of Sarah, Rebekah, and Rachel, respectively) as instances in which divine activity precipitates conception.

92. Menn, *Judah and Tamar*, 89.

93. Only in one other instance previous to Gen 38 does the root יסף appear in a context of childbearing: the birth of Abel in 4:2.

clashes with recollection. The solely human nature of Judah's wife's childbearing implies that these births are not a part of the divine promise.

Procreative Sequence (לקח and בוא)

After the birth of his third son, Judah resumes the initiative as subject of the story.[94] The motivic elements that follow might best be understood as internal to the Tamar interlude; that is, whereas the motifs of migration, marriage, and childbearing alluded to instances earlier in the ancestral narrative, the next motifs allude to the story's own beginning, in particular the procreative sequence that Judah instantiates.

Judah takes (לקח) a wife for Er, his firstborn (v. 6). This act recalls his own procreative initiative (v. 2) and intimates the possibility of an iteration of the procreative process. In the structural terminology of Barthes, taking a wife is a cardinal function, the correlates of which are the husband's going into her and the wife's begetting children.[95] That is, according to the procreative model of Judah and his wife (the man sees, takes, and goes in to his wife, the woman conceives and bears a child, and either party names the child), taking a wife effectively "sows" the narrative seed that reaches "fruition" in the begetting of children.[96] Thus when Judah takes a wife, Tamar, for his firstborn, Er, anticipation is focused upon the question of whether or not Tamar will conceive and bear his children.[97]

Tamar's name (תמר)—lexically equivalent to the word for palm tree—insinuates her fertility.[98] Tamar, then, would appear to be an excel-

---

94. This study considers Judah to be subject in two senses: narratological and actantial. He is the narratological subject inasmuch as it is primarily his gaze, his actions, and his words that move the plot. He is actantial subject inasmuch as his desire drives the plot forward.

95. Barthes explains that a "function," as the "smallest narrative unit" of meaning, is a "term of correlation." A "cardinal function"—a subclass of the function—is not only consecutive (leading from one point to another) but also consequential (bearing upon the meaning of the story), and as such it either initiates or terminates an uncertainty (*Image–Music–Text*, 89, 93–95).

96. Barthes, *Image–Music–Text*, 89.

97. Lambe suggests that the procreative pattern in vv. 1–6 introduces the story as one "about the establishment and continuity of a family," and thus when Judah takes a wife for Er, "[t]he expectation seems to be that Er, the firstborn, will carry on the family where Judah left off" ("Genesis 38," 110).

98. Bird, *Missing Persons*, 202, fn. 13, and Frymer-Kensky, *Reading the Women of the Bible*, 266.

lent choice for Er's wife, sure to follow in the footsteps of Judah's own wife. But Er's death halts the emergent procreative sequence and introduces the story's conflict: namely, Judah's problem of procuring progeny for the continuation of his line. The notice that Er (ער) is evil (רע) in the eyes of God, which offers a basic rationale for the divine death sentence, also offers a play on words that suggests that Judah's representation of the diegetic reality (Er is the only son he names)—as well as what the reader reads—is backwards in the eyes of God. If Judah's initial actions trace the irony of his patriarchal status, this pun accentuates it: Judah cannot see straight, even with regard to his own sons.

After his first son's death, Judah resumes initiative once more and instructs his second son, Onan, to perform his levirate duty. His instruction here conspicuously advances along the procreative sequence from taking (לקח), which he did in the case of his first son Er, to "going in to" (בוא; v. 8), which he enjoins Onan to do. But again, Judah's attempt to replicate the procreative sequence that achieved childbirth in the story's beginning fails, for although Onan obeys the strict sense of Judah's word, he stops short of insemination, precluding the possibility of conception. Thus in this second act of the story, taking (לקח) and going in to (בוא) are *ironized*, for neither act proceeds according to expectation; neither advances the procreative sequence (i.e., seeing, taking, going in to, conceiving, bearing, naming) to the next act. Taking does not lead to a sexual encounter in Er's marriage with Tamar, for God kills Er. Similarly, Onan's repeated sexual encounters—the Hebrew construction (אם-בא) suggests their iterative nature[99]—do not lead to conception, for Onan spills his seed on the ground (and ultimately suffers the same fate as Er). Just as one might conclude that Judah is a failure of a patriarch, so one might too conclude that his sons are failures of his example. Neither follows in his procreative footsteps.

Ancestral Offspring (זרע)

The deaths of Er and Onan point up two other ironic echoes, one of which consists in God's activity. Inasmuch as Judah's command to Onan to establish offspring (זרע) recalls the divine plan for the continuation and proliferation of the ancestral family[100]—זרע is a root that appears

---

99. Wenham, *Genesis 16–50*, 362, notes the frequentative aspect that אם can carry.
100. Alexander, "Genealogies, Seed," 255–70. Alexander argues that זרע is a

overwhelmingly in the context of God's promise to the ancestors[101]—it primes the reader for a measure of that plan's fulfillment. So the fact that God kills Er and Onan, both of whom are ancestral offspring themselves, is doubly ironic. Rather than add to the offspring of the ancestral family as he promised, God does the opposite: he subtracts from Judah's offspring. Heightening this peculiarity is the fact that, until this point, God has consistently protected the ancestral family, as evidenced in both the divine character's promissory declarations (e.g., 15:1; 28:15) and his actions (e.g., 12:17; 35:5). As far as God's relation with the ancestral family is concerned, death as a form of divine judgment has only featured as a threat of retribution against *others'* transgression against the ancestral family (20:7). Within a broader frame of reference, death by divine judgment transpires only as a result of a universal or communal breach of God's ideal of righteousness; never before has it featured in the case of an individual.[102] (Indeed, if God were willing to pardon Sodom, a community of wicked people, for the lives of ten righteous individuals, then it would seem counterintuitive for him to single out wicked individuals in a community such as the ancestral family.) Thus the motif of ancestral offspring is *ironized*. The divine executions of ancestral offspring, Er and Onan, are openly at variance with a number of precedents: they run counter to God's promise of more ancestral offspring, God's protection of the ancestral family, and the hitherto communal nature of death by divine judgment.

Wickedness (רעע) and Destruction/Corruption (שחת)

Er's and Onan's fatalities resound ironically not only in terms of divine activity, but also in terms of the ancestral family's moral character. Although previous ancestral characters engage in a number of dubious acts, none meet the negative evaluation and divine death sentence apportioned to

---

Leitwort, or keyword, that thematically structures Genesis around the divine promise.

101. Up to this point in the ancestral narrative, זרע has appeared in thirty-seven instances, thirty-four of which are in the context of the divine promise. The three exceptions are Gen 19:32, 34 (the story of Lot's daughters) and 24:60 (Rebekah's family blessing).

102. Turner comments on the progression of the divine death sentence: "God's judgment which at first had encompassed the whole world with the Deluge, then narrowed to the communities in the cities of the Plain, is now meted out to individuals in a family" (*Genesis*, 165).

Er and Onan. The notice that both Er and Onan are, or do what is, wicked (רעע) draws a subtle equivalence between them and the other victims of the divine death sentence—namely, the antediluvian earth (minus Noah and his family) and the people of Sodom and the Plain cities. Together with the people of the Flood story, Er and Onan comprise the unique circle of characters in Genesis whose wickedness (רעה) is the object of the LORD's gaze (6:5). And like the people of Sodom, Er and Onan are characterized principally by their wickedness: Er and Onan in their deaths, which finalize them as wicked characters, and the people of Sodom in the narrator's own words (13:13) as well as their own (19:9).

Even more damning of Onan in particular is the motif invoked by his practice of *coitus interruptus*, namely that of destruction and corruption (שחת). The account in Hebrew reads ושחת ארצה, which lacks a direct object: "And he destroyed on/to the ground" (v. 9). Most translations interpret that "seed" (זרע) is the implicit object, as an antecedent can be found in the preceding notice that Onan knew that the offspring, or seed, would not be his. While such a translation helps to smooth out what would otherwise be an awkward construction, it diverts attention away from an intriguing equivalence between Onan's action and the divine judgment and destruction of the antediluvian earth. In the Flood story, שחת commonly collocates with ארץ. The two words appear alongside one another in the LORD's judgment that the earth is corrupt (שחת) (6:11); subsequently in the LORD's articulated decision to destroy (שחת) the earth along with all flesh (6:13); and at the end of the story in the LORD's promise never to destroy (שחת) the earth again (9:11). The echo of these words in Onan's act compounds his negative portrayal, insinuating that he, like the antediluvian earth, acts in a corrupt manner and therefore becomes an object of divine destruction.[103]

So it is that Er and Onan, as ancestral offspring, are *ironized*. It is worth pointing out that the wickedness (רעע) and corruption (שחת) are not themselves the ironized motifs; they are, rather, motivic elements that accentuate the latent motif of ancestral virtue and ironize it. In alluding to both sets of the previous victims of the divine death sentences, the mentions of wickedness (רעע) and corruption (שחת) invoke echoes that clash with the conventional expectations of the ancestral family's

---

103. The only other appearance of שחת in Genesis, interestingly, is in the story of the Plain cities' destruction (13:10; 18:28, 31–32; 19:13–14, 29). Although here it does not collocate with ארץ, it maintains a thematic connection between wickedness and consequent divine destruction.

virtuous conduct (cf. God's expectations in 18:19). Not only are Er and Onan failures in their imitation of their father's procreative model, they also are failures as members of the ancestral family. Thus at this point, one might characterize Judah as a sort of anti-patriarch, and his elder two sons as anti-ancestors, inasmuch as their assumption of these roles diverges considerably from expectation.

Multiplication (רבה)

Following Onan's death, Judah falls victim to ignorance. Unaware of the true cause of his sons' death, he identifies Tamar as the fatal factor. Thus he acts contrary to his own intention, initiating the story's first *peripeteia*. Desiring progeny, he prevents its (immediate) possibility by sending Tamar—the fertile palm—home.

At this juncture in the story, the only immediate possibility of preserving the succession of Judah's lineage lies with Judah and his wife. But immediately after Tamar leaves, the narrator relates: "And the days multiplied [רבה], and the daughter of Shua, the wife of Judah, died" (v. 12). The passage of time here finds intriguing expression by the root רבה, which features in the ancestral narrative almost exclusively in terms of the divine promise of multiplication of offspring.[104] Thus it connotes, if only weakly at this point, the divine assurance of children. Parallel to the previous motif of offspring (זרע), this motif appears *ironized* in the very different circumstances of the Tamar interlude, where God's conduct—killing the first two sons of Judah—seemingly contradicts his promise of multiplying offspring.[105] If one traces Judah's story according to its progression in relation to the divine promise, then Judah has moved not forward, but backwards. As Lambe observes, Judah has reached his "nadir," for he has lost two of his three sons and, in addition, "there is no womb in the family in which to plant fruitful seed. The future of the family, at this point, is jeopardized, and a more radical need for progeny to ensure primogeniture arises."[106]

---

104. Only two of the thirteen instances of רבה in the preceding ancestral narrative fall outside the context of the divine promise: Gen 21:20 and 34:12.

105. The זרע-centered discourse of vv. 8–9 accentuates this incongruity, as up to this point, זרע has appeared overwhelmingly in the context of God's promise. See fn. 101 in the present chapter (p. 208).

106. Lambe, "Genesis 38," 114.

THE TAMAR INTERLUDE 211

Bridal Imagery (צעיף, כסה, נחם, and כלה)

Between the death of Judah's wife and the next momentous event in the story, his encounter with Tamar, are a handful of bridal motifs that recall Isaac's union with Rebekah. Judah responds to his wife's death by being consoled (נחם). Many readers contrast this event with its immediate precedent in Gen 37:35, where Jacob refuses to be consoled (נחם). Fewer trace it further back to the first instance of a character's being consoled after a death: Gen 22:67, where Isaac takes Rebekah as his wife and is consoled (נחם). Of course, by itself Judah's act has little in common with Isaac's, and an equivalence drawn between them seems tenuous at best. But Judah's conduct does not stand by itself in drawing this association; what soon follows corroborates the undercurrent of bridal imagery.

When Tamar is told that Judah is coming to Timnah, she responds in a manner that indexes her character's newly acquired subjectivity—narratological and actantial, in addition to grammatical.[107] Putting aside "the garments of her widowhood (בגדי אלמנותה)" and sitting (ישב) away from her home (v. 14), she effectively announces her autonomy, as her actions directly contravene Judah's prior command that she stay (ישב) at home and be a widow (אלמנה) (v. 11). In addition to discarding her widow's garments, Tamar covers (כסה) herself in a veil (צעיף), an act that recalls the only other character to do likewise: Rebekah, just prior to her meeting Isaac (24:65).[108] Adding to the increasing resonance with Isaac and Rebekah's union are Tamar's choice of location—Enaim, which could connote a body of water and thus hint at an allusion to the courtings of both Rebekah and Rachel[109]—and the narrator's recurrent relational epithet for Tamar, כלה. Obviously meaning "daughter-in-law" in this context, the title can also mean "bride."[110] Like the multiplication-of-offspring motif, the bridal motifs appear *ironized* in their context. It is indeed as

---

107. She becomes a narratological subject in the sense that it now becomes primarily her gaze, her actions, and her words that direct the plot. And she becomes an actantial subject in the sense that it is now her desire—namely, for a child—that motivates the plot.

108. Fewell and Gunn, *Gender, Power, and Promise*, 88; Fentress-Williams, "Location, Location, Location," 20.5.

109. Turner, *Genesis*, 166. Along a similar line of thought, one might conjecture that Judah's journey toward Timnah also hints at the beginning of the "betrothal type-scene"—as outlined by Alter, *The Art of Biblical Narrative*, 51—which begins with the bridegroom's journey into foreign territory, where he meets a girl by a body of water.

110. Fentress-Williams, "Location, Location, Location," 20.5.

bizarre—and unancestral—a betrothal as one could imagine. Judah, a less-than-ideal patriarch, is about to join with one who can hardly (if at all) be considered a matriarch: his כלה, his "bride," is really not a bride but rather his own "daughter-in-law"[111]—and, from his perspective, she is not even his daughter-in-law but rather an anonymous prostitute.

Opening (פקח/פתח)

As sight plays a fundamental role in initiating the plot of the Tamar interlude, when Judah sees the Canaanite daughter and begins his family, so it proves crucial to the second half of the story. Here, though, Tamar's sight, rather than Judah's, dictates proceedings. When she first receives the report that Judah is coming up to Timnah, Tamar is invited to behold (הנה) his approach (v. 13). She sees more than his approach, though. She sees (ראה) through to Judah's deception: Shelah has grown up, yet she still has not been given to him as wife (v. 14). Tamar's insight finds representation not only in the simple narration of what she perceives, but also in her position of interception. She sits at the opening (פתח) of Enaim (עינים), which may refer either to a pair of springs or a pair of eyes. One need not restrict the meaning to one reference or the other, for the plurality of semantic possibilities contributes to the richness of the story's "fraught background." While the reference to a body of water strengthens the associations of the betrothal motifs, the alternative reference to eyes corroborates the sense that Tamar's eyes are now opened.[112] In contrast to her father-in-law, whose lack of perception has failed him in his quest for progeny, Tamar sees clearly.

Read as an indication of Tamar's newfound sight, "the opening of Enaim" suggests an equivalence between Tamar and the only other character in the ancestral narrative whose eyes are opened: Hagar.[113] When

111. Such an incestuous encounter entails death for both parties in priestly law (Lev 20:12).

112. Nowhere else in Genesis does the root פתח refer to the opening of eyes. (It most commonly appears as a noun referring to an entrance or a verb describing the opening of an external object, e.g., a sack or a window.) There are, however, instances elsewhere in the Hebrew Bible. Cf. 1 Kgs 8:29, 52; Neh 1:6; 2 Chr 2:20, 40; 7:15.

113. Before the ancestral narrative, the eyes of the first man and woman are opened (פקח) in Gen 3:7. This instance of eye-opening, however, differs from Hagar's (21:19) in its passive construction: whereas God opens (*qal* stem) Hagar's eyes, the eyes of the first humans are opened (*nifal* stem). Based on this evidence, divine eye-opening assumes a positive connotation while passive eye-opening assumes a negative one.

Hagar and Ishmael run out of water in the wilderness, and Hagar despairs of her son's impending death, a divine messenger proclaims salvation and then God opens (פקח) her eyes to see a well of water (21:19). The slight lexical difference (between פתח and פקח) notwithstanding, the resemblance in situation is notable: both Hagar and Tamar are outsider women (Hagar as an Egyptian, Tamar as a stranger who appears in the land of Canaan) who have been evicted from the ancestral household, and for both characters the opening of their eyes proves instrumental to the resolution of their unfavorable circumstances. Furthermore, Tamar's positioning at the opening of Enaim (עינים; possibly "two springs") on the way (דרך) to Timnah mirrors Hagar's first flight into the wilderness, in which the divine messenger finds her by the spring (עין) on the way (דרך) to Shur (16:7). In addition to the structural resemblances, there is also a notable thematic resonance. Just as Tamar's story is fraught with the power of sight, so too is Hagar's story. Hagar's manner of beholding Sarai (16:5–6) and what Sarah herself beholds in Hagar's son, Ishmael (21:9–10), precipitate both of Hagar's wilderness wanderings, and various elements of her wilderness theophanies emphasize the significance of sight—notably her position at the עין (16:7), which carries connotations of its other meaning ("eye"); her claim that she has seen God and God has seen her (16:13);[114] and God's opening of her eyes so that she sees a well of water (21:19).

The motif of opening extends beyond the opening of eyes. More recently in the narrative—in the two instances of פתח which immediately precede its usage in the Tamar interlude—God opens the wombs of Leah and Rachel, in each case resolving an apparent procreative conflict (29:31; 30:22).

Read as an allusion to both womb- and eye-opening, the "opening of Enaim" identifies Tamar with several noteworthy women before her: Hagar, Rachel, and Leah. Yet inasmuch as the motif connotes the necessity of divine agency to the resolution of otherwise inscrutable obstacles, it is *ironized*. It is out of place in the Tamar interlude. God does not open Tamar's eyes; she sees for herself. Neither does he open her womb; indeed, as her name suggests, infertility is not the problem. (Furthermore,

---

Applied to the Tamar interlude, the result is ambiguous: in its noun form (and in a different lexical root, פתח), its implication for the active/passive nature of Tamar's newfound sight is indeterminate. Are her eyes opened completely on her own accord, or do they open as a result of some form of divine prompting?

114. See fn. 85 in ch. 3 (p. 106)

God's brief cameo earlier in the story heightens the irony inasmuch as his conduct initiates rather than resolves the procreative problem.)

Excursus: The Tamar Interlude as "Sight-Bound" and Tamar's Recourse to Visual Semiotic Means

The pun of פתח עינים, "opening of eyes," flags not only motivic associations of divine acts of eye- and womb-opening. It also points up the determinant play of sight in the Tamar interlude—Tamar sees the reality of the situation, Judah sees only the appearance—a significant point worth further exploration, considering its strong resonance throughout the Joseph story. Indeed, immediately preceding and following the Tamar interlude are other instances in which a discrepancy in what characters see determines the course of events. Joseph's brothers present Jacob with Joseph's bloodied coat, thereby leading him to see (or recognize) what they know to be false: that Joseph is dead. Potiphar's wife retains Joseph's garment, which she knows to be a sign of Joseph's continence, as visual evidence to substantiate her story of Joseph's sexual advance, thus ensuring Joseph's imprisonment. Later when Joseph's brothers arrive in Egypt, Joseph recognizes them but they do not recognize him, and Joseph exploits this unevenness of perception in order to submit them to an ordeal of his design.

The general narrative style throws into deep relief the import of sight in the Tamar interlude, because in biblical narrative, dialogue commonly directs narration. That is, what characters say determines, in part if not in full, what characters do. Thus Robert Alter asserts the general "primacy of dialogue" in biblical narrative: dialogue "is so pronounced that many pieces of third-person narration prove on inspection to be dialogue-bound, verbally mirroring elements of dialogue which precede them or which they introduce. Narration is thus often relegated to the role of confirming assertions made in dialogue."[115] In the book of Genesis, the primacy of dialogue manifests itself in two basic ways: in the "open, intersubjective" modality of narrative initiated by God's unresolved promises and in the "closed, object-oriented" modality derived from character discourse that directs the various subplots toward closure.[116] In either

---

115. Alter, *The Art of Biblical Narrative*, 65.

116. This basic division of narrative modalities (as found in Genesis) is proposed in White, *Narration and Discourse*, 107.

case—whether toward an open or closed future—character dialogue moves the plot forward.

But in the Tamar interlude, dialogue is decidedly subordinate to sight.[117] What characters see precipitates what characters do (and what they say). A brief inventory of the main events in the story demonstrates the primacy of sight.[118] The story begins after Judah sees (ראה) the daughter of a Canaanite man, Shua, and initiates a procreative pattern (v. 2). The procreative pattern, however, is disrupted by death: Judah's sons Er and Onan die because of how God sees them (they are, or do what is, evil "in the eyes of the LORD"; vv. 7, 10).[119] Later, after Tamar has been sent home,[120] she is called to see (הנה) that her father-in-law is going to a sheep-shearing event (v. 13), and she subsequently sees (ראה) that Judah has not kept his word (v. 14). She plants herself in Judah's path, veiled and covered—ambiguously enough that the reader does not know whether it is a prostitute's guise or merely a cover for anonymity—and for the second time Judah's sight (ראה) leads to a procreative act (vv. 15–18). The story retains its suspense concerning Tamar's undisclosed plan as she resumes her widow's appearance and Judah's friend Hirah cannot find (מצא) her. Judah is then summoned to see (הנה) his daughter-in-law's pregnancy (v. 24). After he decrees her death, she invites him to recognize (נכר) his pledge items (v. 25). His recognition (נכר) secures Tamar's life as well as the lives of the twins to whom she subsequently gives birth (vv. 26–30).

Setting the primacy of sight in the Tamar interlude into even deeper relief is the general failure of the spoken word. As the ancestral subject whose actions direct much of the story, Judah talks the most. His words,

---

117. Menn, *Judah and Tamar*, 44–45. Menn observes the significance of perception and knowledge throughout Gen 38.

118. It should be noted that a few instances of sight in Gen 38 do not literally precede dialogue, but rather result from it—particularly when characters are called to see something (vv. 13, 24, 25). In each case, however, the dialogue does not itself precipitate action; rather, it serves to invite a perception which will, in turn, precipitate action. Thus, in two of the cases (vv. 13, 24), the report is anonymous—perhaps drawing attention away from the act of reporting to the contents of the report—and its primary purpose is to direct the gaze (הנה) of the recipient to an important detail—upon which s/he later acts. In the third case, it is not the spoken word but rather the perception it invokes that determines what the addressed character does (v. 25).

119. One might also argue that Onan's knowledge (ידע) is a form of perception.

120. The motive for Judah's decision to send Tamar home is revealed through spoken word, rather than sight. Nonetheless, his speech is clearly a sort of interior monologue and thus serves to outline his perception of events. In this sense, perception remains the precipitant of action.

however, meet with very little success. In fact, until his pronouncement at the story's denouement, his every word is either disobeyed or qualified by another character's word. Onan disobeys his command to raise up offspring for Er. Tamar disobeys (albeit temporarily) his command to remain a widow in her father's house. In his roadside encounter with Tamar—whom he mistakes at the time as a prostitute—his verbal advance is rebuffed with a request for payment and his suggestion for payment is adjusted to include a pledge. Even his resignation at not retrieving his pledge items—"let her keep [the pledge items] for herself" (v. 23)—meets with failure, as in the next scene Tamar returns the items to him, an act which also effectively overturns his command that she be burned. In summary, Judah's words fail. We might surmise that the primary reason for this is his ignorance. In a story where perception governs the plot, Judah's lack of perception undermines his words. He addresses his words to situations he does not understand and to characters who have or come to have a position of superior knowledge, and thus his words fail to exercise mastery over their intended objects.

While it is noteworthy, the sight-boundedness of the Tamar interlude is not unparalleled. It particularly recalls the sight-bound segments of other stories in the ancestral narrative that feature lead women characters. While it would be remiss to draw any strong conclusions without further study, a brief reflection on these similarities may prove informative with regard to the semiotic role of sight in the story-world of the ancestral narrative and may illumine the place of Tamar among characters who exercise a similar play with sight.

Before the Tamar interlude, sight plays a determinative role in the stories of each main female character, from the first woman to Dinah. What the first woman sees (ראה)—namely, that the tree (of the knowledge of good and evil) is good for food, and that it is a delight to the eyes (עינים) (3:7)—precipitates her and her husband's eating the forbidden fruit. Sarai as an object of sight—beautiful in appearance (מראה; 12:11) and someone whom the Egyptians see (ראה; 12:12, 14)—catalyzes the encounter between Abram and the Egyptians. Later, what Sarai implicitly sees and entreats Abram to see (הנה; 16:2)—her barrenness as the ostensible result of divine restriction—activates the attempt at surrogate childbirth. The attempt meets its unfavorable conclusion when Hagar sees (ראה; 16:4) that she has conceived, a perception that leads her, in turn, to have a lessened regard for Sarai—"her mistress was lessened in her eyes (עינים)" (16:4). It is Sarai's implicit recognition of Hagar's lessened regard for her that determines her humbling treatment of Hagar, which leads Hagar to flee into the wilderness, where she experiences a theophany, the significance of which, in her own words, seems to consist in both God seeing her and her seeing God (16:13).[121] The second Hagar interlude proceeds according to a similar sight-determined sequence, as again what Sarah sees (ראה)—Ishmael playing (or "Isaacing"; 21:9)—motivates the plot: she demands Hagar and Ishmael's expulsion. Hagar's wilderness experience again highlights the consequence of sight. First leading her to distance herself from her son—lest she "look on" (ראה ב-) his death (21:16)—sight then ensures her and Ishmael's survival: God opens her eyes (עינים) and she sees (ראה) a well of water (21:19).

In the next event involving a woman, Rebekah as an object of sight—as exceedingly pleasant of appearance (מראה; 24:16)—attracts Abraham's servant's attention and secures her selection as the leading candidate for Isaac's wife. (Many readers focus on the alleged divine validation of the servant's selection, but it is important to observe that the servant retains the power of decision: in 24:14, he stipulates of God, "Let the girl to whom *I say* . . . be her whom you have appointed." Thus Rebekah's appearance, which catches the servant's attention, is the decisive initial factor in her becoming Isaac's wife.) Next, Rebekah as an object of sight—again pleasant of appearance (מראה; 26:7)—factors into Isaac's sister-wife scheme, which is foiled when Abimelech sees (ראה) Isaac playing about with her (26:8). Although Rebekah's scheme to have Jacob receive Isaac's blessing does not explicitly engage the signification of sight (touch is the more pressing concern; cf. 27:11–12, 15–16), it nonetheless exploits Isaac's blindness (cf. 27:1). Similarly, Rebekah's father exploits Jacob's lack of sight in the evening darkness in order to deceive him into first marrying Leah; the significance of sight in this episode is highlighted by Jacob's realization (הנה) in the morning that he has been with Leah, not Rachel (29:25).

In a manner parallel to the strife between Sarah and Hagar, Rachel and Leah's "baby wars" in Gen 30 revolve around what they see: first Rachel sees (ראה) her barrenness, implicitly juxtaposed to Leah's fertility, and thus envies her sister and seeks equal status through surrogacy (30:1); then Leah sees (ראה) that she has stopped bearing children, and she too seeks more children through surrogacy (30:9).[122] Lastly, both

---

121. See fn. 85 in ch. 3 (p. 106).

122. Also, like their matriarchal predecessors Rebekah and Sarai, Rachel and Leah are both characterized by their appearance in one way or another (Rachel as beautiful;

what Dinah sees and her being seen profoundly shapes the story of the ancestral encounter with the Hivites. Going out to look on (ראה ב-) the daughters of the land (34:1), Dinah becomes the object of Shechem's sight (ראה; 34:2). Although Dinah does not receive the same characterization as her matriarchal forebears, who are described as beautiful, her being seen nonetheless precipitates male desire, which in turns drives the plot along—in this case, into violent conflict.

In contrast to the significant role of sight in the stories of these women, stories that involve only male characters appear more often to originate from and proceed according to the signification of speech. The archetype of this tendency is the episode of Sarah's burial in Gen 23. Abraham and the Hittites comprise the exclusively male cast of characters. Apart from Abraham's bowing before them and the actual weighing out of silver and transfer of property, the exchange between Abraham and the Hittites, including that between Abraham and Ephron the Hittite, proceeds solely by the semiotic means of speech. The narrative does not proceed by any verbs of sight (e.g., ראה); and only twice are "eyes" (עינים) mentioned, both times as metonym for the Hittites' presence (23:11, 18). In distinct contrast, the narrative abounds with speech (e.g., אמר, ענה) and hearing. Of Genesis' six mentions of ears (אזנים) as instruments of hearing, three appear in this one episode (23:10, 13, 16).[123] Instead of the common entreaty (הנה נא) ("behold [please]"), which is conspicuously absent, Abraham and the Hittites repeatedly—five times in total—implore one another, "Listen to me/us (שמעני/שמענו)" (23:6, 8, 11, 13, 15). Their dialogue comes to a close when finally one of the parties—Abraham—listens, or rather "agrees" to the terms of the other (שמע אל; 23:16).

The point of this general distinction between the semiotic means of speech and sight is not to gender either means in positivist fashion. Many counterexamples exist: the narrative spotlights both Sarai and Rebekah as they overhear conversations (18:10; 27:5); Sarah, Rebekah, and Leah each make decisive verbal demands of their husbands (21:10; 27:46—28:1; 30:16); Judah acts on what he sees (37:25-26), Joseph's brothers exploit what their father sees (37:32-33), and Joseph schemes according to the

---

Leah's eyes as "tender," translated alternately as "lovely" or "weak"). In their cases, however, it is indeterminate whether (and if so, how) their appearance affects the story. In other words, the narrative does not explicitly identify Rachel's beauty as the cause of Jacob's love.

123. The other three—20:8; 44:18; 50:4—transpire in dialogues comprised exclusively of male characters.

dynamic of recognition/non-recognition (42:8)—to name but a few instances. Rather, the distinction may suggest more broadly that speech and sight as semiotic means are generally hierarchized according to the scale of power among characters. Characters that assume more authoritative positions—such as the inhabitants over against the sojourner, the husband over against the wife, or most broadly the man over against the woman—naturally resort to command or proclamation as a means of seeking their end. Characters in subordinate positions—often female characters—unable to achieve their ends through decree, are represented as quieter but craftier: even as they are seen, they too see, and occasionally take recourse to the semiotic means of sight through which they can deceive those in positions of power.[124]

A number of matriarchal motifs echo ironically in the Tamar interlude. The dynamic of sight, however, echoes with affirmation, showing Tamar to resemble the matriarchs (and other women in Genesis). Inasmuch as the matriarchs become a part of the ancestral story by sight—by being seen, by seeing, and by making others to see (or not see)—Tamar parallels them. Seeing the reality of Judah's intention and making herself to be seen anonymously (whether she intends to pose as a prostitute is indeterminate),[125] she ultimately opens Judah's eyes, making him to see what before he could not see. She—like Sarah, Leah, and Rachel, and most of all Rebekah—is a game-changer in terms of what she sees, how she is seen, and how she makes others see. Her play with sight subverts Judah's play with words. Bal's summary regarding the opposition between Tamar's visual and Judah's verbal semiotic means is fitting: "Tamar uses the semiotic means, the signs that are left at her disposal, to take over. Her response to Judah's initiative to lie is an initiative to bring out the truth."[126]

Procreative Sequence: Part II (ראה, נתן, בוא, and הרה)

The second encounter between Tamar and Judah houses not only external motifs but also, as before in vv. 6 and 8, motifs internal to the story. Again the Tamar interlude alludes to its own procreative model—the man

---

124. Although it is not the only means of deception, sight clearly stands in Genesis as the preferred mode.

125. The narrative relates the effect of, rather than the motive for, her change of attire (vv. 14–15).

126. Bal, "Tricky Thematics," 149–50.

seeing (ראה), taking (לקח), coming in to (בוא אל), and the woman conceiving (הרה), bearing (ילד), and naming (קרא)—and again the allusions appear *ironized*. But whereas Judah's attempt to jumpstart an iteration of the procreative sequence on the level of his sons fails and introduces the story's main conflict, here his unwitting act—not intended for procreation—succeeds and initiates a resolution to the procreative conflict.

The context of Judah and Tamar's encounter insinuates that their seeing one another will initiate another attempt at the procreative sequence. Judah goes up (עלה; v. 12) to Timnah with Hirah, sees a woman (ראה; v. 15), and turns aside to her (נטה; v. 16). Similarly, at the start of the story, he goes down (ירד; v. 1), turns aside (נטה; v. 1) to Hirah, and sees a woman (ראה; v. 2)—from which the procreative sequence proceeds. Drawing from the same lexical paradigms that preceded the initial procreative sequence, Judah's actions hint at the possibility of the sequence's iteration.[127]

When Judah encounters Tamar, presumably at her station at Enaim, he sees her (ראה; v. 15), though in quite a different way than she has just seen her situation (ראה; v. 14). He does not see things as they really are: instead, owing to Tamar's different garb, he sees her as a prostitute. (The narrative appears to delight in reminding us of Judah's ignorance: first, in v. 15, he considers her a prostitute, and then in v. 16, the narrator affirms that he does not know that she is his daughter-in-law.) The unconventional circumstances in which Tamar and Judah perceive one another ironizes seeing (ראה) as the initial act of the procreative sequence, for although seeing operates here as catalyst for procreation, it does so in rather unexpected fashion. First, Tamar's seeing prods against the patriarchal norm whereby a man's desire instigates sexual union.[128] It is ultimately a woman's seeing, rather than a man's, that initiates this procreative encounter. Second, Judah's seeing pales in comparison to the seeing by which he began the story. That is, here he does not see a woman suitable for marriage, for procreation (contra 38:2), but rather a prostitute. His failure to recognize her as his daughter-in-law only heightens the irony of his seeing. Judah's seeing signifies as much what he does *not*

---

127. Cf. Menn, *Judah and Tamar*, 22. Menn identifies journeying alone, veering aside, and male companionship as three motifs associated with the initiation of the procreative sequence.

128. The immediate reference for this norm would be 38:2, but one might also look to Shechem in 34:2 and possibly to Pharaoh and the Egyptians in 12:15 (in which the occurrence of a consequent sexual act is indeterminate).

see as what he does: he does not see his כלה (38:16), either "bride" or "daughter-in-law."

Judah's first words to Tamar—"Come, please, let me come in to you (אבוא אליך)"—confirm the likelihood of the procreative sequence's resumption. Tamar's response prompts a negotiation of price and pledge, and only once she agrees upon the items that Judah is to give (נתן) her do they join together. Whereas earlier taking (לקח) followed seeing (ראה) and precipitated sexual union (בוא), the altered economy of sexual relations in this scenario replaces it with its paradigmatic opposite, giving (נתן). Having first appeared in the roles of wife and daughter-in-law, Tamar has since shifted identities to widow and ultimately here to prostitute, and yet it is precisely as a prostitute that she is able to turn the tables and take what is hers. No longer is she an object that Judah takes upon seeing (v. 6), nor is she a commodity promised to be given (v. 14) to a man. Tamar's subjectivity thus shows the procreative sequence here to be further *ironized* inasmuch as her conduct ruptures the procreative sequence's expectation of the male subject's acquisition. Rather than taking (לקח) Tamar, Judah gives (נתן) to her the pledge items, the promise of a future payment, and ultimately a son. In other words, if anyone does the taking in this scene, it is Tamar.

Tamar's conception—which drives the procreative sequence along, leaving only birth (ילד) and naming (קרא) unfulfilled—highlights the distinctiveness of Tamar's initiative among biblical women: ותהר לו (v. 18). A *hapax legomenon*, this phrase bears resemblance to the common phrase for a woman's bearing a child to her husband, ילד ל- (e.g., 17:21; 30:17). But whereas the latter clearly represents a woman's bearing a child to or for her husband, the former phrase retains an element of ambiguity that allows for multiple interpretations. It could mean that the woman conceives "for" (or "to") the man.[129] The majority of translations, however, opt for the alternative—namely that the woman conceives "by" the man. While the first option implies the man's priority as the beneficiary to whom the achievement matters most, the second suggests that the man is an instrument by which the woman achieves her own end. The ambiguity in v. 18 thus speaks to the shared (actantial) subjectivity of Tamar and Judah, inasmuch as both seek a common end. In the context of Tamar's subjectivity, however, and taking into account what seems semantically

---

129. This study has only been able to find one English translation that follows this route: Young's Literal Translation.

smoothest, the second translation prevails, expressing that Tamar has achieved her objective—through the means provided by Judah—and showing the procreative sequence to be *ironized* in this encounter. This is anything but a normal procreative sequence. Contrary to expectation, it is a woman who drives this act of procreation.

Matriarchal Initiative

It is important to acknowledge, of course, that Tamar's initiative is not entirely at odds with precedent. Previous matriarchs seek to circumvent procreative difficulties through their own initiative. Most notably, Sarah, Rachel, and Leah all appropriate handmaids as surrogate mothers. Inasmuch as Tamar's initiative recalls theirs, however, it is *ironized*. In her rather different circumstances, Tamar does not employ another woman as a surrogate. Instead she becomes her own surrogate, "posing as another woman herself."[130]

Corroborating the irony of Tamar's initiative is the resonance between her conduct and that of Lot's daughters, a resonance that, in one sense, is stronger than any matriarchal correspondence. Although Tamar's initiative initially likens her to the matriarchs, she, unlike the matriarchs, "is not a barren wife. Indeed, after a certain point, Tamar is not a wife at all."[131] Tamar is, rather, a daughter-in-law. This distinction in turn points to a different precedent for Tamar's story: the story of Lot's daughters. The two stories follow a remarkably comparable trajectory. Both parties suffer the death of "suitable sexual partners"; take initiative that involves "secrecy and deception"; and sidestep the procreative dilemma by means of "an older relative from the previous generation"—"thus invoking the common theme of incest."[132] Furthermore, the marked gender inversion of procreative initiative in Tamar's union with Judah resonates with a similarly striking reversal in the case of Lot's daughters, who "'go into' (ותבא, Gen 19:33; ובאי, Gen 19:34) their father and 'lie' (ונשכבה,

---

130. Menn, *Judah and Tamar*, 95.

131. Menn, *Judah and Tamar*, 94.

132. Menn, *Judah and Tamar*, 97. See also Jackson, "Lot's Daughters and Tamar as Tricksters," 30–35. Jackson offers a more in-depth exploration of the parallels. In addition to the basic similarities noted by Menn, Jackson points out that the stories focus on the relationship between a daughter and father figure, involve characters who are effectively widows and widowers, play on the difference between sexual and cognitive knowledge (ידע), and present trickster characters as the protagonists.

Gen 19:32; וַתִּשְׁכַּב, Gen 19:33; שְׁכָבְתִּי, Gen 19:34; שִׁכְבִי, Gen 19:34; וַתִּשְׁכַּב, Gen 19:35) with him."[133] These parallels with Lot's daughters throw into further relief the contrast between matriarchal initiative and Tamar's conduct. Tamar, this irony would suggest, is as much of a matriarch as Lot's daughters, which is to say—at least according to traditional interpretation—not at all.

Interrupted Childbearing (הרה and ילד)

In contrast to Judah's wife, Tamar does not enjoy a routine, unhindered childbearing experience. Bearing (ילד) does not immediately follow upon conceiving (הרה). Tamar thus joins the company of the other two women in Genesis whose childbearing experiences are interrupted: Hagar and Rebekah. In their stories, the interval between conception and birth (16:4–14; 25:22–23) consists primarily in a divine revelation that affirms the significance of the impending birth. Unlike Hagar and Rebekah, however, Tamar receives no divine word between the time of her conception and childbirth. Tamar, like Judah's wife, evokes parallels with previous wives of the patriarchs—parallels in which the matriarchal motifs are *ironized*, for they foreground a basic difference in Tamar's (as also in Judah's wife's) experience: God is not present.

Righteousness (צדק)

Three months after Judah's encounter with the woman on the roadside, and after his unsuccessful attempt via Hirah to pay her and to retrieve his pledge items, he is called to see (הנה) that Tamar has conceived from fornication (זנונים) (v. 24).[134] Again ignorant to the full reality underlying appearances, he sentences Tamar to be burned. As his command moves toward realization, however, Tamar reveals the pledge items and asks Judah to recognize (נכר) to whom they belong (v. 25). Judah recognizes (נכר), but the text lacks a direct object, thus raising the question: what

---

133. As Menn notes, "Elsewhere in the Bible, these verbs denoting sexual activity appear with masculine subjects" (*Judah and Tamar*, 98).

134. Bird, *Missing Persons*, 205. Bird observes the ironic double-standard of Judah's actions, which is flagged by a lexical equivalence (זנה): when he identifies an anonymous prostitute (זנה) by the roadside, he makes a proposition; when he hears that his daughter-in-law has committed an act of fornication (זנה), he issues a death-sentence.

exactly does Judah recognize? Himself? (Tamar's construction would suggest as much—"to *whom* . . . ?") The pledge items? Who his daughter-in-law is (and has been)? How he has wronged her in neglecting his (apparent) levirate obligation? Perhaps the ambiguity of what or whom Judah recognizes plays on the breadth of Judah's ignorance. That is, so much of what Judah has seen, he has mistaken; there is much for him to recognize. If this truly does serve as a recognition scene for Judah, a time for the opening of his own eyes, then it may be impossible to limit his recognition to any one element.

Once Judah's eyes are opened and he can see things as they are, he pronounces that Tamar is more righteous (צדק) than he is. Immediately Judah's words might assume an ironic tone, as his questionable conduct throughout the story—withholding Tamar from Er, joining with an apparent prostitute—diminishes the worth of the pronouncement. How much is it really saying to say that Tamar has been more righteous than Judah? Even so, the motif of righteousness is further *ironized* in the context of its associations. The root צדק almost always indexes a character's relationship with God.[135] (Indeed, the only other characters to whom righteousness is attributed by another, either a character or the narrator, are Noah and Abraham,[136] both of whom enjoy a close rapport with the divine character.) More specifically, it connotes the ancestral–divine relationship: as God muses earlier in an interior monologue, צדקה characterizes how the ancestral family should conduct itself in order to keep the way of God so that God may fulfill his promise to Abraham (18:19). Heard alongside these undertones, the motif of righteousness rings hollow in Judah's proclamation. The story's deviations from ancestral precedent and God's absence from Tamar's plight intimate that her righteousness—unconventional in itself[137]—falls short of its lofty precedents.

---

135. E.g., Gen 6:9; 7:1; 14:18; 15:6. The root צדק functions otherwise (before Gen 38) only in 30:33, where the term applies to the relation between Jacob and Laban.

136. Abimelech does refer to his people as righteous, but more in a manner that identifies them as a part of his own person rather than as separate others (20:4).

137. Posing as a prostitute to have sexual relations with one's father-in-law (if this were indeed Tamar's intention) hardly suggests itself as the conventional picture of righteousness.

Twin Childbirth (תאומים)

The Tamar interlude ends with the birth of twins. Numerous readers have noted the parallel between this account and its only precedent, the twin births of Esau and Jacob (תאומים; 25:24; 38:27).[138] Menn explores the correspondence between the two scenes:

> Each refers to the time of delivery for the mother (לדתה, Gen 38:27; ללדת, Gen 25:24), contains an exclamation of visual surprise (והנה, Gen 38:27; 25:24), and notes that there were twins in the woman's belly (תאומים בבטנה, Gen 38:27; תומם בבטנה, Gen 25:24). Following these opening announcements, the focus in each case turns directly to the twins, who become the main subjects of the action, and away from the mother, who is usually the subject of the verbs in birth scenes.[139]

Menn also identifies a number of common words and themes, including "attention to the actions of the 'hand'" as a determinant of birth order, the color red, and a name connoting "disruption and prominence."[140]

Menn speculates that the correspondence, taken as an "intentional allusion," "legitimates Tamar, whose impersonation of a prostitute and unconventional conception through intercourse with her father-in-law may otherwise devalue her in the reader's mind."[141] The absence of divine involvement, however, challenges this reading—which in any case appears to derive in part from a retrospective perspective that accounts for "Tamar's position as the ancestress of an important lineage"[142]—and suggests the opposite, namely that Tamar's conduct and its consequences are not divinely legitimated. In other words, the twin childbirth motifs allude to a divinely ordained birth and are thus *ironized* in the circumstances of Tamar. As conspicuous as God is in Rebekah's conception and course of childbearing, so he is absent in the same phase preceding Zerah and Perez's births.

---

138. Menn, *Judah and Tamar*, 90. Menn observes that the births of Esau and Jacob and Zerah and Perez are the only two depictions of twin births in the Hebrew Bible.

139. Menn, *Judah and Tamar*, 90.

140. Menn, *Judah and Tamar*, 91.

141. Menn, *Judah and Tamar*, 94.

142. Menn, *Judah and Tamar*, 94.

The Direction of Allusion

As the foregoing exploration has demonstrated, the ancestral birth narrative motifs are incongruous with the Tamar interlude. Thus the question presents itself: what attitude does the story take toward the motifs that it cites? What is the direction of allusion? Are the motifs ironized by the story? Does the story show the motifs to be lies, suggestions that mislead from the story's reality? Or do the motifs themselves ironize the story? Do they suggest that the story is not as it appears, that there is more to it than meets the eye?

A simple example of irony might help to illustrate the directional variability of incongruous allusions. Consider that a family's house has been burned to the ground and that, upon returning to the site one year after the fire, one family member quotes the old adage, "There's no place like home." One can easily interpret the adage as being *ironized* by circumstance. Expressed in the context of the destroyed house (which here connotes home), the quoted proverb fails to resonate with its full meaning. The family member, rather, conveys a measure of dissociation toward the idea that this "home" is a place treasured above all others. The adage, however, can also be interpreted as *ironizing* the circumstance. In a sense, the ironic quotation marks that enclose the adage turn inside out: the circumstance becomes that which is quoted, ironized. In this case, the adage conveys a measure of dissociation toward the expected disappointment attendant on the destruction of a house, suggesting that even in this unpleasant circumstance the "home" remains a place treasured above all others. Perhaps the immaterial—memories, associations, and so on—elevates the home above the fate of its material existence.

Like this adage, the motifs in the Tamar interlude can aim ironically in opposite directions. If the motifs are ironized by the story, then they function as allusions to dissociate the Tamar interlude from the typical ancestral birth story. Their motivic associations fail to take root, and the story exposes them as frauds, as intruders with no real claim to the story. By rejecting the motifs, the story rejects the fullness of their meaning. The failed motifs, in this case, imply a failed ancestral birth story, where each analogous component falls short of the original. The motifs suggest that the story is something of a parody of an ancestral birth narrative—where "parody" means an imitation that fails to live up to the original, that is, an imitation that is evaluated negatively in relation to the original.

If, on the other hand, the motifs ironize the story, then they function as allusions to suggest the story's illusion. That is, the ironic quotation marks turn inside out, and the assumptions and expectations that previous stories have invested the motifs with combat the assumptions and expectations of the present story. The motifs insist that there is more than meets the eye, that the story (strictly speaking) does not tell the whole story. They populate the story with memories, associations, and connotations that transform the story. What first sounds like a rather unancestral story resounds with motivic undertones and overtones that indicate otherwise.

It remains, then, to explore the Tamar interlude's relation to the collection of motifs. How might the motifs be ironized? How might they ironize? The first question leads to a reading of the Tamar interlude as a parody of an ancestral birth narrative, in the sense of a substandard imitation. The interlude's failure to live into the ancestral associations of the motifs would render it a sort of exception that proves the rule in terms of ancestral identity. As a decidedly unancestral story, it would accentuate and reinforce ancestral identity. The second question, conversely, points the way forward for reading a thematic development of ancestral identity. The motifs would trace the outlines of an ancestral story around what appears to be an unancestral episode, thus reconfiguring what passes for ancestral.

A Parody of an Ancestral Birth Narrative

As the preceding exploration of the ancestral motifs in the Tamar interlude demonstrates, the motifs, when taken individually, are ironized by the incongruous circumstances of the story. The assumptions and expectations that inhabit each motif clash with the reality of the story, and the motifs are unable to find full embodiment. The ironized motifs thus stage a sort of parody: Judah, God, and Tamar become the cast of a stunted, distorted ancestral birth narrative.

As a patriarch, Judah falls short on several points. As the motifs of patriarchal migration and marriage make clear, Judah diverges from the precedent of his forebears: he migrates, but turns aside to a foreign man rather than to the worship of God; he marries, but against the endogamous ideal of his grandfather and great-grandfather. His manner of relations, both divine and human, does not command respect in terms of patriarchal precedent. One might add to these shortcomings his parenting and his manner of relating to Tamar. His first two sons, both of whom fail to fulfill his hope for another generation of offspring, are the first (and only) ancestral characters singled out by God for their wickedness. Then, after Judah's first wife dies, he "turns aside" again (38:16), this time in an encounter redolent with bridal motifs that are ironized against the backdrop of a rather bizarre conjugal union, if one can even call it that. Although Judah and Tamar's union ultimately yields what previous ancestral unions have—continuation of the family line—Judah is completely ignorant of the event's significance in any appropriate sense. He perceives the encounter neither as marriage, nor even as a reunion with his own daughter-in-law: rather, in his ignorance, he sees only a prostitute. Whereas in previous betrothals, the identities of both parties are foregrounded in a scene of recognition (24:63–67; 29:9–20), here the encounter—at least from Judah's perspective—is one of anonymity and insignificance. Compounding the irony of this bridal scene are the internal motifs of the procreative sequence. Several noteworthy changes to the sequence flag Tamar's initiative and dominance, implying that Judah now cannot do even the one thing that earlier he had done successfully—procreate. Thus Judah fails as a patriarch: he does not acknowledge God, he does not marry endogamously, the bridal scene in which he appears is anything but a proper ancestral marriage, and his procreative agency shifts hands to a woman.

Tamar assumes a position in the parodic cast through her sheer difference from matriarchal precedent. Ethnically and familially unidentified, her origin presumably lies outside the ancestral family (the story's setting would suggest that she is Canaanite).[143] While she admittedly resembles the matriarchs in her initiative and cunning—particularly in her exploitation of the semiotic means of sight—her lack of divine endorsement and the utterly unconventional means by which she achieves her ends sets her apart. Whereas God helps previous matriarchs, his character ostensibly opposes Tamar. Killing her first two partners, he apparently absconds when Tamar might be said to need him most. That Tamar receives Judah's approbation and attribution of righteousness underscores

---

143. Menn speculates that the absence of explicit identification "may actually reflect the narrator or redactor's attempt to shield Tamar and her relations with Judah from the pejorative force of the biblical laws and narratives condemning intermarriage with Canaanites" (*Judah and Tamar*, 54).

the strangeness of her character. Tamar's righteousness, on the surface of things, is certainly of a different sort than Noah's and Abraham's.

God takes his place in the parodic cast in a rather different way than Judah and Tamar. Whereas their *actions* foreground their limitations, God's relative *absence* accentuates another sense of shortcoming. The several cases of childbearing are perhaps the most notable instances of divine absence. The spate of childbirths that Judah's wife enjoys at the story's beginning draws parallels with the matriarchs' childbirths, particularly Leah's, and yet they differ in one key way: the divine character is not implicated in any way. Similarly, Tamar's course of childbearing parallels Hagar's and Rebekah's in multiple ways, but again Tamar's case is distinguished by the absence of God. Tamar's procreative quandary further distinguishes this difference inasmuch as the resolution, which in past procreative dilemmas has originated from divine intervention, comes solely by means of her own work. God's character falls short of expectations not only in his absence in the procreative and childbearing process, but also in his brief cameo appearance. Instead of multiplying ancestral offspring, God deducts from their numbers—killing Er and Onan. Thus, in several ways, God assumes a position that is lacking in comparison to his typical relationship to the matriarch and patriarch: not implicated in the childbearing process, and absent from the resolution to the procreative conflict, he appears only in order to subtract from, rather than multiply, the ancestral offspring.

Together, Judah, Tamar, and God embody the Tamar interlude's parody of an ancestral birth narrative. This is what a birth narrative looks like when the patriarch is unpatriarchal, the matriarch is a presumably foreign woman lacking divine support, and God is antagonistic and absent to the procreative plight. This, in other words, is anything but an ancestral birth narrative.

Thus the difference of the Tamar interlude, by showing what is unancestral, would serve to rigidify ancestral identity. In particular, the parodic illustrations of Judah, Tamar, and God would reinforce the traditional representation of matriarchal and patriarchal identity[144]—which

144. The narrative never identifies characters as "matriarch" or "patriarch." These titles are interpretive labels. This study applies them not in a positivist fashion—that is, it does not set about the project of identifying the mothers and fathers of a specific lineage—but rather heuristically, as a way of referring to a certain construction of character. That is, by identifying an attribute as "matriarchal" or "patriarchal," it associates that attribute with a type of character, a type, furthermore, that takes root in the first mothers and fathers of the ancestral lineage. Cf. Nicol, who entertains the narrative

includes patriarchal and matriarchal relations to the divine—and the ideal of endogamy. In contrast to Judah, a true patriarch demonstrates and inculcates an appreciation for God and refrains from mixing with foreigners. In contrast to Tamar, a true matriarch comes from within the family and enjoys divine aid in her procreative plight. In contrast to Judah and Tamar's union, a true ancestral union is endogamous.

Thematic Development: Ancestral Self-Identity

The incongruity between the Tamar interlude and the individual motifs yields a basic proposition: that the Tamar interlude is a parody of an ancestral birth narrative. Ironic quotation marks enclose each motif, pointing out that it does not accord with its narrative context and resolving it by doubting or rejecting its motivic implications. Yet these ironic quotation marks, like quotation marks in general, are not entirely stable.

Voloshinov, who took great interest in the relation between the quoting context and the quoted text in instances of reported speech, explains that in some cases, "the verbal dominant may shift to the reported speech, which in that case becomes more forceful and more active than the authorial context framing it. This time the reported speech begins to resolve, as it were, the reporting context, instead of the other way around."[145] Transposing this observation to the situation of motifs, one might reach a similar conclusion: if the motifs achieve a level of coherence that rivals the narrative that cites them, then they might offer a semantic alternative to that narrative. The motifs might resolve the narrative, rather than vice versa. Bakhtin affirms this potential shift from ironized (or "parodied") discourse to ironizing discourse:

> [A] heightening of activity on the part of the [parodied] discourse is also possible. When parody senses a fundamental resistance, a certain strength and depth to the parodied words of the other, the parody becomes complicated by tones of hidden polemic. Such parody already has a different sound to it. The

---

invitation to compare elements with their perceived precedents: "At [the] second or subsequent occurrence [of a narrative element], the reader 'remembers' that such a feature has been encountered already and may be invited to reflect upon the earlier occurrence(s) as an element of narrative context" ("Story-Patterning in Genesis," 224).

145. Voloshinov, *Marxism and the Philosophy of Language*, 121.

parodied discourse rings out more actively, exerts a counterforce against the author's intentions.[146]

Bakhtin in effect acknowledges the irrelevance of intention. Regardless of what an author or narrator might be argued to mean, the consistency and cogency of ironized elements may afford them a power of their own, may facilitate their transformation into a "counterforce." Thus, regardless of how one reads the narrator in the Tamar interlude, if the ancestral birth narrative motifs coalesce in a meaningful narrative of their own, then they might be read not to serve the purpose of parody but instead to offer a counternarrative to it. They would contest the embedding narrative that casts them as misfits and argue that it is the embedding narrative, the parodic appearance of things, that is ironic.

The numerous ancestral motifs of the Tamar interlude indeed take on a different tone, or become "complicated by tones of hidden polemic," when heard cumulatively, in concert, rather than as isolated motifs. As incongruous as the motifs are with the plot, so they are congruent with one another. Like the intermeshed teeth in a series of gears, their motivic associations form a consistent, coherent semantic alternative to the depiction of a rather unancestral episode.[147] Together the motifs reminisce about ancestral birth narratives in which the patriarch, the matriarch, and God all play important roles in preserving the ancestral lineage. The motifs of patriarchal migration and marriage recall the divinely affirmed sojourns of Abraham, Isaac, and Jacob, and the marriages of Isaac and Jacob to women hailing from a different land. The motif of matriarchal initiative, in collaboration with the significance of sight in Tamar's experience, echoes the self-motivated character of the matriarchs. The numerous motifs of childbearing, as well as the motifs of bridal imagery and twin-bearing that invoke specific memories of Rebekah and Isaac's marriage, conjure up stories of divinely affirmed childbirth. The motifs of offspring, multiplication, and opening bring to mind the divine promise

---

146. Bakhtin, *Problems of Dostoevsky's Poetics*, 198.

147. It is worth pointing out that other studies have highlighted the motivic associations between Gen 38 and other stories in the ancestral narrative and have come to a similar conclusions, namely that the motifs in Gen 38 are ironizing rather than ironized. Perhaps the best example of such a study is Jackson's "Lot's Daughters and Tamar as Tricksters." Focusing more on patriarchal hegemony than on ancestral identity, she postulates that the motifs in Gen 38 (and in the story of Lot's daughters) collaborate with those in other stories of female tricksters (e.g., Rebekah, Leah, Rachel) to present a comic vision that subverts the patriarchal structures that dominate the ancestral narrative.

of multiplied offspring and the divine agency facilitating that promise, overcoming the procreative complications that beset the matriarchs. The motif of righteousness recollects its previous exemplars and particularly the divine prescription of righteousness as the mode of ancestral conduct by which God's promises will be realized. Marriage, matriarchal initiative, childbearing, the divine promise of offspring and divine agency facilitating it, righteousness as an ancestral trait—these images of past matriarchs and patriarchs materialize in the collaboration of the motifs, offering the pieces to a compelling counternarrative to what is ostensibly an unancestral story. Invoking these interrelated ancestral birth stories, the motifs can be read as a collective *ironizing* force, inverting the ironic quotation marks and thus questioning the proposition that the Tamar interlude is a parody of an ancestral birth story.[148]

The way that the ancestral birth narrative motifs collaborate and ironize what appears to be an unancestral story might be further illumined with a brief analogy. The cumulative ironizing effect of the motifs is like the effect of the following description: "It is covered in fur, but it's not a cat. It has a tail, but it's not a cat. It has whiskers, but it's not a cat. It pounces on mice, but it's not a cat." And so on. While the description insists, "It's not a cat," the descriptive contents, when taken together, suggest that it *is* a cat. So too the repeated failure of the individual motifs of the Tamar interlude insists on one thing while the motifs' collaboration suggests another. That is, the interlude continually contests the ancestral birth narrative motifs—insisting that the narrative is not an ancestral birth story—while the motifs collectively propose the contrary.

As a collective ironizing force, the ancestral birth narrative motifs not only transform the interlude. They are themselves transformed and thereby contribute to the thematic development of the ancestral narrative. Just as an episode of a sonata-rondo weds assorted motifs from the refrains in a new and unfamiliar context, thus contributing to their and the refrains' development, so the Tamar interlude may be heard to join together various ancestral birth narrative motifs in its own peculiar circumstance, in the process developing new associations and implications for the ancestral birth narrative. Heard as elements of a genuine, if rather

---

148. Tarlin, "Tamar's Veil," 174–81. Tarlin effectively observes the interpretive possibility of reading the irony of Gen 38 in two directions, though she reads not in terms of ancestral identity but rather the Israelite system of patriarchy. For her, Gen 38 can be a parodic comedy that affirms Israelite patriarchy (in spite of its less-than-ideal patriarch), or a satire that implies its eventual doom.

strange, ancestral birth narrative, the motifs realize new possibilities within themselves. They partake in new harmonies and melodic progressions. The motifs of patriarchal migration and matriarchal procreative conflict, for instance, culminate in exogamous union rather than a divine event. The matriarchal motifs of marriage and childbearing find association with a presumably Canaanite woman rather than a woman from within the ancestral family. The motifs of offspring, multiplication, and opening here mark the potential for procreative conflict to proceed in a manner opposite to expectations: rather than deriving from the human problem of barrenness and finding resolution through divine intervention, it derives from God, who kills Er and Onan, and finds resolution in the human agency of Tamar. Thus, even as the motifs join together and show the interlude to be a part of the ancestral story, their own transformation stretches the conventional boundaries of the ancestral story by developing its themes.

In particular, the motifs ironize two thematic cornerstones of ancestral self-identity: first, the traditional embodiment of matriarchal and patriarchal identity, which includes matriarchal and patriarchal relations to the divine character, and second, the ideal of endogamy. Both themes are founded on the distinction between ancestral insider and outsider, and therefore both themes give way as the motifs present a counternarrative that "relate[s] and relativize[s]" the traditional identities of ancestral insiders and outsiders.[149] As the motifs assume new thematic relations and associations, they invite a dynamic reconfiguration of the boundaries that delineate what is matriarchal and patriarchal and what is a proper mode of preserving the ancestral lineage.

This reconfiguration transpires circuitously. First, the motifs, which individually appear ironized, depict the interlude's characters as outsiders. Then, as the motifs cohere with one another and the story transfigures

---

149. Hutcheon explores irony's "transideological" character, its ability to be interpreted as destructive ("seen to finalize and exclude") and constructive. She comments that among its more constructive uses is its function "to relate and relativize" (*Irony's Edge*, 17). It is worth noting, furthermore, that Hutcheon characterizes irony not only as transideological but also as trans-affective. Citing Voloshinov, *Marxism and the Philosophy of Language*, 81, 103, she observes that irony accentuates the "evaluative accent" that a context gives its utterance. In summary, then, irony is intended and interpreted to have alternately constructive and destructive political effects as well as to evaluate positively and negatively. The variability of the motifs' irony in the Tamar interlude—are the motifs ironized or ironizing?—illustrates well irony's transideological and trans-affective character.

into an ancestral birth narrative, they show the characters to be in fact insiders. While this study has already reviewed the ironic capacities of the motifs—how they can be both ironized and ironizing—it is worth briefly attending to their circuitous effect on the identity of the characters in order to illumine the thematic reconfiguration at work.

At first, heard against the tones of the ironized motifs, the cast of the Tamar interlude seems to consist of ancestral outsiders, characters at variance with their matriarchal and patriarchal precedents. Judah, the closest thing to an insider by virtue of his heritage, goes outside his family, outside the practice of acknowledging God in migration, and outside the bounds of his forefathers' marriage prohibition; later he goes outside the conventional procreative sequence, as Tamar takes control and dictates its proceedings. Judah's sons push Judah's family even further to the outside: by acting in a manner with strong parallels to the wickedness of the antediluvian earth and the people of the Plain cities, they incite God to act toward the ancestral family in a way contrary to precedent. Er and Onan essentially effect the conversion of their family from insider to outsider, inasmuch as their actions lead to the opposite of traditional ancestral–divine relations. Instead of fulfilling his promise to deliver offspring to the ancestral family, God delivers death. Tamar is the most obvious outsider, assuming this role in multiple senses. Entering the story as an outsider with no ethnic or familial identification, she finds herself pushed further outside through expulsion from the ancestral family, at which point she takes on the liminal identity of a prostitute. God does not resolve her dilemma; she takes matters into her own hands. Furthermore, one might consider God himself to be an outsider, as he acts outside—that is, against—the promise of increased ancestral offspring. He is also an outsider in his absence; he is literally outside the narration of most of the story.

As the motifs begin to harmonize, they collectively cast these outsider characters together in a story that looks more and more like an ancestral birth narrative, thus suggesting that the characters are more than meets the eye, that they may even be insiders. Despite defining these characters more by their divergence from ancestral motifs, by their difference from ancestral identity,[150] than by any positive identity,[151] the Tamar interlude embraces their difference. If it were to identify its bizarre plot as an ancestral birth narrative, it would arguably diminish its characters' difference, suggesting the characters to be more of an anomaly, an exception that proves the rule, rather than representative parts of the ancestral birth narrative. Through irony, the interlude says—or rather says without saying—that this difference is meaningful. Thus the circumstances of Tamar, Judah, and a non-present God are not a parody, nor do they merely point back to the archetypal roles of the ancestral birth narrative. The ancestral birth narrative, rather, is suggestively stretched by them. Even as the motifs harmonize and show the interlude to be a part of the ancestral story, they also realize new thematic possibilities and show how matriarchal and patriarchal identity and the ancestral mode of preserving the lineage can be reconfigured. Judah, despite his foibles and unorthodox mixing with people of the land, becomes a "patriarch"; Tamar, despite her presumably non-ancestral background and her uncommon relations, becomes a "matriarch"; their one-time union, despite its exogamous nature, is affirmed; and, furthermore, God, despite his absence and seemingly antagonistic behavior, would appear to trust in the unconventional agencies of this patriarch and matriarch.

This ironic stretching of matriarchal and patriarchal identity pervades the refrains of the ancestral narrative. Hearing the episode of the Tamar interlude provokes a rehearing of the themes of self-identity elsewhere in the narrative. The irony of the interlude suggests a negative

150. This idea originates in Sharp's treatment of Tamar's femininity. Sharp employs Judith Butler's concept of the feminine as difference rather than identity. In the case of Gen 38, each character finds form in the motifs that allude to previous matriarchs and patriarchs. Taken individually, each motif is ironized in its context. The characters of Gen 38 appear different from those to whom the allusions point.

151. It is noteworthy that several narrative absences leave the characters undefined in key ways: the absence of Tamar's ethnic identity, the absence of indication of Judah's place among Jacob's sons (in contrast to the more or less explicit mentions of filial hierarchy in the Abraham and Jacob stories), and the absence of God in the resolution to the procreative dilemma. In themselves, these absences are negative. They offer no positive determination to the relevant aspects of the characters' identity. (E.g., God's narrative absence is not the same thing as the narrative explicitly relating, "God was absent from the scene.") The interplay between these absences and the invocation of a number of interrelated ancestral birth stories stretches the possibilities for interpretation. Perhaps Tamar is a Canaanite, but perhaps she is also a "matriarch." Perhaps Judah conducts himself contrary to his forefathers' ideals and is not selected explicitly as an heir to the promise, but perhaps he is nonetheless a "patriarch." Perhaps God is not present in the way that he typically is, but perhaps he is not determinately absent.

evaluation of these themes' conventional significance and invites a more inclusive perspective on ancestral self-identity calibrated along the examples of Judah and Tamar. Although the extent of this study will not allow for a full exploration of how this new perspective might illumine the rest of the ancestral narrative, it is worth running through a few examples to demonstrate the interlude's ironic effect on the narrative refrains' representations of patriarchal and matriarchal identity and endogamy.

Proceeding from the hint of Judah's patriarchal status, one might consider the idea that he is in fact more of a patriarch than Isaac and Jacob inasmuch as his behavior conforms more than theirs to God's original call to Abram to leave his "land" and "kindred" (12:1). Isaac and Jacob's marriages adhere to their own predilection for endogamy, but arguably contravene the original divine call. Their wives come from the land and kindred of their forefather Terah.[152] Besides conforming to the original divine call, Judah's behavior also complies with what might be considered the original patriarchal mode of interethnic relations. Abram assimilates with the people of the land, as is apparent in his alliance with the Amorite brothers, Aner, Eshcol, and Mamre (14:13, 24; cf. the ancestral station at Mamre's oaks in 18:1, 35:27) and his shared terms of theological discourse with King Melchizedek of Salem (both speak of the divine as "God Most High [אל עליון]"; 14:18, 22). More than Isaac or Jacob, Judah too mixes with the inhabitants of the land—associating with Hirah the Adullamite, marrying a Canaanite, and joining with the unidentified Tamar. In more ways than one, Judah's conduct adheres to patriarchal precedent better than the conduct of the preceding patriarchs themselves.

Proceeding from the hint of Tamar's matriarchal status, one might consider that non-ancestral background is more integral to the matriarchal position than it first appears. Tammi J. Schneider observes a contrast between the narrative presentation of the wives of Terah's sons, Abram and Nahor. The narrative details the history of Nahor's wife, Milcah: she is the daughter of Haran, quite possibly the same Haran as Terah's third son. She would appear to come from within the family, then, and thus Milcah's marriage to her would qualify as endogamous. Sarai, on the other hand, is "an outsider" with no history (and no apparent future).[153]

152. Brett, *Genesis*, 50. Brett sees the equivalence of language in God's call in 12:1 and Abraham's instruction to his servant in 24:4 as an implicit indictment of Abraham's endogamous preference: whereas God told him to leave his land and kindred, he tells his servant to return to his land and kindred (to retrieve a wife for Isaac).

153. Schneider, *Sarah*, 17–18. Cf. Jeansonne, *The Women of Genesis*, 14. See also

This seed of ambiguity concerning Sarai's origin feeds speculation as to why Abraham shows little regard for her safety. (Is it because she can bear no sons? Or is it because she is not from the family, not as valued as those who are?—e.g., Lot, whose safety may be seen as the primary reason for Abraham's plea for Sodom [cf. 18:23–33, 19:29].) It also suggests, however, that Tamar, more than Rebekah, Rachel, and Leah, conforms to matriarchal precedent: like Sarai, she is presumably an outsider, as she remains familially (and ethnically) unidentified. Like Judah, Tamar's character echoes more resonantly with the original outline of ancestral identity, suggesting that she is even more matriarchal than the matriarchs themselves.[154]

Proceeding from the hint of affirmation of Judah and Tamar's exogamous union, finally, one might consider that endogamous marriage may not have as strong roots in precedent as the forefathers' predilection for it suggests. Most notably, the divine character never prescribes endogamy; indeed, the initial call to Abram to leave his land and kindred would suggest divine indifference, if not opposition, to the idea.[155] In addition, other notable men in the ancestral family marry either exogamously or ambiguously in terms of familial relation. For instance, besides his union with Hagar, Abraham takes the familially unidentified Keturah for a wife (25:1); Joseph takes the Egyptian Asenath as wife (41:45) and fathers two sons who later receive Jacob's blessing (48:20); and perhaps most intriguingly, Simeon, whose violence against the Hivites might be interpreted as ethnic exclusivism, has a Canaanite wife (46:10). Endogamy as a rule, it would appear, crumbles when scrutinized in terms of its lack of divine endorsement and its subtle incorporation into ancestral practice.

Frymer-Kensky, "Sarah 1/Sarai," 150–51. Frymer-Kensky problematizes the common counterargument to Sarah's outsiderness—namely, that Abraham identifies her as his half-sister—by pointing out that the narrative identifies her as Terah's daughter-in-law rather than daughter (11:31).

154. The argument for Tamar's ancestral affinities, if not her matriarchal exemplarity, is not uncommon, but it rarely sustains the comparison beyond a few similarities. For an extended argument, see Kim, "A Literary-Critical Analysis," 221–48, 274–75. Kim which explores a number of the thematic elements indicated in this study—including the procreative dilemma, hidden origins of genealogy, trickery, veiling, and the birth of twins—and proposes the idea of Tamar as "the fifth matriarch." For other, shorter cases, see Sharp, *Irony and Meaning*, 93; Menn, *Judah and Tamar*, 94; Frymer-Kensky, *Reading the Women of the Bible*, 276; Turner, *Genesis*, 168; Brett, *Genesis*, 114.

155. Brett, *Genesis*, 91.

Thus the Tamar interlude contributes to the ancestral narrative's thematic development. Invoking a host of motifs from ancestral birth narratives, it defamiliarizes them and thereby invests them with new meaning. The motifs no longer contain matriarchal and patriarchal identity and ancestral marriage within the same boundaries as before. They ironize the traditional formulations of identity—the formulations according to which the Tamar interlude appears unancestral—and suggest a reconfiguration. Their suggestion pervades the ancestral narrative. Wherever motifs such as the barren matriarch, the migrating patriarch, or ancestral marriage are heard or reheard, there too are heard overtones of Tamar, Judah, and their renowned union, rupturing the conventional definitions of ancestral self-identity and inviting a reconsideration of what it means to be matriarchal and patriarchal and to marry ancestrally.

Summary

Conventional readings naturalize the Tamar interlude by treating it as a key to a principal concern of the surrounding narrative. They find resolution to the question of agency—who is in control of events, God or humans?—in the events of the interlude, which are read to showcase divine providence, a wholly human drama, or, conversely, a story that disregards the causes of events in favor of their effects, namely those that determine the matter of ancestral inheritance. A host of motifs within the interlude, however, suggests that the story is more than an interpretive key to the embedding narrative, that it assumes a significance of its own. Alluding to previous ancestral birth narratives, albeit in defamiliarized fashion, the collective of motifs cast the Tamar interlude as its own kind of ancestral birth narrative. The noticeable difference between the Tamar interlude and other ancestral birth narratives invite an ironic reading. Either the distorted motifs reveal the interlude to be a stunted imitation, a failure of a birth narrative. Or they ironize the original contours of the ancestral birth narrative, relativizing them and suggesting their own reconfiguration. The latter reading finds confirmation particularly in the accumulation and congruence of the motifs in the Tamar interlude. Together they may be heard as a harmonized countermelody, a strain that objects to the traditional representation of matriarchal and patriarchal identity and the concomitant ideal of endogamy.

Conclusion

Having advanced a poetics of the interlude and a hermeneutics of irony, and demonstrated how these might contribute to close readings of the strange stories of Hagar, Dinah, and Tamar, this study now approaches its end. This conclusion duly assumes the task of summarizing this study, remarking on its implications for further research, and drawing to a close with one final word.

What Are the Strange Stories Doing in the Ancestral Narrative?

The ancestral narrative is a story about the ancestral family. It blends together tales of scheming mothers, contending brothers, genealogical others, sojourning, and confrontation with the land's occupiers, harmonizing them all under the interests of the ancestral family as it marches forward toward the divine promises. The stories of Hagar, Dinah, and Tamar, however, ring dissonantly against this narrative backdrop. Their strangeness—their disjunction with the surrounding plot and their alternative subjectivities—unsettles the natural unification of the ancestral narrative. Thus the strange stories commonly assume the title "interlude." These stories stand out. They are different. It follows, then, to ask: just what are they doing in the ancestral narrative?

As this study has demonstrated, interpretation traditionally neglects the full ramifications of this question. It answers, in effect, that the stories are not so strange, that they in fact serve to reinforce the ancestral interests of the narrative, albeit indirectly. Their difference accentuates fundamental concerns of the ancestral narrative, which are often concerns of ancestral identity. According to traditional interpretation, the Hagar interlude foregrounds the special ancestral–divine relationship and the covenantal line that proceeds through Isaac. The Dinah interlude underscores the ultimately exclusivist mode of relations that is to govern the ancestral family's way of living in the promised land. And the Tamar interlude draws attention to the question of divine and human agency and how that plays out in the resolution to the Joseph story.

Moving beyond these traditional readings—which more often than not derive from a quest for original meaning, for the stories' foundational significance—this study embarks on a story of reading that both accounts for conventional interpretation and pushes forward into new territory. That is, it acknowledges how the strange stories have structured interpretation in the past, how previous readers have made sense of the stories, but it also considers how the stories resist conventional interpretation, how alternative interpretations might make better sense out of the stories' strangeness. Indeed, this study strives to attend to the stories' strangeness and to resurrect the question of the stories' narrative function. It privileges their alternate subjectivities and heeds their narratological peculiarities—the *mise en abyme* of sojourn in the Hagar interludes, the voice of the evaluative comments in the Dinah interlude, and the collection of ancestral birth narrative motifs in the Tamar interlude. And it investigates how the stories relate to the ancestral narrative through their appropriation of common ancestral motifs.

Interludes, Irony, and Ancestral Identity

Observing that common ancestral motifs assume unfamiliar associations in the strange stories, this study accordingly submits a thesis that explores how the strange stories defamiliarize the ancestral narrative. In simplified form, the thesis is that *the strange stories might be read as interludes that ironize ancestral identity.* The contribution of this thesis to biblical studies might be summarized along the lines of its radicality—that is, according to the way that this thesis stems from the same roots as traditional interpretation but culminates in different results.[1] In terms of its poetics of the interlude (ch. 1), its hermeneutics of irony (ch. 2), and its close readings of ancestral identity (chs. 3–5), it shares with conventional readings the same starting point, the same roots. But then it diverges to explore other possibilities nurtured by these roots.

---

1. This study identifies its interpretation as "radical" in the sense of the word's derivation from the Latin *radix*, or "root."

In terms of poetics, it picks up on interpretation's tendency to identify the stories as "interludes." Scrutinizing the conceptual possibilities of interlude, particularly as they are outlined in the analogy to music, it advances a more robust sense of interlude, one that takes its cue from the especially suggestive model of the sonata-rondo episode. Whereas traditional scholarship distinguishes the strange stories as interludes in the sense that they are intermediately positioned and secondary in terms of significance, this study demonstrates that they may qualify as interludes in a fuller way. Like the sonata-rondo episode, the Hagar, Dinah, and Tamar interludes are not only intermediate and secondary, but also contrastive and developmental. That is, through their alternate subjectivities they assume a significance of their own, a sort of native significance, that contrasts with the interests of the primary narrative. But they also harbor within themselves thematic strains from the primary narrative, strains that they situate in new relations—new harmonies and melodic progressions. God appears in unexpected relations with characters outside the ancestral family, the land and its inhabitants assume unimagined relations with the ancestral family, and the family's lineage unfolds in unplanned ways. Thus the interludes develop key ancestral themes by showing how they might sound differently than they do in the primary narrative, by exposing their potential to mean differently.

In terms of hermeneutics, this study begins with the common interpretive assumption that these strange stories have something to say about the ancestral family. But whereas conventional interpretation reads the interludes as confirming ancestral identity, this study proceeds from its poetics of the interlude—which appreciates the thematic development in the stories—to demonstrate how that thematic development might be illumined by a hermeneutics of irony. Defining irony as a mode of discourse that consists in quoting a prior proposition and implying a negative judgment toward it, this study points out that the thematic development of each interlude houses significant ironic potential. By invoking ancestral motifs but defamiliarizing them against the backdrop of new, incongruous settings, the interludes invite reevaluation of their meaning. When the interludes resound central ancestral motifs, such as sojourn, the promises of land and universal blessing, and endogamy, they do so in contexts that cast doubt on the motifs' previous associations. Perhaps sojourn does not signify the ancestral family's exclusive status as God's privileged partner; perhaps the promises of land and universal blessing are not as inconsistent as they first appear; perhaps endogamous relations are not the ideal. Irony says what it does not mean. Perhaps when these interludes restate familiar motifs, they mean something different—even contrary—to what was meant before.

In terms of its close readings, this study starts with an illustration of how interpretation conventionally naturalizes the interlude. It retraces previous readings to see how they align the interlude with the interests of the surrounding narrative—how they represent the interlude as a foil, commentary, or key on an important ancestral theme. Then, following a poetics of the interlude that privileges the stories' ironic potential, it introduces alternative readings that expose the stories' subversive capacities. In these readings, ancestral identity looks quite differently than it did before.

In each case, the ironic readings take as their starting point a narratological peculiarity that resists the conventional reading—the *mise en abyme* of Hagar's sojourn, the echo of Dinah's brothers' voice in the evaluative comments on the narrative level, and the collection of ancestral birth narrative motifs in Tamar's story. The readings then trace how these narratological oddities work in concert with the stories' alternative subjectivities to ironize ancestral identity. The presumably exclusive nature of the special divine-ancestral relationship crumbles as the *mise en abyme* of Hagar's sojourn repositions the sojourner, whoever that is, at the center of divine attention and relationship. The brothers' recommendation for an exclusivist mode of relations collapses when the narrator's ironic ventriloquizing of their voice is heard to challenge their perspective and invite a more inclusive alternative, one not unlike that proposed by Shechem and the Hivites. The established matriarchal and patriarchal identities, along with the ideal of endogamy, founder as certain ancestral birth narrative motifs reassemble around the presumably Canaanite Tamar and the wayward Judah in an arrangement that envisions more inclusive matriarchal and patriarchal identities and allows for exogamous relations. In summary, what before looked like an exclusive ancestral identity shows porous and shifting boundaries and opens itself to more inclusive reformulations. Irony relativizes the conventional definition of ancestral identity; the ancestral family's relationships to God, to the land and its inhabitants, and to itself assume a more provisional, permeable character.

Implications for Further Study

Of this study's three main points of focus—the interlude, irony, and ancestral identity—two are already familiar faces within current studies of Genesis. First, recent biblical scholarship has devoted increasing attention to irony, and Genesis in particular has enjoyed much of the spotlight. Sharp's comprehensive survey of irony in the biblical text registers the prominence of Genesis in studies of biblical irony. She finds in Genesis several points worth investigation, including the incongruities of the creation stories, which subvert the stability of discourse; the significance of foreign rulers in the sister-wife stories and the Joseph saga, which ironizes patriarchal claims to power and morality; and the figure of the prostitute, which upsets the institution of patriarchy.[2] Thus she concludes: "Genesis is rife with ironies."[3] Second, recent interest in textual constructions of Israelite and ancestral identity has spurred exploration of the various ways that Genesis might be read to represent identity. The opposing cases presented by Brett, who reads a subversion of both ancestral covenant identity and other forms of exclusivism and dominance,[4] and Heard, who reads a buttressing of covenant identity,[5] perhaps best exemplify this interest, as their dialogue reveals a lively diversity of thought centering in the question of ancestral identity.

Scholarship's acquaintance with questions of irony and identity means that this study does not so much pioneer a new path in this territory; rather, it extends its own voice into a lively dialogue. It speaks against some voices, and joins with others in its implications. On the matter of irony, this study supports the position that the narrative of Genesis—and biblical narrative by extension—meaningfully employs verbal irony. Against Sternberg and likeminded scholars who would wish

---

2. Sharp, *Irony and Meaning*, 35–42, 51–61, 89–97.

3. Sharp, *Irony and Meaning*, 242.

4. Brett summarizes the direction of his argument: "[A]s I have argued, the subtext of the narrative repeatedly throws into question any notion of *covenant* that is rigorously exclusive.... We can at least infer... that the editors of Genesis are rarely content to leave any claim of superiority unchallenged, whether the claim be on superior birth, or on the exclusive favour of the covenant, or on the purity of endogamous marriage" (*Genesis*, 84).

5. Heard summarizes his take: "It is the narrative fact of separateness by divine design... that is the key to Genesis's ideological success" (*The Dynamics of Diselection*, 183). In other words, ancestral/Israelite identity and privilege derive from an inscrutable divine selection, that is, the covenant between God and his people.

to stabilize the biblical narrative, to delimit it to an original meaning that a conscientious, competent reader would not fail to miss,[6] this study exposes loose threads in the narrative where the narrator's straightforwardness becomes questionable. All it takes is one instance of irony to destabilize the entire narrative. In this study, the irony of Hagar's sojourn inaugurates a suspicion of irony, and the Dinah and Tamar interludes validate it, as they further expose the conflicting impulses in the narrative and their capacity for irony. Others who have taken a similar tack in uncovering narrative dissimulation in Genesis include Brett, whose reading of ancestral identity detects within the text an "intentional hybridity" of different voices that puts "the authority of the dominant voice into question";[7] Miles and Bloom, who read a conflicted divine character at once "lofty, unwavering" and "intimate, volatile, and prone to dark regrets and darker equivocations";[8] and countless feminists who read a subversion of patriarchy in many of the stories involving matriarchs and other women.[9] The implication of this study and readings such as these, then, is the variability of interpretation. Whether their object be ancestral identity, the character of God, the institution of patriarchy, or another theme yet to be explored, readings that demonstrate meaningful thematic incongruities attest to the openness of interpretation, the manner in which the words of the narrative may be legitimately read to different effect.

On the matter of identity, this study promotes the viewpoint that Genesis sketches an inclusive and unresolved ancestral identity. It opposes the common interpretation that the ancestral identity prefigures the

---

6. Sternberg posits that the narrator "is absolutely and straightforwardly reliable" and does not engage in verbal irony. This notion forms an integral part of his concept of the biblical text as a "foolproof composition," that is, a text that guides its readers to a common ground. He summarizes: "[T]he Bible is difficult to read, easy to underread and overread and even misread, but virtually impossible to, so to speak, counterread" (*The Poetics of Biblical Narrative*, 51).

7. Brett, *Genesis*, 22.

8. Miles, *God*, 38. Cf. Bloom, who suggests that the "high, even exalted irony that is the continuous condition of the Book of J" centers in "the representation of Yahweh as at once human-all-too-human, even childlike, even childish, and yet Yahweh and none other, which is to say, wholly incommensurate even with himself" (*The Book of J*, 25–26).

9. E.g., Trible, *Texts of Terror*; Exum, *Fragmented Women*; Fewell and Gunn, *Gender, Power, and Promise*; Davies, *The Dissenting Reader*; Jeansonne, *The Women of Genesis*; Frymer-Kensky, *Reading the Women of the Bible*; Schneider, *Mothers of Promise*; Jackson, *Comedy and Feminist Interpretation of the Hebrew Bible*.

relatively exclusive formulations of Israelite identity. The interpretation that the ancestral family is a pure lineage that is specially chosen by God for exclusive inheritance of the land appears to derive its strength from retrospection—that is, from reading subsequent narrative elements back into the narrative of Genesis—or theological premises. In other words, because definitions of Israelite identity often insist (sometimes violently so) on the separateness of the people of Israel, or because God's involvement in biblical narrative seems to reflect a pattern of divine election, readers assume an exclusive ancestral identity. This study, however, situates itself alongside readings whose close attention to the particularity of Genesis yields a very different understanding. In addition to Brett's interpretation of intentional hybridity, other less narratologically inclined readings observe a basic disjunction between the cultural and religious practice of the ancestral family in Genesis and that of Israel in the narrative that follows. Moberly, for instance, who reads with an interest in historical-critical matters, observes the "non-Israelite" subjectivity that inheres in much of the ancestral narrative: "[T]here is much in the patriarchal stories that is not told in Israel's terms but retains its own distinctiveness."[10] The primary implication of this study and readings such as Moberly's is to maintain the particularity of ancestral identity, to differentiate it from Israelite identity. It is to remind the familiar reader not to get ahead of herself, to remain open to unfamiliar aspects of the ancestral family. Israel realizes the potential of ancestral identity in one way, but the ancestral narrative itself intimates other possibilities.

Thus, this study's investigation of irony and ancestral identity does not so much raise questions as it does suggestions. It points out paths that have already been cleared and affirms the value of beginning an interpretive venture on them. Nevertheless, this study also trailblazes a new path, and in the process it raises questions about how trekkers may continue this path beyond the endpoint of this study. This new path, along with the questions it raises for further research, proceeds from the innovation of a poetics of the interlude. If the "interludes" of Hagar, Dinah, and Tamar can be read according to a richer conceptualization, one that appreciates the interlude's developmental capacity, then what about other "interludes" in Genesis? This study limited its analysis to the strange stories of Hagar, Dinah, and Tamar because they distinguish themselves in their alternate

10. Moberly, *Genesis 12–50*, 15–16. Elsewhere Moberly gives an account of "patriarchal religion," much of which registers the difference between ancestral identity and later Israelite identity (*Genesis 12–50*, 84–87).

subjectivity; that is, not only do they deviate from the ancestral plotline, they also grant a considerable level of attention to non-ancestral subjects. But there are other strange stories in the narrative, stories that for one reason or another prompt scholars to identify them as "interludes." Might not they, like the stories of Hagar, Dinah, and Tamar, harbor within them elements that develop and determine the surrounding narrative? Might not they defamiliarize a familiar aspect of the narrative, just as the stories of Hagar, Dinah, and Tamar defamiliarize the ancestral family?

Two prime candidates for subjection to a poetics of the interlude are the "interlude" of Lot and Sodom,[11] which interrupts the covenantal progress in Abraham's story, and the "interlude" of Isaac in Gerar,[12] which obtrudes on the Jacob cycle's drama of fraternal conflict. Are these just "mere" interludes,[13] diversions that must be naturalized according to their surroundings? Or might they be interludes in the fuller sense of the concept? Already scholarship has noted that both stories host several key motifs from the primary narrative of Genesis. The question revolves around how these motifs play out in the interlude. Do they confirm the associations conferred upon them by the primary narrative, or does their defamiliarized appearance contest these associations and carry with it new motivic implications?

Alter acknowledges that the story of Lot and Sodom appears to constitute an "interruption" in Abraham's story, but posits that it is, to the contrary, a "major thematic nexus."[14] In addition to making the common observation that the Lot and Sodom interlude echoes the motif of hospitality, which is foregrounded just before in the story of Abraham's reception of the divine visitors, Alter also points out that a motivic matrix of justice, propagation, and sight energizes the story. These motifs hark back to previous stories in Genesis, where sight and blindness mark matters of sexual morality, and reflect the fact that propagation is "conditional ... on moral behavior."[15] Interpreting the configuration of these motifs in the Lot and Sodom interlude as a commentary on the

---

11. E.g., Jeansonne, *The Women of Genesis*, 24; Brettler, *How to Read the Bible*, 58.

12. E.g., Brodie, *Genesis as Dialogue*, 295; Rendsburg, *The Redaction of Genesis*, 56; Fishbane, *Text and Texture*, 47.

13. Vrolijk protests the identification of Gen 26 as "a mere interlude," registering the sense that the interpretation of these stories as interludes diminishes their narrative significance (*An Examination*, 76).

14. Alter, "Sodom as Nexus," 32.

15. Alter, "Sodom as Nexus," 31–34.

implicit moral conditions of God's covenantal promise (in Gen 17), Alter ultimately reads the interlude as "monitory."[16] A certain justice—a certain sense of what is right and wrong—is taken for granted, and the story falls into place as a warning, as an ancestral how-*not*-to guide. So Alter comments: "The biblical writers will rarely lose sight of the ghastly possibility that Israel can turn itself into Sodom."[17] In this sense, the interlude serves as a foil and does little to develop the narrative.

Nevertheless, Alter's reading hints at the possibilities for reading the story within a poetics of the interlude. In a story so starkly narrated, without any evaluative comments indicating how the strange events are to be judged—from the Sodomites' aggression against the visitors and Lot's offer of his own virgin daughters, to the divine destruction of the Plain cities and Lot's daughters' incestuous seductions—there remains an abundance of interpretive space in which to explore the motifs, and particularly the motif of justice. Indeed, rather than confirming a sense of justice, the interlude might be posing the question, "What is justice?" Following a story in which God expects justice from Abraham (18:19) and Abraham expects justice from God (18:23–32), the narrative itself seems poised for an illustration of justice. What the interlude offers, instead, is a bizarre story that, devoid of the narrator's judgment, defamiliarizes justice. It is difficult to argue that the Sodomites have acted justly. But what about Lot? What about God? The interlude moves justice from the realm of discourse to the realm of action and—true to the dictum, "easier said than done"—confronts the reader with a messy story to untangle.

Numerous scholars have also observed a thematic resonance in the interlude of Isaac in Gerar. Many point out its correspondence to a distinctive type-narrative variously identified as the "sister-wife" or the "endangered ancestress" story.[18] Like Abraham in Gen 12:10–20 and 20:1–18, Isaac sojourns in a foreign territory, passes off his wife as his sister, and answers to the local ruler when the ruse is discovered. Others who have sought to assimilate the "interlude" into its immediate narrative context draw attention to its structural sequence of conflict, expulsion, and reconciliation, which anticipates Jacob's experience.[19] While both of these lines of reading acknowledge the interlude's invocation of themes

16. Alter, "Sodom as Nexus," 36.
17. Alter, "Sodom as Nexus," 36–37.
18. Exum, *Fragmented Women*, 13.
19. Brodie, *Genesis as Dialogue*, 295.

from the primary narrative, they domesticate the interlude. They read it as an interpretive key that shows the likeness between Isaac and his father or, conversely, between Isaac's experience and his son's.

A possibility for reading the story within a poetics of the interlude, however, subsists in the noted resemblance between Isaac and Abraham. Abraham dominates the narrative in a manner that is especially striking for a deceased character. His memory is such a consistent presence—his name appears eight times in the story—that one might say he haunts the story. Abraham's recollection is never more than a step away from Isaac. The famine that precipitates Isaac's sojourn draws a comparison to the famine that precipitated Abraham's (26:1), God's promises to Isaac explicitly recall God's original promise to Abraham (26:3, 5, 24), and Isaac digs the same wells that Abraham did and gives them the same names (26:15, 18).

On one level, the continual reference to Abraham seems to confirm Isaac as the legitimate covenantal heir of this father: he follows in his father's footsteps in a number of ways. But juxtaposed with marked reminders of the difference between Isaac and Abraham, the haunting presence of Abraham may push in an opposing direction. At the story's beginning, the narrative relates that the famine is "separate from" (מלבד) the famine of Abraham's time (26:1). When Isaac digs the same wells as his father and confers upon them the same names, the herders of Gerar contend with him and he renames the wells (26:18–22). The story then concludes with a covenant and exchange of oaths between Isaac and Abimelech (26:26–33) that parallels the agreement between Abraham and Abimelech (21:25–32). Isaac, in other words, must make peace anew on his own terms with Abimelech; the covenant and oaths of his father were no longer in effect. (That both stories etiologize Beersheba, furthermore, suggests the individual significance of each story.) The invocation of Abraham's memory, set side by side with the conspicuous distinction between Isaac's story and Abraham's, may function therefore not to confirm Isaac but rather to ironize a sense of patriarchal traditionalism—a sense that might be found elsewhere in certain patriarchal customs, such as endogamy and burial at Machpelah. That is, Isaac follows Abraham's example in a number of ways. His digging anew the old wells of Abraham, which the Philistines had stopped up, and his choice to give them the same names epitomize the attempt to repeat the past. Yet life is different now, as Isaac finds out. He must contend with the local herders over the wells. That he renames the wells in light of their new significance suggests a subversion of holding onto the past. The patriarchal traditionalism that might motivate customs such as endogamy and burial at Machpelah might not rest in the good graces of the narrative as much as it would have seemed.

The examples of these two "interludes" demonstrate that a poetics of the interlude might yet have more to offer to the interpretation of Genesis. And while the confines of this study limit it to the narrative of Genesis, the possibility of reading other biblical narrative within a poetics of the interlude must also be considered. Indeed, wherever biblical scholars identify a story as an "interlude," the invitation is made.

Concluding Remarks

It remains now for this study to draw to a close. Yet it must do so with its tongue in cheek, with the self-awareness that here it engages in an irony of its own. For to advance a conclusion is to finalize interpretation, and this is an endeavor upon which a hermeneutics of irony frowns. Irony resists resolution. It never says exactly what it means, but instead what is *not* meant, or rather, what is meant to be challenged and brought into dialogue. So it is that this study advances a conclusion that acknowledges its inconclusiveness. It puts forward a provisional conclusion, one whose heuristic value consists in summarizing the significance of this study.

This story of reading has demonstrated that the strange stories of Hagar, Dinah, and Tamar can be read as interludes according to a more comprehensive sense of the concept—a sense sketched out in analogy to the sonata-rondo episode. These strange stories can be read to transcend the limits imposed by their traditional subjection to the primary narrative. Instead of reading the primary narrative to determine the strange stories, the strange stories can be read to determine the primary narrative. Appropriating ancestral motifs from the primary narrative and showing them in new thematic relations, they *develop* key ancestral themes. As the etymological roots of "develop" would suggest, the strange stories indeed "unfold" or "unfurl" themes from the primary narrative. They reveal thematic trajectories that would otherwise stay hidden within the folds of the primary narrative.

In each case of unfolding, the strange story highlights the ancestral theme's ironic capacity. It stages the theme in a context that features an alternate subjectivity, a context that defamiliarizes the theme, conferring upon it new associations and contesting its conventional significance. The Hagar story unravels the theme of the ancestral–divine relationship. By associating sojourn, a fundamental ancestral motif that evokes the ancestral family's unique participation in the divine plan, with an outsider, the Hagar story plays on the possibility that the ancestral family's special relationship with God may be porous, that it may be inclusive of outsiders, that it may in fact be better reconfigured as God's special relationship with the sojourner, whoever that is. The Dinah interlude unfurls the theme of the ancestral family's relationship to the land and its inhabitants. By ventriloquizing an exclusivist configuration of motifs relating to the land, the families of the earth, and intermarriage in a suggestively ironic fashion, the Dinah interlude challenges such a mode of relations and invites consideration of a more inclusive way, like that suggested by Shechem and the Hivites. The Tamar interlude unwinds the theme of ancestral self-identity. By hosting a collective of motifs that allude to the ancestral birth narratives—and thereby framing the drama of an outsider matriarch, a wayward patriarch, and an exogamous union as an ancestral birth narrative—the Tamar interlude objects to the traditional limitations of matriarchal and patriarchal identity and endogamous union, and encourages a less rigid formulation of ancestral self-identity.

Thus the interludes of Hagar, Dinah, and Tamar demonstrate that their strangeness need not be *reduced* or naturalized according to the ancestral themes that govern the primary narrative, but rather may be read to *produce* new understandings of those themes. Far from being "between the play," the interludes epitomize play as, through their irony, they give old ancestral themes new life and entertain possibilities for an ancestral identity that exceeds its own boundaries.

Bibliography

Ackerman, James S. "Joseph, Judah, and Jacob." In *Literary Interpretations of Biblical Narratives*, edited by Kenneth R. R. Gros Louis, 85–113. Nashville: Abingdon, 1982.

Aczel, Richard. "Hearing Voices in Narrative Texts." *New Literary History* 29 (1998) 467–500.

———. "Throwing Voices." *New Literary History* 32 (2001) 703–5.

———. "Understanding as Over-hearing: Towards a Dialogics of Voice." *New Literary History* 32 (2001) 597–617.

Alexander, T. D. "Genealogies, Seed and the Compositional Unity of Genesis." *Tyndale Bulletin* 44 (1993) 255–70.

Alter, Robert. *The Art of Biblical Narrative*. New York: Basic, 1981.

———. "Sodom as Nexus: The Web of Design in Biblical Narrative." *Tikkun* 1 (1986) 30–38.

Amit, Yairah. *Reading Biblical Narratives: Literary Criticism and the Hebrew Bible*. Translated by Yael Lotan. Minneapolis: Fortress, 2001.

Amos, Clare. "Genesis." In *Global Bible Commentary*, edited by Daniel Patte et al., 1–16. Nashville: Abingdon, 2004.

Apel, Willi, ed. *Harvard Dictionary of Music*. 2nd ed. London: Heinemann Educational, 1970.

Arnold, Bill T. *Genesis*. New Cambridge Bible Commentary. Cambridge: Cambridge University Press, 2009.

Auerbach, Erich. *Mimesis: The Representation of Reality in Western Literature*. Translated by Willard R. Trask. Princeton: Princeton University Press, 1953.

Bakhtin, Mikhail. *The Dialogic Imagination: Four Essays by M. M. Bakhtin*. Edited by Michael Holquist. Translated by Caryl Emerson and Michael Holquist. University of Texas Press Slavic Series 1. Austin: University of Texas Press, 1981.

———. *Problems of Dostoevsky's Poetics*. Edited and translated by Caryl Emerson. Theory and History of Literature 8. Minneapolis: University of Minneapolis Press, 1984.

Bal, Mieke. *Death & Dissymmetry: The Politics of Coherence in the Book of Judges*. Chicago Studies in the History of Judaism. Chicago: The University of Chicago Press, 1988.

———. *Lethal Love: Feminist Literary Readings of Biblical Love Stories*. Indiana Studies in Biblical Literature. Bloomington, IN: Indiana University Press, 1987.

———. *Narratology: Introduction to the Theory of Narrative*. 3rd ed. Toronto: University of Toronto Press, 2009.
———. "Tricky Thematics." *Semeia* 42 (1988) 133–55.
Bar-Efrat, Shimon. *Narrative Art in the Bible. Understanding the Bible and Its World*. London: T. & T. Clark, 2004.
Barenboim, Daniel, and Edward W. Said. *Parallels and Paradoxes*. London: Bloomsbury, 2002.
Baroni, Raphaël. "Tellability." In *Handbook of Narratology*, edited by Peter Hühn, John Pier, Wolf Schmid, and Jörg Schönert, 447–54. Narratologia 19. New York: de Gruyter, 2009.
Barth, Karl. *Church Dogmatics*. Edited by G. W. Bromiley and T. F. Torrance. Translated by G. W. Bromiley et al. 14 vols. Edinburgh: T. & T. Clark, 1936–62.
Barthes, Roland. *Image–Music–Text*. Translated by Stephen Heath. New York: Hill and Wang, 1977.
———. *The Semiotic Challenge*. Translated by Richard Howard. New York: Hill and Wang, 1988.
Bechtel, Lyn M. "Dinah." In *Women in Scripture: A Dictionary of Named and Unnamed Women in the Hebrew Bible, the Apocryphal/Deuterocanonical Books, and the New Testament*, edited by Carol L. Meyers, Toni Craven, and Ross Shepard Kraemer, 69–71. Boston: Houghton Mifflin, 2000.
———. "What If Dinah Is Not Raped? (Genesis 34)." *Journal for the Study of the Old Testament* 62 (1994) 19–36.
Beecher, Henry Ward. *Life Thoughts*. 1st and 2nd series. London: Blackwood, 1858.
Belfiore, Elizabeth. "περιπέτεια as Discontinuous Action: Aristotle 'Poetics' 11. 1452a22–29." *Classical Philology* 83 (1988) 183–94.
Berlin, Adele. "Literary Approaches to Biblical Literature: General Observations and a Case Study of Genesis 34." In *The Hebrew Bible: New Insights and Scholarship*, edited by Frederick E. Greenspahn, 45–75. Jewish Studies in the 21st Century. New York: New York University Press, 2008.
———. *Poetics and Interpretation of Biblical Narrative*. Bible and Literature Series 9. Sheffield, UK: Almond, 1983.
Bird, Phyllis. *Missing Persons and Mistaken Identities: Women and Gender in Ancient Israel*. Minneapolis: Fortress, 1997.
Bloom, Harold. *The Book of J*. Biblical Hebrew translated by David Rosenberg. New York: Vintage, 1991.
———, ed. *Jonathan Swift*. Bloom's Classic Critical Views. New York: Bloom's Literary Criticism, 2009.
Blyth, Caroline. "Terrible Silence, Eternal Silence: A Feminist Re-reading of Dinah's Voicelessness in Genesis 34." *Biblical Interpretation* 17 (2009) 483–506.
Bobin, James, dir. *The Muppets*. 2011. Santa Barbara, CA: Walt Disney, 2012. DVD.
Booth, Wayne C. *The Rhetoric of Fiction*. 2nd ed. London: Penguin, 1991.
———. *A Rhetoric of Irony*. Chicago: The University of Chicago Press, 1974.
Brett, Mark G. *Genesis: Procreation and the Politics of Identity*. Old Testament Readings. London: Routledge, 2000.
Brettler, Marc Zvi. *How to Read the Bible*. Philadelphia: Jewish Publication Society, 2005.
Brodie, Thomas L. *Genesis as Dialogue: A Literary, Historical, & Theological Commentary*. Oxford: Oxford University Press, 2001.

Brooks, Cleanth. *The Well-Wrought Urn: Studies in the Structure of Poetry*. New York: Harcourt Brace, 1947.
Brown, Francis, S. R. Driver, and Charles A. Briggs. *A Hebrew and English Lexicon of the Old Testament*. Oxford: Clarendon, 1907.
Brueggemann, Walter. *Genesis*. Interpretation. Atlanta: John Knox, 1982.
Buber, Martin. *Schriften zur Bibel*. Munich: München Kösel, 1964.
Camp, Claudia V. *Wise, Strange, and Holy: The Strange Woman and the Making of the Bible*. Journal for the Study of the Old Testament Supplement Series 320. Gender, Culture, Theory 9. Sheffield, UK: Sheffield Academic Press, 2000.
Caplin, William E. *Classical Form: A Theory of Formal Functions for the Instrumental Music of Haydn, Mozart, and Beethoven*. New York: Oxford University Press, 1998.
Carden, Michael. "Genesis/Bereshit." In *The Queer Bible Commentary*, edited by Deryn Guest, Robert E. Goss, Mona West, and Thomas Bohache, 21–60. London: SCM, 2006.
Chatman, Seymour. *Story and Discourse: Narrative Structure in Fiction and Film*. Ithaca, NY: Cornell University Press, 1978.
Childs, Brevard S. *Introduction to the Old Testament as Scripture*. Philadelphia: Fortress, 1979.
Clark, Katerina, and Michael Holquist. *Mikhail Bakhtin*. Cambridge: Belknap Press of Harvard University Press, 1984.
Clark, Jr., Ronald R. "The Silence in Dinah's Cry." *Restoration Quarterly* 49 (2007) 143–58.
Clarke, Adam. *The Holy Bible, Containing the Old and New Testaments: The Text Carefully Printed from the Most Correct Copies of the Present Authorized Translation, Including the Marginal Readings and Parallel Texts, with a Commentary and Critical Notes, Designed as a Help to a Better Understanding of the Sacred Writings*. 7 vols. New York: Ezra Sargent, 1811.
Clifford, Richard J. "Genesis 38: Its Contribution to the Jacob Story." *Catholic Biblical Quarterly* 66 (2004) 519–32.
Clines, David J. A. *The Theme of the Pentateuch*. 2nd ed. Journal for the Study of the Old Testament Supplement Series 10. Sheffield, UK: Sheffield Academic Press, 1997.
Cohn, Dorrit. "Metalepsis and Mise en Abyme." Translated by Lewis S. Gleich. *Narrative* 20 (2012) 105–14.
Cohn, Robert L. "Negotiating (with) the Natives: Ancestors and Identity in Genesis." *Harvard Theological Review* 96 (2003) 147–66.
Colebrook, Claire. *Irony*. The New Critical Idiom. London: Routledge, 2004.
Cosmides, Leda, and John Tooby. "Consider the Source: The Evolution of Adaptations for Decoupling and Metarepresentations." In *Metarepresentations: A Multidisciplinary Perspective*, edited by Dan Sperber, 53–115. New York: Oxford University Press, 2000.
Culler, Jonathan. *Literary Theory: A Very Short Introduction*. Oxford: Oxford University Press, 1997.
———. "Omniscience." *Narrative* 12 (2004) 22–34.
———. *On Deconstruction: Theory and Criticism after Structuralism*. 25th anniv. ed. London: Routledge, 2008.
———. *The Pursuit of Signs: Semiotics, Literature, and Deconstruction*. London: Routledge, 2001.

———. *Structuralist Poetics: Structuralism, Linguistics and the Study of Literature*. 1975. Reprint, London: Routledge, 1992.
Currie, Mark. *Postmodern Narrative Theory*. Transitions. New York: St. Martin's, 1998.
Dane, Joseph A. *The Critical Mythology of Irony*. Athens: University of Georgia Press, 1991.
Davies, Eryl W. *The Dissenting Reader: Feminist Approaches to the Hebrew Bible*. Aldershot, UK: Ashgate, 2003.
Dozeman, Thomas B. "The Wilderness and Salvation History in the Hagar Story." *Journal of Biblical Literature* 117 (1998) 23–43.
Earl, Douglas. "Toward a Christian Hermeneutic of Old Testament Narrative: Why Genesis 34 Fails to Find Christian Significance." *Catholic Biblical Quarterly* 73 (2011) 30–49.
Elleström, Lars. *Divine Madness: On Interpreting Literature, Music, and the Visual Arts Ironically*. Lewisburg, PA: Bucknell University Press, 2002.
Eslinger, Lyle. *Into the Hands of the Living God*. Bible and Literature Series 24. Journal for the Study of the Old Testament Supplement Series 84. Sheffield, UK: Sheffield Academic Press, 1989.
Exum, J. Cheryl. "The Accusing Look: The Abjection of Hagar in Art." *Religion and the Arts* 11 (2007) 143–71.
———. *Fragmented Women: Feminist (Sub)versions of Biblical Narratives*. Journal for the Study of the Old Testament Supplement Series 163. Sheffield, UK: JSOT, 1993.
Fentress-Williams, Judy. "Location, Location, Location: Tamar in the Joseph Cycle." *Bible & Critical Theory* 3 (2007) 20.1–20.8.
Fewell, Danna Nolan, and D. M. Gunn. *Gender, Power, and Promise: The Subject of the Bible's First Story*. Nashville: Abingdon, 1993.
———. "Tipping the Balance: Sternberg's Reader and the Rape of Dinah." *Journal of Biblical Literature* 110 (1991) 193–211.
Fish, Stanley. *Doing What Comes Naturally: Change, Rhetoric, and the Practice of Theory in Literary and Legal Studies*. Post-Contemporary Interventions. Durham, NC: Duke University Press, 1989.
Fishbane, Michael. *Text and Texture: Close Readings of Selected Biblical Texts*. New York: Schocken, 1979.
Fludernik, Monika. "New Wine in Old Bottles? Voice, Focalization, and New Writing." *New Literary History* 32 (2001) 619–38.
Fokkelman, J. P. *Narrative Art in Genesis: Specimens of Stylistic and Structural Analysis*. 2nd ed. Biblical Seminar 12. 1991. Reprint, Eugene, OR: Wipf and Stock, 2004.
Foucault, Michel. "What Is an Author?" In *Language, Counter-Memory, Practice: Selected Essays and Interviews*, edited by Donald F. Bouchard, 113–38. Ithaca, NY: Cornell University Press, 1977.
Fowler, Roger. *Linguistic Criticism*. 2nd ed. Oxford: Oxford University Press, 1996.
Fox, Everett. "Can Genesis Be Read as a Book?" *Semeia* 46 (1989) 31–40.
Fretheim, Terence E. *Abraham: Trials of Faith and Family*. Studies on Personalities of the Old Testament. Columbia: University of South Carolina Press, 2007.
Friedman, Richard Elliott. *The Hidden Face of God*. San Francisco: Harper, 1995.
Frye, Northrop. *The Great Code: The Bible and Literature*. 1982. Reprint, Toronto: Penguin, 1990.
Frymer-Kensky, Tikva. *Reading the Women of the Bible: A New Interpretation of Their Stories*. New York: Schocken, 2002.

———. "Sarah 1/Sarai." In *Women in Scripture: A Dictionary of Named and Unnamed Women in the Hebrew Bible, the Apocryphal/Deuterocanonical Books, and the New Testament*, edited by Carol L. Meyers, Toni Craven, and Ross Shepard Kraemer, 150–52. Boston: Houghton Mifflin, 2000.

Genette, Gérard. *Narrative Discourse*. Translated by Jane E. Lewin. Oxford: Cornell University Press, 1980.

Gibson, John C. L. *Genesis*. 2 vols. Daily Study Bible. Philadelphia: Westminster, 1982.

Gide, André. *Journals 1889–1949*. Edited and translated by Justin O'Brien. Lives and Letters. Harmondsworth, UK: Penguin, 1967.

Goetschius, Percy. *Lessons in Music Form: A Manual of Analysis of All the Structural Factors and Designs Employed in Musical Composition*. Boston: Ditson, 1904.

Goldin, Judah. "Youngest Son or Where Does Genesis 38 Belong?" *Journal of Biblical Literature* 96 (1977) 27–44.

Goldingay, John. "The Patriarchs in Scripture and History." In *Essays on the Patriarchal Narratives*, edited by A. R. Millard and D. J. Wiseman, 11–42. Leicester, UK: IVP, 1980.

Golka, Friedemann W. "Genesis 37–50: Joseph Story or Israel-Joseph Story?" *Currents in Biblical Research* 2 (2004) 153–77.

Good, Edwin M. *Irony in the Old Testament*. 2nd ed. Sheffield, UK: Almond, 1981.

Gossai, Hemchand. *Power and Marginality in the Abraham Narrative*. 2nd ed. Princeton Theological Monograph Series 130. Eugene, OR: Pickwick, 2010.

Gribble, David. "Narrative Interventions in Thucydides." *The Journal of Hellenic Studies* 118 (1998) 41–67.

Gruber, Mayer I. "A Re-Examination of the Charges against Shechem Son of Hamor." Translated by Marian Broida. Unpublished paper. Exchanged personally.

Gunn, David M., and Danna Nolan Fewell. *Narrative in the Hebrew Bible*. New York: Oxford University Press, 1993.

Habel, Norman C. *The Land Is Mine: Six Biblical Land Ideologies*. Overtures to Biblical Theology. Minneapolis: Fortress, 1995.

Hackett, Jo Ann. "Rehabilitating Hagar: Fragments of an Epic Pattern." In *Gender and Difference in Ancient Israel*, edited by Peggy L. Day, 12–27. Minneapolis: Fortress, 1989.

Hamilton, Victor P. *The Book of Genesis: Chapters 1–17*. New International Commentary on the Old Testament. Grand Rapids: Eerdmans, 1990.

———. *The Book of Genesis: Chapters 18–50*. New International Commentary on the Old Testament. Grand Rapids: Eerdmans, 1995.

Hammer, C., ed. *Rhetores Graeci ex recognitione Leonardi Spengel*. 2 vols. Leipzig: Teubner, 1894.

Heard, R. Christopher. *Dynamics of Diselection: Ambiguity in Genesis 12–36 and Ethnic Boundaries in Post-Exilic Judah*. Semeia Studies 39. Atlanta: Society of Biblical Literature, 2001.

Hepokoski, James, and Warren Darcy. *Elements of Sonata Theory: Norms, Types, and Deformations in the Late-Eighteenth-Century Sonata*. Oxford: Oxford University Press, 2006.

Holland, Glenn S. *Divine Irony*. London: Associated University Presses, 2000.

Huddlestun, John R. "Divestiture, Deception, and Demotion: The Garment Motif in Genesis 37–39." *Journal for the Study of the Old Testament* 98 (2002) 47–62.

Hughes, Paul Edward. "Seeing Hagar Seeing God: Leitwort and Petite Narrative in Genesis 16:1–16." *Didaskalia* 8 (1997) 43–59.
Humphreys, W. Lee. *The Character of God in the Book of Genesis: A Narrative Appraisal*. Louisville: Westminster John Knox, 2001.
Hutcheon, Linda. *Irony's Edge: The Theory and Politics of Irony*. London: Routledge, 1995.
Hyman, Ronald T. "Final Judgment: The Ambiguous Moral Question That Culminates Genesis 34." *Jewish Bible Quarterly* 28 (2000) 93–101.
Iser, Wolfgang. *The Implied Reader: Patterns of Communication in Prose Fiction from Bunyan to Beckett*. Baltimore: Johns Hopkins University Press, 1974.
Jackson, Melissa. *Comedy and Feminist Interpretation of the Hebrew Bible: A Subversive Collaboration*. Oxford Theological Monographs. Oxford: Oxford University Press, 2012.
―――. "Lot's Daughters and Tamar as Tricksters and the Patriarchal Narratives as Feminist Theology." *Journal for the Study of the Old Testament* 26 (2002) 29–46.
Jacobs, Mignon R. "Love, Honor, and Violence: Socioconceptual Matrix in Genesis 34." In *Pregnant Passion: Gender, Sex, and Violence in the Bible*, edited by Cheryl A. Kirk-Duggan, 11–35. Atlanta: Society of Biblical Literature, 2003.
Jeansonne, Sharon Pace. *The Women of Genesis: From Sarah to Potiphar's Wife*. Minneapolis: Augsburg Fortress, 1990.
Joüon, Paul. *A Grammar of Biblical Hebrew*. Edited and translated by Takamitsu Muraoka. 2 vols. Subsidia Biblica 14. 1991. Reprint, Roma: Editrice Pontificio Istituto Biblio, 2005.
Kaminski, Carol M. *From Noah to Israel: Realization of the Primaeval Blessing After the Flood*. London: T. & T. Clark, 2004.
Kaminsky, Joel S. *Yet I Loved Jacob: Reclaiming the Biblical Concept of Election*. Nashville: Abingdon, 2007.
Kennedy, Elisabeth Robertson. *Seeking a Homeland: Sojourn and Ethnic Identity in the Ancestral Narratives of Genesis*. Biblical Interpretation 106. Boston: Brill, 2011.
Kerman, Joseph, and Gary Tomlinson, with Vivian Kerman. *Listen*. 5th ed. New York: Bedford/St. Martin's, 2004.
Kierkegaard, Søren. *The Concept of Irony, with Continual Reference to Socrates*. Translated by Lee M. Capel. Midland Book 111. Bloomington, IN: Indiana University Press, 1965.
Kille, D. Andrew. "Jacob: A Study in Individuation." In *Psychology and the Bible: From Genesis to Apocalyptic Vision*, edited by J. Harold Ellens and Wayne G. Rollins, 65–82. Vol. 2 of *Psychology and the Bible: A New Way to Read the Scriptures*. Psychology, Religion, and Spirituality Series. Westport, CT: Praeger, 2004.
Kim, Dohyung. "A Literary-Critical Analysis of the Role of Genesis 38 within Genesis 37–50 as Part of the Primary Narrative (Genesis–2 Kings) of the Hebrew Bible." PhD Diss., University of Sheffield, 2010.
Klein, Lillian R. *The Triumph of Irony in the Book of Judges*. Bible and Literature Series 14. Sheffield, UK: Almond, 1988.
Kozar, Joseph Vicek. "When 'Circumfession' Is Not Enough: Understanding the Murder of the Newly Circumcised Shechemites Subsequent to Shechem's Rape of Dinah (Genesis 34)." *Proceedings—Eastern Great Lakes and Midwest Biblical Societies* 23 (2003) 55–64.

Kruschwitz, Jonathan. "The Type-Scene Connection between Genesis 38 and the Joseph Story." *Journal for the Study of the Old Testament* 36 (2012) 383–410.
Kugler, Robert, and Patrick Hartin. *An Introduction to the Bible*. Grand Rapids: Eerdmans, 2009.
Kunin, Seth Daniel. *The Logic of Incest: A Structuralist Analysis of Hebrew Mythology*. Journal for the Study of the Old Testament Supplement Series 185. Sheffield, UK: Sheffield Academic Press, 1995.
Labov, William, and Joshua Waletzky. "Narrative Analysis: Oral Versions of Personal Experience." In *Essays on the Verbal and Visual Arts*, edited by June Helm, 12–44. Seattle: University of Washington Press, 1967.
Lambe, Anthony J. "Genesis 38: Structure and Literary Design." In *The World of Genesis: Persons, Places, Perspectives*, edited by Philip R. Davies and David J. A. Clines, 102–20. Journal for the Study of the Old Testament Supplement Series 257. Sheffield, UK: Sheffield Academic Press, 1998.
Levenson, Jon. "The Universal Horizon of Biblical Particularism." In *Ethnicity and the Bible*, edited by Mark G. Brett, 143–69. Biblical Interpretation 19. Leiden: Brill, 1996.
Liedke, G. "דין." In *Theological Lexicon of the Old Testament*. Edited by Ernst Jenni and Claus Westermann. Translated by Mark E. Biddle. Peabody, MA: Hendrickson, 1997. Accordance 9.
Lubbock, Percy. *The Craft of Fiction*. 1921. Reprint, London: Cape, 1965.
Margolin, Uri. "Narrator." In *Handbook of Narratology*, edited by Peter Hühn, John Pier, Wolf Schmid, and Jörg Schönert, 351–69. Narratologia 19. New York: de Gruyter, 2009.
Marshall, Celia Brewer. *Genesis*. Interpretation Bible Studies. Louisville: Geneva, 1998.
Mbuvi, Amanda Beckenstein. "Belonging in Genesis: Biblical Israel and the Construction of Communal Identity." PhD diss., Duke University, 2008.
McAfee, Gene. "Chosen People in a Chosen Land." In *The Earth Story in Genesis*, edited by Norman C. Habel and Shirley Wurst, 158–74. The Earth Bible 2. Sheffield, UK: Sheffield Academic Press, 2000.
McKinlay, Judith E. "Sarah and Hagar: What Have I to Do with Them?" In *Her Master's Tools? Feminist and Postcolonial Engagements of Historical-Critical Discourse*, edited by Caroline Vander Stichele and Todd C. Penner, 159–77. Global Perspectives on Biblical Scholarship 9. Atlanta: Society of Biblical Literature, 2005.
Menn, Esther Marie. *Judah and Tamar (Genesis 38) in Ancient Jewish Exegesis: Studies in Literary Form and Hermeneutics*. Supplements to the Journal for the Study of Judaism 51. Leiden: Brill, 1997.
Miles, Jack. *God: A Biography*. New York: Vintage, 1996.
Moberly, R. W. L. *Genesis 12–50*. Old Testament Guides. Sheffield, UK: Sheffield Academic Press, 1992.
Muecke, D. C. *Irony*. Critical Idiom 13. London: Methuen, 1970.
Ngan, Lai Ling Elizabeth. "Neither Here Nor There: Boundary and Identity in the Hagar Story." In *Ways of Being, Ways of Reading: Asian American Biblical Interpretation*, edited by Mary F. Foskett and Jeffrey Kah-Jin Kuan, 70–83. Saint Louis: Chalice, 2006.
Nicol, George G. "Story-Patterning in Genesis." In *Text as Pretext: Essays in Honour of Robert Davidson*, edited by Robert P. Carroll, 215–33. Journal for the Study of the

Old Testament Supplement Series 138. Sheffield, UK: Sheffield Academic Press, 1992.
Niditch, Susan. "Genesis." In *Women's Bible Commentary*, edited by Carol A. Newsom, Sharon H. Ringe, and Jacqueline E. Lapsley, 13–29. 3rd ed. Louisville: Westminster John Knox, 2012.
Nikaido, Scott K. "Hagar and Ishmael as Literary Figures: An Intertextual Study." *Vetus Testamentum* 51 (2001) 219–42.
Noble, Paul R. "A 'Balanced' Reading of the Rape of Dinah: Some Exegetical and Methodological Observations." *Biblical Interpretation* 4 (1996) 173–204.
———. "Esau, Tamar, and Joseph: Criteria for Identifying Inner-biblical Allusions." *Vetus Testamentum* 52 (2002) 219–52.
Noske, Frits. *The Signifier and the Signified: Studies in the Operas of Mozart and Verdi.* The Hague: Nijhoff, 1977.
Okoye, James C. "Sarah and Hagar: Genesis 16 and 21." *Journal for the Study of the Old Testament* 32 (2007) 163–75.
Paris, Christopher T. "Narrative Obtrusion in the Hebrew Bible." PhD diss., Vanderbilt University, 2012.
Parry, Robin A. "Feminist Hermeneutics and Evangelical Concerns: The Rape of Dinah as a Case Study." *Tyndale Bulletin* 53 (2002) 1–28.
———. *Old Testament Story and Christian Ethics: The Rape of Dinah as a Case Study.* Paternoster Biblical Monographs. Milton Keynes, UK: Paternoster, 2004.
Pascal, Roy. *The Dual Voice: Free Indirect Speech and Its Functioning in the Nineteenth-Century European Novel.* Manchester: Manchester University Press, 1977.
Provan, Iain, V. Philips Long, and Tremper Longman III. *A Biblical History of Israel.* Louisville: Westminster John Knox, 2003.
Pyper, Hugh S. *The Unchained Bible: Cultural Appropriations of Biblical Texts.* Library of Hebrew Bible/Old Testament Studies 567. London: T. & T. Clark, 2012.
Rashkow, Ilona N. "The Rape(s) of Dinah (Gen. 34): False Religion and Excess in Revenge." In *The Destructive Power of Religion: Violence in Judaism, Christianity, and Islam*, edited by J. Harold Ellens, 53–80. Models and Cases of Violence in Religion 3. London: Praeger, 2004.
Reis, Pamela Tamarkin. "Hagar Requited." *Journal for the Study of the Old Testament* 87 (2000) 75–109.
Rendsburg, Gary. *The Redaction of Genesis.* Winona Lake, IN: Eisenbrauns, 1986.
Richards, I. A. *Principles of Literary Criticism.* 2nd ed. London: Harcourt, 1926.
Ron, Moshe. "The Restricted Abyss: Nine Problems in the Theory of Mise en Abyme." *Poetics Today* 8 (1987) 417–38.
Rosen, Charles. *Sonata Forms.* New York: Norton, 1980.
Rosenberg, Joel. *King and Kin: Political Allegory in the Hebrew Bible.* Indiana Studies in Biblical Literature. Bloomington, IN: Indiana University Press, 1986.
Schlegel, Friedrich. *Philosophical Fragments.* Translated by Peter Firchow. Minneapolis: University of Minneapolis Press, 1991.
Schmidt-Beste, Thomas. *The Sonata.* Cambridge Introductions to Music. Cambridge: Cambridge University Press, 2011.
Schneider, Tammi J. *Mothers of Promise: Women in the Book of Genesis.* Grand Rapids: Baker, 2008.
———. *Sarah: Mother of Nations.* New York: Continuum, 2004.

Scott, Derek B. "Bruckner's Symphonies—A Reinterpretation: The Dialectic of Darkness and Light." In *The Cambridge Companion to Bruckner*, edited by John Williamson, 92–107. Cambridge: Cambridge University Press, 2004.

Sharon, Diane M. "Some Results of a Structural Semiotic Analysis of the Story of Judah and Tamar." *Journal for the Study of the Old Testament* 29 (2005) 289–318.

Sharp, Carolyn J. *Irony and Meaning in the Hebrew Bible*. Indiana Studies in Biblical Literature. Bloomington, IN: Indiana University Press, 2009.

Shemesh, Yael. "Rape Is Rape Is Rape: The Story of Dinah and Shechem (Genesis 34)." *Zeitschrift für die alttestamentliche Wissenschaft* 119 (2007) 2–21.

Shklovsky, Viktor. "Art as Technique." In *Russian Formalist Criticism: Four Essays*, translated and edited by Lee T. Lemon and Marion J. Reis, 3–24. Regents Critics Series. Lincoln, NE: University of Nebraska Press, 1965.

Ska, Jean Louis. *"Our Fathers Have Told Us": Introduction to the Analysis of Hebrew Narratives*. Subsidia Biblica 13. Roma: Editrice Pontificio Instituto Biblico, 1990.

Slepian, Barry. "The Ironic Intention of Swift's Verses on His Own Death." *Review of English Studies* 14 (1963) 249–56.

Soanes, Catherine, and Angus Stevenson, eds. *Oxford Dictionary of English*. 2nd rev. ed. Oxford University Press, 2010. eBook ed.

Speiser, E. A. *Genesis*. 3rd ed. Anchor Bible 1. Garden City, NY: Doubleday, 1982.

Sperber, Dan, and Deirdre Wilson. "Irony and the Use-Mention Distinction." In *Radical Pragmatics*, edited by Peter Cole, 295–318. New York: Academic, 1981.

———. *Relevance: Communication and Cognition*. Oxford: Blackwell, 1986.

Stein, Leon. *Structure and Style: The Study and Analysis of Musical Forms*. Exp. ed. Princeton: Summy-Birchard Music, 1979.

Sternberg, Meir. "Biblical Poetics and Sexual Politics: From Reading to Counterreading." *Journal of Biblical Literature* 111 (1992) 463–88.

———. *The Poetics of Biblical Narrative: Ideological Literature and the Drama of Reading*. Indiana Studies in Biblical Literature. Bloomington, IN: Indiana University Press, 1987.

Tarlin, Jan William. "Tamar's Veil: Ideology at the Entrance to Enaim." In *Culture, Entertainment and the Bible*, edited by George Aichele, 174–81. Journal for the Study of the Old Testament Supplement Series 309. Sheffield, UK: Sheffield Academic Press, 2000.

Thirlwall, Connop. "On the Irony of Sophocles." In *The Philological Museum*, Vol. 2, edited by Julius Charles Hare, 483–537. Cambridge: J. Smith, 1833.

Todorov, Tzvetan. *Introduction to Poetics*. Translated by Richard Howard. Theory and History of Literature 1. Minneapolis: University of Minnesota, 1981.

Todorov, Tzvetan, and Arnold Weinstein. "Structural Analysis of Narrative." *NOVEL: A Forum on Fiction* 3 (1969) 70–76.

Treacy-Cole, Diane. "Women in the Wilderness: Rereading Revelation 12." In *Wilderness: Essays in Honour of Frances Young*, edited by R. S. Sugirtharajah, 45–58. Library of New Testament Studies 295. London: T & T Clark, 2005.

Trible, Phyllis. "Ominous Beginnings for a Promise of Blessing." In *Hagar, Sarah, and Their Children: Jewish, Christian, and Muslim Perspectives*, edited by Phyllis Trible and Letty M. Russell, 33–69. Louisville: Westminster John Knox, 2006.

———. *Texts of Terror: Literary-Feminist Readings of Biblical Narratives*. Overtures to Biblical Theology 13. Lyman Beecher Lectures 1981–82. Philadelphia: Fortress, 1984.

Turner, Laurence A. *Announcements of Plot in Genesis.* Journal for the Study of the Old Testament Supplement Series 96. Sheffield, UK: JSOT, 1990.
———. *Genesis. Readings: A New Biblical Commentary.* Sheffield, UK: Sheffield Academic Press, 2000.
Van Dijk-Hemmes, Fokkelien. "Tamar and the Limits of Patriarchy: Between Rape and Seduction (2 Samuel 13 and Genesis 38)." In *Anti-Covenant: Counter-Reading Women's Lives in the Hebrew Bible,* edited by Mieke Bal, 135–56. Bible and Literature Series 22. Sheffield, UK: Almond Press, 1989.
Van Wolde, Ellen. "Does Inna Denote Rape? A Semantic Analysis of a Controversial Word." *Vetus Testamentum* 52 (2002) 528–44.
———. "Love and Hatred in a Multi-Racial Society: The Dinah and Shechem Story in Genesis 34 in the Context of Genesis 28–35." In *Reading From Right to Left: Essays on the Hebrew Bible in Honour of David J. A. Clines,* edited by J. Cheryl Exum and H. G. M. Williamson, 435–49. Journal for the Study of the Old Testament Supplement Series 373. London: Sheffield Academic Press, 2003.
———. "Who Guides Whom? Embeddedness and Perspective in Biblical Hebrew and in 1 Kings 3:16–28." *Journal of Biblical Literature* 114 (1995) 623–42.
Voloshinov, V. N. *Marxism and the Philosophy of Language.* Translated by Latislav Matejka and I. R. Titunik. Studies in Language 1. New York: Seminar, 1973.
Von Rad, Gerhard. *Genesis: A Commentary.* Translated by John H. Marks. Rev. ed. Old Testament Library. London: SCM, 1972.
Vrolijk, Paul D. *An Examination into the Nature and Role of Material Possessions in the Jacob-Cycle (Gen 25:19—35:29).* Vetus Testamentum Supplements 146. Leiden: Brill, 2011.
Walsh, Richard. "Person, Level, Voice: A Rhetorical Reconsideration." In *Postclassical Narratology: Approaches and Analyses,* edited by Jan Alber and Monika Fludernik, 35–57. Theory and Interpretation of Narrative Series. Columbus, OH: Ohio State University Press, 2010.
Warrack, John Hamilton, and Ewan West, eds. *The Concise Oxford Dictionary of Opera.* 3rd ed. Oxford Paperback Reference. Oxford: Oxford University Press, 1996.
Wenham, Gordon J. *Genesis 1–15.* Word Biblical Commentary 1. Waco, TX: Word, 1987.
———. *Genesis 16–50.* Word Biblical Commentary 2. Dallas: Word, 1994.
Westermann, Claus. *Genesis 12–36: A Commentary.* Translated by J. J. Scullion. Minneapolis: Augsburg, 1985.
White, Hugh C. "The Joseph Story: A Narrative Which 'Consumes' Its Content." *Semeia* 31 (1985) 49–69.
———. *Narration and Discourse in the Book of Genesis.* Cambridge: Cambridge University Press, 1991.
White, John J. "The Semiotics of the Mise-en-Abyme." In *The Motivated Sign,* edited by Olga Fischer and Max Nänny, 29–53. Iconicity in Language and Literature 2. Amsterdam: Benjamins, 2001.
Williamson, Paul R. *Abraham, Israel and the Nations: The Patriarchal Promise and Its Covenantal Development in Genesis.* Journal for the Study of the Old Testament Supplement Series 315. Sheffield, UK: Sheffield Academic Press, 2000.
Wilson, Deirdre. "The Pragmatics of Verbal Irony: Echo or Pretence?" *Lingua* 116 (2006) 1722–43.

Wilson, Deirdre, and Dan Sperber. *Meaning and Relevance*. New York: Cambridge University Press, 2012.

———. "On Verbal Irony." *Lingua* 87 (1992) 53–76.

Winterbottom, M., ed. *M. Fabi Quintiliani Institutionis oratoriae libri duodecim*. 2 vols. Oxford: Clarendon, 1970.

Wünch, Hans-Georg. "Genesis 38—Judah's Turning Point: Structural Analysis and Narrative Techniques and Their Meaning for Genesis 38 and Its Placement in the Story of Joseph." *Old Testament Essays* 25 (2012) 777–806.

Yamada, Frank M. "Dealing with Rape (in) Narrative (Genesis 34): Ethics of the Other and a Text in Conflict." In *The Meanings We Choose: Hermeneutical Ethics, Indeterminacy and the Conflict of Interpretations*, edited by Charles H. Cosgrove, 149–65. Journal for the Study of the Old Testament Supplement Series 411. London: T. & T. Clark, 2004.

Yamanashi, Masa-aki. "Some Issues in the Treatment of Irony and Related Tropes." In *Relevance Theory: Applications and Implications*, edited by Robyn Carston and Seiji Uchida, 271–80. Pragmatics and Beyond New Series 37. Amsterdam: Benjamins, 1998.

Zakovitch, Yair. *"And You Shall Tell Your Son—": The Concept of Exodus in the Bible*. Jerusalem: Magnes, 1991.

Zunshine, Lisa. *Why We Read Fiction: Theory of Mind and the Novel*. Theory and Interpretation of Narrative. Columbus, OH: Ohio State University Press, 2006.

www.ingramcontent.com/pod-product-compliance
Lightning Source LLC
Chambersburg PA
CBHW051518230426
43668CB00012B/1652

"Musical composition, ventriloquy, narrative mimicry, and irony form Jonathan Kruschwitz's analytical constellation to reassess the morally unsettling and hermeneutically controversial stories of Hagar, Dinah, and Tamar in the book of Genesis. Often seen as narrative cul-de-sacs enforcing a rigid construction of Israelite ancestral identity and destiny, these interludes are shown in Kruschwitz's careful reading to be integral to a more expansive and dynamic understanding of communal identity. This is truly a timely interpretation in a world currently fraught with social exclusivism."
—DANNA NOLAN FEWELL, John Fletcher Hurst Professor of Hebrew Bible, Drew University, and author of *The Children of Israel: Reading the Bible for the Sake of Our Children*

"Jonathan Kruschwitz enriches our reading of Genesis, focusing on three stories often treated as diversions from its central narrative. In addition to a nuanced treatment of irony, he explores how structures developed by classical composers suggest parallels for biblical scholars. This elegant and timely study shows how these stories disrupt the dichotomy between insider and outsider to present a more inclusive understanding of identity, highly relevant to contemporary concerns."
—HUGH S. PYPER, Emeritus Professor of Biblical Interpretation, Sheffield Institute for Interdisciplinary Biblical Studies, University of Sheffield

"Observing that the accounts of Hagar, Dinah, and Tamar all resist harmonization with the main storyline, Kruschwitz applies the concepts of the musical interlude and irony to highlight elements of the overall ancestral account that would otherwise be overlooked. For example, Hagar embodies the 'porous inclusion of outsiders' implicit in the sojourner theme of Genesis. Evidencing a refined literary sensibility, Kruschwitz's study will become a benchmark in the study of the Bible's ancestral narratives."
—MARK E. BIDDLE, Acting Dean, Sophia Theological Seminary

"Weaving together perspectives from musicology and irony, Jonathan Kruschwitz offers an incisive analysis of the stories of Hagar, Dinah, and Tamar, who each in her own right has made her way into the ancestral narrative. Insightful, wise, and thoroughly convincing, Kruschwitz's reading of these strange stories as interludes to the ancestral narrative demonstrates the importance of listening carefully to the new thematic overtones bestowed upon us by these interludes that forever changes how we view the dominant storyline."

—L. Juliana Claassens, Professor of Old Testament, Stellenbosch University, South Africa

"Jonathan Kruschwitz weaves together a discerning reading of Genesis with a winsome knowledge of music composition in order to explain how the stories about Hagar, Dinah, and Tamar offer an ironic view on the most important themes in the ancestral narrative. Kruschwitz's skilled readings helpfully challenge received ideas, invite the reader to their own fresh engagement with familiar texts, and demonstrate the power of a critically informed, interdisciplinary hermeneutic."

—C. A. Strine, Senior Lecturer in Ancient Near Eastern History & Literature, University of Sheffield